W9-AWV-775

VISUAL QUICKSTART GUIDE

JAVA 2

FOR THE WORLD WIDE WEB

Dori Smith

Peachpit Press

Visual QuickStart Guide
Java 2 for the World Wide Web
Dori Smith

Peachpit Press

1249 Eighth Street
Berkeley, CA 94710
(510) 524-2178 · (800) 283-9444
(510) 524-2221 (fax)

Find us on the World Wide Web at: www.peachpit.com

To report errors, please send a note to errata@peachpit.com

Peachpit Press is a division of Pearson Education

Editor: Nancy Davis
Production coordinator: Lisa Brazieal
Compositors: Jude Levinson, Owen Wolfson
Proofreader: Anne Gillick
Indexer: Emily Glossbrenner
Cover design: The Visual Group

ISBN: 0-201-74864-9

0 9 8 7 6 5 4 3 2 1

Printed and bound in the United States of America

Dedication

To Tom Negrino—not only could I not have done this book without you, but without you, I couldn't even have imagined it. Thanks for being my best friend, biggest cheerleader, and true love.

Thanks!

Thanks are especially due to the best editor in the world, Nancy Davis, for never losing faith in this book, and for her help in translating Geek to English.

Lisa Brazieal did the tough production work of turning a variety of files and formats into something that was suitable for print. That this book looks like a book at all is due to her talent and skill. Thanks are also due to Nancy Ruenzel and Marjorie Baer of Peachpit for their support and patience.

Paul Devine and Cliff Vick helped to update this book from Java 1.0 to Java 2—thanks, guys! Cliff also did a great job as tech editor; any technical mistakes still remaining are my own.

Thanks are due to my agent, David Rogelberg of Studio B, for his hard work and good advice.

It's uncommon to thank doctors in the acknowledgements of a book, but given that I had two separate cancer scares during its writing, I feel I owe a debt of gratitude to Drs. Pile and Shapiro. Thanks for keeping your heads while I was losing mine.

Thanks all around to the Wise-Women's Web Community http://www.wise-women.org who never fail to inspire me.

As always, to Sean Smith, World's Best Kid™, who has patience that someday, all books will come to an end.

This book contains no coffee puns.

TABLE OF CONTENTS

TABLE OF CONTENTS

INTRODUCTION

Welcome to the wonderful world of Java!

As programming languages go, Java is a relative newcomer that has achieved widespread popularity in an amazingly short amount of time. This is because it's much simpler than many other languages, while still being extremely useful due to its cross-platform capabilities.

Most books on Java expect you to have some programming background. Unlike those others, this book doesn't make that assumption. We'll take it slow and easy, with lots of examples that build on previous examples. When you finish this book, those other books that might as well have been in Greek should now make sense.

What is Java?

Java first gained widespread notice in 1996, when it burst upon the new Web scene with an amazing amount of hype. At the time, it wouldn't have surprised me to see headlines claiming that Java was the cure for cancer or that it would solve world hunger.

The hype then died down and gave rise to the perception that Java was a flop. This couldn't have been further from the truth. Java didn't fulfill all its expectations simply because nothing could have. Perception has finally started to catch up with reality, and Java is now seen as a useful piece of the Web programming puzzle.

Java is just a programming language and, in fact, always was. What's different about Java is that it's a great programming language: very small, useful, and cross-platform. There are a few gotchas involving vendors, versions, browsers, and platforms, though, and those will be covered in Chapter 1.

Who this Book is For

This book is primarily aimed at two groups of people: Web programming students and Web designers. Don't worry, though—if you're not in one of these two groups, the nice people at the bookstore won't refuse to sell it to you, and you'll probably still find it useful. However, if you are in one of these groups, you should find it right up your alley.

In any case, I've made the assumption that you already know something about the Web and HTML. For example, I'm expecting that you at least understand HTML tags well enough to be able to understand the code in your pages. If you don't, there are a number of excellent books out there; I recommend *HTML 4 for the World Wide Web, 4th Edition: Visual QuickStart Guide* by Elizabeth Castro as a great place to start.

Web programming students

Thanks to the format of the Visual QuickStart Guides, many teachers have found that they make good textbooks, and the students like the price and weight.

One word of caution, though: I've seen plenty of emails from students attempting to disguise their homework assignments as questions about this book. Don't even try it, okay?

Web designers

You learned HTML and it wasn't too hard.
Then, you surprised yourself when JavaScript
wasn't anywhere near as hard as you thought
it would be. Now, you're wondering if maybe
you should try something a little harder and
check out Java. Welcome! This book will do
several things for you:

◆ It will help you learn the basics of Java, so
you can see if you want to take on writing
Java yourself.

◆ It will teach you the best ways to use Java
programs that other people have written.

◆ It will help you talk to Java programmers
in their own language. Yep, you'll learn
how to speak geek with the best of 'em.
I've found that people who've decided
that they want to outsource their Java
work are much happier with the end
result when they're able to communicate
with their programmers.

◆ And lastly, it'll give you one more skill set
to help get those jobs. In a tough economy,
you need everything possible going for
you. Adding Java to your repertoire might
be just the thing that makes your résumé
or portfolio stand out from the others.

About this Book

This book uses some formatting tricks that should make it easier for you to understand what's going on.

In the step-by-step instructions that make up the bulk of the book, I've used a special type style to show when I'm talking about code, like this:

```
<APPLET>
```

```
public class Applet1 extends Applet
```

In the illustrations that accompany the text, I've highlighted the parts of the applets that I'm discussing in red, so you can see at a glance what I'm referring to.

Because book pages are narrower than monitors, some of the lines of code are too long to fit on one line of the book. When this happens, I've broken the line of code into segments and inserted an arrow to indicate that it's a continued line. Here's an example:

```
g.drawString("This is a very long message
→ to display on the screen", 100 , 25);
```

The illustrations that you'll see in this book fall into three categories, which I've called Listings, Applets, and Figures. A listing is an HTML file which contains a tag that refers to a Java file. An applet is the Java program itself. Figures are the screenshots, that is, what you'll see on the screen when you load the HTML file into your browser.

Don't Type that Code!

Some books give you a long listing of code and expect you to type it all in. In this day and age, that's way too old-fashioned. It was hard enough for me to do the typing; you shouldn't have to do it also. So I've created a companion Web site for this book that contains all of the HTML and Java files used here, ready for you to either download or copy and paste into your own pages.

Of course, in the unlikely event that any mistakes happened to slip into print, those will be listed on the site also. You can find all this at

`http://www.dori.com/java/`

If you have any comments or questions about this book, please send me e-mail at `java2@dori.com`. But please, don't send me your files. Given the rapidly increasing number of viruses, I never open attachments from people I don't know (I'm sure your files are fine; it's those other people I have to worry about). Instead, post the files to your Web site, and then send me a URL in your e-mail.

WHAT IS JAVA?

In 1995, the World Wide Web went from something that only college students and a few geeks knew about into a massive fad that everyone who was anyone had to be on. And if you were on the Web, you had to put up your own home page, generally with an obnoxious background, an "Under Construction" graphic, and links to the three people you knew who also had pages on the Web.

Pretty soon, people said, "there's gotta be more to Web page building than this." Java hit the scene (via the release of Netscape 2.0) at the beginning of 1996, and the Web hasn't been the same since.

A Short History Lesson

Several years ago (several decades in Web time) the Next Big Thing was going to be set-top boxes. Set-top boxes are, simply, a box made to sit on top of your television set, with the purpose of making your television viewing experience more "interactive."

Sun Microsystems was working on a language for set-top boxes that it called Oak. In order for this new language to work, it had to be small (so that commands could quickly be sent from the cable company to your TV and vice versa) and portable (so that it would work with different cable companies). To fill the bill, James Gosling of Sun created Oak as a subset of C++.

Like most Next Big Things, set-top boxes went nowhere. But when the Web hit, Sun realized that, in Oak, they had a language that could work over the Web, allowing people to move away from those boring, static, flat pages. In a major marketing move, Sun renamed Oak "Java," and the hype began.

One of Sun's original selling points for Java was "Write Once, Run Anywhere," usually abbreviated as WORA. In theory, you'd be able to code your program once, and it would then run on any machine with Java support. Sun is responsible for Java on Windows and Unix, while Apple handles the Macintosh. Microsoft originally had a contract with Sun to work on Java, but that agreement headed to court in October 1997.

Microsoft then introduced Visual J++ for Windows, a programming language extremely similar to Java, but with a few added benefits in return for giving up compatibility with other platforms. When J++ fizzled, Microsoft settled with Sun in January 2001. For those developers who had an investment in J++ code, Microsoft created J# (read as "J Sharp"), which allows recompilation of J++ code to run on their new .NET platform. Microsoft also declined to ship Java with either Windows XP or Internet Explorer 6; thankfully, though, it can be downloaded directly from Sun.

For those who like to keep up with geek politics, you can follow the Java wars via these links:

```
http://java.sun.com/aboutJava/
http://www.microsoft.com/java/
http://www.javalobby.org/
```

The Next Big Thing

There's always a Next Big Thing. Over the last few years, it's been set-top boxes, multimedia, and most spectacularly of all, push technology. NBTs make life easy on tech columnists (who just have to write about how things are going with the current NBT) and corporate MIS departments (who can always get more money out of management by claiming they're working on the current NBT).

While most NBTs go nowhere, they rarely completely die out. For example, the set-top box concept appears to be making a comeback in the TiVo and Replay DVRs (Digital Video Recorders), albeit in a scaled-back version.

Current NBTs, as of this writing, are XML (eXtensible Markup Language) and surfing the Web via your cell phone—you make the call!

Why Learn Java?

Why should a non-programmer learn a programming language?

The sidebar shows one example of the many help wanted ads that have crossed my desk. When you read it, it's clear that the opening is for a design/marketing person, until you get to the last paragraph. Along with everything else this company wants, the requirements state that the candidate must know Java.

As Web work has progressed, the line between programmers and designers has blurred. It's common for people who don't consider themselves programmers to be working with JavaScript and CGI. Knowing Java adds another tool to your toolbox. You at least need to understand when (and when not!) to use Java—and if you can code it, too, you're a star.

If you're a programmer, this applies even more to you. Java is a fast growing field for Web developers, and it isn't showing signs of slowing down. Adding Java to your résumé will increase your opportunities.

Java skills are most important of all for freelancers and consultants. If you add Java to your list of skills, you're a much more attractive candidate to clients.

Common Java Myths

There are a number of common myths about what Java is, and what Java isn't. I'll set a few of them straight here.

Myth: Java is related to JavaScript

As described above, Java was designed at Sun Microsystems. JavaScript, on the other hand, was created by Netscape to be a client-side scripting addition to HTML, and was originally named LiveScript. When Java took off in a huge way, the smart folks at Netscape

continued

Help Wanted—Creative Director

The Creative Director responds to design requests from merchandising and marketing staff for projects typically requiring fast turnaround time. The Director needs to develop current in-house creative capabilities for quick-turn projects and will manage an outside agency when additional skills are needed or for longer term projects.

Current knowledge of Web design technologies and ability to measure and improve site performance are critical elements of the job. The position involves significant interaction with the Engineering staff for site development, performance and production.

Reporting to the VP of Merchandise Management, the position has the following responsibilities:

Brand Image: Being the "keeper of the brand" from the creative services point of view. Translating corporate marketing strategy into site design principles and standards, appealing to a wide range of customer segments and integrating branding messages across all media, including Web and print.

User Interface Design: Building a user interface with world-class site navigation, designing with a look and feel consistent with the brand, influencing buyer behavior, and basing design decisions on usability lab findings.

Marketing Campaign Design: Designing ad campaigns for customer acquisition and installed base marketing, including banner ad design, e-mail production and print media.

Qualifications: A successful Creative Director with more than five years of experience and a well-rounded portfolio, including management of a major Web site. Hands-on supervision of a production team is a must, and required technical skills include copywriting, HTML, Java, and Photoshop. Additionally, proven talent in user interface design and brand marketing is critical.

figured out how to get some of that buzz for themselves—by renaming LiveScript "JavaScript." It worked quite well from the hype standpoint, but has confused people ever since.

If you want to know more about JavaScript, I recommend looking at *JavaScript for the World Wide Web, 4th Edition: Visual QuickStart Guide* by Tom Negrino and me (Peachpit Press, 2001).

Myth: Java should be written JAVA

Java isn't an acronym, it's a word. Although I did once hear a claim that it "might" stand for "Just Another Vague Acronym"....

Myth: Java is just for the Web

In general, when people think of Java they think of little doodads running in browser windows over the Internet. And for the most part, that's the aspect of Java that most people are familiar with (and primarily what this book will cover). The actual name for these doodads is *applets*. They're not standalone applications; they can't run by themselves and need a browser.

However, you can write perfectly acceptable applications with Java. Why would you want to? Well, because it's a small, simple, cross-platform language. And while this book is called *Java 2 for the World Wide Web*, almost all of the concepts (except for those specifically having to do with browsers) also apply to stand-alone applications.

Figure 1.1 A DEC PDP-11. You won't be needing one of these.

Myth: Java is just on the client side

Some people who think that Java is just for the Web go further and think that Java is only on the client side; in other words, that it can only be run inside a browser. This couldn't be further from the truth.

One of the big growth areas for Java at the moment is in *servlets*. These, like applets, are mini-programs that run as part of another application, in this case, a Web server. And again, the reason for doing this is that Java is small, simple, and cross-platform. If you write one useful servlet, you can run it as part of Unix, Windows, and Macintosh servers. This aspect of Java will be covered in Chapter 13.

Myth: You have to learn another programming language first

For a programming language, Java is fairly easy to learn. There are a number of people who claim that you should learn C, or C++, or even Pascal first. I've found one thing in common with all of these people: They always recommend the language that *they* learned first.

Again: for a programming language, Java is fairly easy to learn. It's an excellent way to start learning object-oriented concepts, without a lot of the garbage that's in, for example, C++. If you learn Java first, you won't have to then unlearn all those bad habits. Consequently, this book doesn't make any comparisons like "For those of you who know SmallTalk, *this* is similar to *that*." For one thing, there are excellent books out there that will teach you Java when you already know another language; for another thing, all the SmallTalk programmers I know think that everyone should stop using Java and switch to SmallTalk instead.

Besides, if I recommended that you all learn programming the way I did, well, there aren't a lot of PDP-11s running BASIC anymore...and I won't even talk about DEC-10 assembler on punch cards (**Figure 1.1**).

What You'll Need

If you learned HTML or JavaScript, you probably didn't need to buy any new tools. A text editor was enough to get you started, with the possible later addition of a visual Web design tool. With Java, on the other hand, you're likely to need something more.

That something more is usually referred to as an *integrated development environment* (or IDE) or sometimes as a *compiler*. If you're on Windows, Linux, or Solaris, you might try your luck with the free Java 2 SDK offered by Sun:

`http://java.sun.com/j2se/1.3/`

While it is free, it's not exactly friendly to novices. If you want some handholding, or you're on a different platform, you'll want to check out Appendix A, which includes a list of other development environments available (some of which are also free).

✔ Tip

- Given that there are so many different IDEs available, this book doesn't try to cover creating applets with each. The IDE you choose won't teach you Java, but it should tell you at least how to load it on your system and get started. And after that, you have this book.

Java's Different Versions

As this book will focus primarily on writing Java 2 applets, you'll need to make sure that your browser (and those of your site's visitors) support Java 2. Unfortunately, many do not.

But, you might wonder, "Java 2 has been out since 1998—don't most people have browsers newer than that?"

Yes, and no. It's not quite that simple.

But first, a little history: there have been four major releases of Java so far: 1.0, 1.1, 1.2, and 1.3. When Java 1.2 was released, Sun changed the name of the language from Java to Java 2. So, while you might think that Java should have gone from 1.1 to 2.0, Sun didn't do anything that simple. Instead, they kept the new name with the old numbering, leading to the different versions being Java 1.0, Java 1.1, Java 2 1.2, and Java 2 1.3. Clear as mud, huh? Given that, what this book covers is Java 2, which means versions 1.2 and forward.

The responsibility for who makes sure that a browser can handle Java 2 has varied over the years. At this point in time, Sun supports Windows and various flavors of Unix (including Solaris and Linux) and Apple supports Macintoshes. At points in the past, Netscape browsers came with their own versions of Java unable to run anything else, and this didn't end until Netscape Communicator 4.76.

Because of the legal battles over Java between Microsoft and Sun, there are also some restrictions on what Microsoft can ship. Legally, Microsoft cannot/will not (depending on who you talk to) ship anything after Java 1.1.

And to make matters worse, Apple made the decision that they would only support Java 2 on Mac OS X, not on any previous versions of their Mac OS.

continued

Consequently, if one of your applet's users has an older version of the Mac OS, or an older version of Netscape, or a version of Windows with Microsoft's version of Java, it's entirely likely that they won't be able to run your Java 2 applet.

If that's the case, you're not completely out of luck. Appendix D covers the differences between versions. With that, you should be able to take this book's applets and rewrite them for earlier versions of Java.

JAVA'S DIFFERENT VERSIONS

2

JAVA BASICS

One of the reasons that many people find computer programming intimidating is the large amount of jargon and buzzwords used by those "in the know." In this chapter, I'll explain commonly used Java jargon and concepts in plain English, with a minimum of Three Letter Acronyms (TLAs, for short).

Introducing the Amazing Java Virtual Machine

One of the most commonly used acronyms in Java is *JVM*, which stands for Java Virtual Machine. Understanding why the JVM exists is the key to understanding what's so special about Java.

Take a look at **Figure 2.1**, which shows how normal programs work. If you want to run Microsoft Word on a PC, you need to buy the Wintel version. If you want to run it on a Mac, you need to buy the Mac version. If you buy the wrong version for your machine, your computer just won't be able to read what's on the disks. Programs that are machine-specific are said to be in *machine code*.

Java programs, on the other hand, look at the world differently, as shown in **Figure 2.2**. In order to run Java, your machine needs a piece of software called a Java Virtual Machine, or JVM. If you've ever run a Java applet or application on your computer, or if you have a modern browser, you've already got a JVM.

Java programs don't talk directly to your computer. Instead, they talk to the JVM, and the JVM talks to your computer. You can think of the JVM as a translator between the Java code and your computer, which is why Java code is referred to as *interpreted* code instead of *compiled* (machine-specific) code. The JVM is machine-specific code that runs on your computer. Its sole purpose in life is to take Java programs and convince your computer that they're really programs made to run on your particular machine.

As far as the Java program is concerned, the JVM might as well be the computer itself, since that's as close to the hardware as it gets. That's why it's called a "virtual machine."

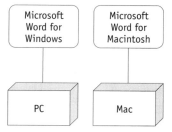

Figure 2.1 This is how normal compiled programs expect the world to look.

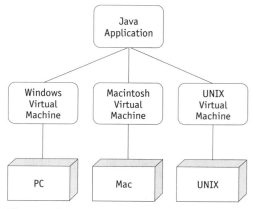

Figure 2.2 But a Java program can run on any hardware, so long as there's a Java Virtual Machine running on it.

Java Security

One of the main reasons for Java's popularity is that it's secure. This means that someone cannot write a Java applet which, when run through your browser, will delete files from your hard drive or e-mail your credit card numbers.

Java manages this using the concept of the *sandbox*. When Java applets are restricted to playing in the sandbox, there's a long list of things that they can't do on a browser's machine. Java applets cannot read, write, delete, rename, or check for the existence of files. They cannot list or create directories, nor can they check to see if a given file name is a file or directory. They also cannot print or create a network connection to a computer other than the one from which the code itself was loaded.

This changes, to some degree, in later versions of Java. Appendix D has more information on these capabilities, but for the most part, this book will stay inside the sandbox.

Java Files

When you start writing a Java program, you'll begin by creating an `AppletName.java` file in your development environment. This file, with the name ending in `.java`, will contain the source code that you type in, as shown in **Figure 2.3**.

When you compile your program, a new file will be created, one that ends with `.class`. This file is the one that's understood by the JVM. It contains something called *bytecodes*, which are the result of the compilation of your program and serve as the input to the JVM. **Figure 2.4** looks like garbage to us, but it's everything the JVM needs to know.

When you upload your applet to your server, you only need to upload the `.class` file. It may seem odd that you don't need to upload the file that you actually worked on, but you don't have to (unless you want the world to be able to see your source code!).

Figure 2.3 Here's what the code for HelloWorld.java looks like.

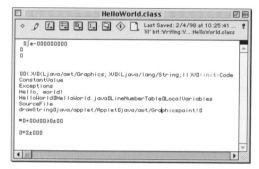

Figure 2.4 And here's what HelloWorld.class looks like; HelloWorld.java has been translated into bytecodes that the JVM can understand.

Figure 2.5 This cat object's name is Pixel. His Web site is at http://www.pixel.mu/.

Figure 2.6 This gone-but-not-forgotten cat object's name was Mutant Alien From Hell...really, it was.

Buzzword Bingo

The following sections will help you understand some Java-related terms that we will use throughout this book.

Object

Close your eyes and picture a cat in your mind. Think about four legs, paws, and fur. That abstract idea in your head is a `cat` object. Unless (like me at this moment) you have a cat sitting in your lap right now, it's a completely abstract object; in other words, that cat doesn't actually exist. That's okay, it's still a `cat` object.

To know what objects Java has that you can play with, check out `http://java.sun.com/ j2se/1.3/docs/api/overview-summary.html`. It contains documentation for all the objects that come with Java 1.3. If you need any other objects, you'll have to create them yourself. Luckily, that's not too difficult.

Instance

In order for you to pet that cat you're thinking of, it's got to be an actual cat. In Java, this is referred to as an *instance* of an object. The object itself is an abstract idea. In order for it to exist, you have to create an instance. You can have multiple instances of an object; **Figures 2.5** and **2.6** show two instances of the `cat` object. You'll learn how to create instances of objects in your code starting in Chapter 4.

For example, say you want to build a desk. You know just what you want the desk to look like, so you draw a picture on a piece of paper as a blueprint. That picture is an object: it's not a desk, but it can be used to create a desk. You can then create several identical desks, all from that one blueprint. You can give the blueprint to a friend, and they can create a desk (or several desks)

continued

BUZZWORD BINGO

just like yours. Copies can be made of your blueprint, and people all over the world can create more desks. The desks that are built are instances of that desk object that you designed when you drew the picture.

Java, for example, contains a `Font` object. In order to create a font that you can work with, you need to create an instance of the `Font` object. This is done by adding a line to your applet:

```
Font f = new Font("TimesRoman",
→ Font.BOLD,24);
```

This creates a new instance (named `f`) of the `Font` object. That new font is then set to the font of 24 point Times Roman Bold.

Instantiate

This is one of the ugliest, most confusing words in Java, and all it means is "to create an instance of." If you instantiate a cat object, in English, it just means that you create another cat. If you instantiate a desk, it means that you got out the hammer, nails, and lumber, and built another real-world desk.

Instantiation/Instantiating

These are just more ways of referring to the process of creating an instance.

Method

The things that objects can do are called *methods*. It might be helpful for you to think of objects as nouns and methods as verbs. For instance, you could check to see if a `cat` object `isPurring()`. Note the parentheses; they indicate that you're referring to a method, not an object.

Dot syntax

Now that we have these objects and methods, how are they put together? Java uses something called dot syntax, which JavaScript users should find familiar.

What's Buzzword Bingo?

Buzzword Bingo is a game popularized by Scott Adams' comic strip "Dilbert." You and your coworkers each take 24 random examples of commonly used business jargon and put them onto a card with a Bingo game grid. Then you take the cards into a meeting with management and check off a square every time someone uses the phrase. Whoever fills up a row, column, or diagonal on their card first is the winner.

Many Java books read like someone trying to force a quick end to a game of Buzzword Bingo. This book has a goal of trying to explain its terms, rather than just assume that you've picked them up while reading other programming books (which also assumed that you had learned its terms from other programming books, and so on).

You can put objects and their methods together by simply combining them with periods (or dots). This is called *dot syntax*. Here are some examples:

`cat.isPurring()`

`desk.hasDrawers()`

`Font.getSize()`

Instance variables

Objects have instance variables. For that `cat` object, the instance variable `numberOfLegs` is four. Note that instance variables are different from methods: There are no parentheses, because no action is taking place.

Instance variables describe something about the object. For example:

`cat.numberOfLegs` contains how many legs this cat has.

`desk.typeOfWood` contains what material the desk is made of.

`Rectangle.height` is an actual Java instance variable that contains the height of a rectangle object.

Objects can consist of combinations of objects

Java starts with little tiny objects, and puts them together to create big, complex objects. This means that if you have something complex, you can break it down into simple components. Take `desk.typeOfWood` from our previous example. The value of that object would be just a short piece of text, which Java calls a *string*. Strings are objects in their own right, with their own methods, such as `length()`. So, you could refer to `desk.typeOfWood.length()` to get the length of the name of the type of wood that the desk is made out of.

continued

An example from Java is `userCheckbox.`
`getCurrent().getLabel()`. In this example
there are a group of checkboxes (called
`userCheckbox`), which have been set up to
be radio buttons. To find out which radio
button is currently selected, we look
at `userCheckbox.getCurrent()`. That just
returns a checkbox to us, not a name, so
we need to look at the check box's label.
Calling the `getLabel()` method on
`userCheckbox.getCurrent()` gives us the
value we need.

As you may have noticed, objects are always
listed from the most general to the most specific. Each object after the dot limits what the
object refers to and makes it more precise.

Class

If you combine an object with all its associated instance variables and all its associated
methods, you have a *class*. So far, we've discussed the `cat` object. If you take everything
you know about the `cat` object, along with its
associated instance variables (`numberOfLegs`,
`eyeColor`, `noseColor`, `furLength`) and its associated methods (`isPurring()`, `isEating()`,
`isSleeping()`), you'll have the class `Cat`.
When you create a `cat` object, you're creating
an instance of the `Cat` class, and all of its
associated instance variables and methods
are available to your code.

If you created the `cat` object and its methods, you know what the `cat` class contains.
Otherwise, you'll need to refer to documentation, based on what the `cat` class extends
(see below).

An actual Java example is a `Rectangle`, which
has instance variables `x` and `y` (designating
the starting points), as well as `height` and
`width`, and methods such as `isEmpty()`.

`Font` is another class, which contains the
methods `getFont()`, `getSize()`, and
`getStyle()`.

Constructors

Constructors are another part of a class; you call them to create an object. You could create a new `cat` object by calling `Cat("Pixel")`. You can create a new `font` object by calling `Font("Helvetica",Font.Italic,36)`.

Alternatively, you could create a new `Rectangle` either by calling `Rectangle(x,y,width,height)`, or by calling `Rectangle(point,dimension)`. A class can have several different constructors, i.e., several different ways to create the same object.

A group of checkboxes could be created by calling:

`new Checkbox("Breakfast");`

`new Checkbox("Lunch");`

`new Checkbox("Dinner");`

or by calling:

`new Checkbox("Breakfast",true);`

`new Checkbox("Lunch",false);`

`new Checkbox("Dinner",false);`

The former uses the default value (not checked) for whether the checkbox is checked or not, the latter style explicitly sets whether the checkbox is checked or not.

Inheritance

Java derives a great deal of its power from the concept of inheritance. For instance, you may have a class `HousePet`, which includes the methods `isEating()` and `isSleeping()`. Then you can create the classes `Cat` and `Dog`, and have them *inherit* everything that's in `HousePet`, including those two methods.

Extends

When one class gets its characteristics from another through inheritance, it is said to *extend* that class. `Cat` extends the class `HousePet`, so `Cat` can also be referred to, then, as a *subclass* of `HousePet`.

In Java, for example, `Dialog` extends `Window`. This means that a dialog box is a specific type of a window. `Dialog` inherits everything that `Window` contains, but a few methods are then added to `Dialog` that apply only to dialog boxes.

In this book, we'll be primarily writing applets, so almost everything we do will be extending the Java class `java.applet`. Consequently, our applets will inherit everything that Java provides the `Applet` class, as a starting point for everything that we write.

Package

A group of related classes is called a package.

AWT

AWT stands for Abstract Windowing Toolkit. The AWT package is used to display information in a window, which means that we'll be seeing a lot of it in this book.

JDK

JDK stands for Java Development Kit. Each version of the JDK is associated with a version of Java; for example, Java 1.0 is also referred to as JDK 1.0.

Using Java
on Your Pages

You don't actually have to know Java to put Java applets on your pages. You can get applets from any number of places, and just use the HTML `applet`, `object`, and/or `embed` tags to place them where you want them. In this chapter, we'll look at where to get applets on the Web (often for free) and how to place them on your pages.

Using the APPLET Tag on Your Pages

Surprisingly, you can make extensive use of Java applets on your Web pages without ever learning the Java language. **Listing 3.1** is an example of an HTML file that uses the `applet` tag to add an applet to the Web page.

To place a Java applet on your Web page with the Applet tag:

1. `<applet code="HelloWorld.class"`
   `→ width="200" height="50">`

   The `applet` tag is a part of HTML. The attributes we're using here are `code` (the name of the applet's class file), and `height` and `width` (which tell the browser how much room the Java applet will take up on the page). **Table 3.1** contains a list of `applet` attributes.

   In this case, we're calling the `HelloWorld` applet. The class file (described in Chapter 2) is named `HelloWorld.class`. The width is 200 pixels and the height is 50 pixels. **Figure 3.1** shows what the applet looks like on a Web page.

2. `</applet>`

   This ends the `applet` tag.

Listing 3.1 It's really pretty straightforward to add a Java applet to your Web page.

```
                    Listing
<html>
<head>
 <title>Listing 3.1</title>
</head>
<body bgcolor="white">
 <applet code="HelloWorld.class" width="200"
 → height="50">
 </applet>
</body>
</html>
```

Figure 3.1 This is what the HelloWorld applet looks like on a Web page.

Table 3.1

Attributes of the Applet Tag	
ATTRIBUTE	DESCRIPTION
align	The applet's alignment on the Web page (see **Table 3.5**).
alt	Alternate text that should display (but doesn't in most browsers) if the browser doesn't support Java.
code	The name of the applet's class file.
codebase	The directory containing the file referenced in the code attribute. It's unneeded if the applet is in the same directory as the HTML file calling it.
height	The amount of vertical room, in pixels, that the browser will set aside for the applet.
hspace	The amount of horizontal empty space, in pixels, that the browser will put around the applet.
id	A unique identifier for the applet, used by either CSS or JavaScript.
mayscript	Tells the browser whether or not JavaScript is allowed to communicate with this applet. This attribute doesn't take any values; if it exists, the applet is scriptable.
name	The name is a way of identifying the applet for either CSS or JavaScript. Similar to id but available in more browsers.
vspace	The amount of vertical empty space, in pixels, that the browser will put around the applet.
width	The amount of horizontal room, in pixels, that the browser will set aside for the applet.

✔ **Tip**

■ If you have applets that are shared by multiple pages on your site, add the codebase attribute of the applet tag to refer to the applet in a common directory. That way, you don't have to duplicate the file in every HTML directory.

Using the Object Tag on Your Pages

While the applet tag works in most browsers, the W3C deprecated it in HTML 4.0 in favor of the object tag. By this point, enough browsers support object tag that it's the way to go for the future, and consequently, it's what we'll be using for the majority of this book. **Listing 3.2** is an example of an HTML file that uses the object tag to add an applet to the Web page.

The object tag was designed to work with other data types (such as plugins) that aren't natively supported by browsers, so it is a more complex tag in order to be more flexible for the future. **Table 3.2** describes the relevant attributes of the object tag.

To place a Java applet on your Web page with the Object tag:

1. `<object classid="clsid:8AD9C840-044E-` → `11D1-B3E9-00805F499D93" width="200"` → `height="50" codetype="application/` → `java">`

   The object tag is more complex than the applet tag, and requires more attributes. Thankfully, most of the attributes are duplicated in every Java applet, and so, can just be copied and pasted from previous examples you've already done.

   In this case, there are two attributes you've seen before: width and height, and two you haven't: classid and codetype. The classid attribute looks ugly, but it contains a standard value for all applets using the Java 2 plugin (see "The Java 2 Plugin" sidebar for more information about the Java 2 plugin). The codetype attribute contains the MIME type for Java, to tell browsers that the object being loaded should be treated as Java.

Listing 3.2 This applet works with browsers that can handle the newer object tag.

```
<html>
<head>
 <title>Listing 3.2</title>
</head>
<body bgcolor="white">
<object classid="clsid:8AD9C840-044E-11D1-
→ B3E9-00805F499D93" width="200" height="50"
→ codetype="application/java">
 <param name="code" value="HelloWorld.class">
 <param name="type" value="application/x-java-
→ applet;version=1.3">
 <param name="scriptable" value="false">
</object>
</body>
</html>
```

Table 3.2

Attributes of the Object Tag	
Attribute	**Description**
align	The applet's alignment on the Web page (see **Table 3.5**).
classid	Should always be set to "clsid: → 8AD9C840-044E-11D1-B3E9-00805F499D93" to tell the browser that you want to use the Java 2 plugin.
codebase	Per Sun, should be set to "http://java. → sun.com/products/plugin/1.3/ → jinstall-13-win32.cab#Version= → 1,3,0,0", but doing so causes the page to not work in Internet Explorer/Mac (see "The Java 2 Plugin" sidebar).
codetype	Should always be set to "application/ → java".
height	The amount of vertical room, in pixels, that the browser will set aside for the applet.
hspace	The amount of horizontal empty space, in pixels, that the browser will put around the applet.
name	Used to identify the applet for either CSS or JavaScript.
vspace	The amount of vertical empty space, in pixels, that the browser will put around the applet.
width	The amount of horizontal room, in pixels, that the browser will set aside for the applet.

Table 3.3

Name/Value Pairs for the Param Tag	
NAME	**VALUE**
code	The name of the class file for the browser to run.
codebase	Similar to the codebase attribute of the applet tag, this is set to the directory of the class file.
scriptable	Set to true or false to set whether the applet is scriptable from the HTML page.
type	Should be "application/x-java-⇥ applet;version=1.3" or "applica ⇥ tion/x-java-applet". The former specifies a version number and the latter doesn't; choose a version number only if your code requires that the browser support this version of Java.

2. `<param name="code" value=`
   `⇥ "HelloWorld.class">`

Unlike in the `applet` tag, the `object` tag doesn't contain a specific link to the applet being run. Instead, all of that information is put into `param` tags, each of which has a name/value pair. The possible attribute values of the `param` tag are covered in **Table 3.3**. In this line, we're telling the browser that the class file of the applet we want to run is called `HelloWorld.class`.

3. `<param name="type" value=`
   `⇥ "application/x-java-applet;`
   `⇥ version=1.3">`

Here we're telling the browser that, not only is the object being loaded Java, it's a Java 1.3 applet.

4. `<param name="scriptable" value=`
   `⇥ "false">`

The `object` tag uses the `scriptable` parameter to let the Java know whether or not scripting languages can access this applet. In this case, they can't.

5. `</object>`

This ends the `object` tag.

✔ Tip

■ The `param` tag can be used inside the `applet` tag as well as the `object` tag when you want to pass parameters to your applet (as shown later in **Listing 3.7**).

The Java 2 Plugin

Chapter 1 briefly discussed some of the political wars that have gone on over Java. In particular, the one between Sun and Microsoft has led to a change in the way that most browsers now run Java.

It used to be that the version of Java you ran depended on what browser you had. If you had Netscape 3, for instance, you had Netscape's version of their Java Virtual Machine (JVM) and that's all you could have with that browser.

Between the Sun/Microsoft battles and the slowing frequency of browser upgrades, Sun realized that they needed a better way to get newer versions of Java into user's hands. Just waiting for users to download newer browsers wouldn't work, so they started to ship Java as a plugin. This way, an applet could prompt the user (as shown in **Figure 3.2**) to download an updated plugin without having to go through all the hassles of changing to a newer browser.

Sun has specified that the `object` tag should be used for Java applets going forward to allow use of the Java plugin. In addition, they've assigned specific values to certain attributes in order to allow developers to be sure that users have the right version. **Table 3.2**, for instance, shows that Sun says that the `codebase` attribute should be set to the URL of where the user can download the plugin in case they don't have the current version or they don't have Java at all. The bad news is that that URL only works for Windows, Solaris, and Unix. If you have Mac users visiting your page and you have `code-base` set following Sun's spec, their browser will get confused and not run your applet.

The workaround is to leave off the `codebase` attribute all together, and test in some other fashion to see if the user has Java enabled, such as in **Listing 3.4**. Then, if the user doesn't have the right version, ask them to upgrade by going to either `http://java.sun.com/getjava/download.html` (see **Figure 3.3**) or `http://www.apple.com/java/`.

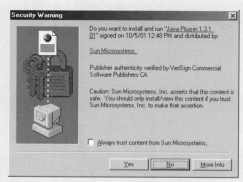

Figure 3.2 If the user has Windows XP and Internet Explorer 6, they may not have Java at all. Here, they're prompted to download the plugin.

Figure 3.3 This page at Sun offers visitors a chance to download the most current Java plugin.

Listing 3.3 Combining the object and embed tags allows your applet to work in the largest number of browsers.

```
                    Listing
<html>
<head>
 <title>Listing 3.3</title>
</head>
<body bgcolor="white">
<object classid="clsid:8AD9C840-044E-11D1-
→ B3E9-00805F499D93" width="200" height="50"
→ codetype="application/java">
 <param name="code" value="HelloWorld.class">
 <param name="type" value="application/x-java-
→ applet;version=1.3">
 <param name="scriptable" value="false">
 <embed type="application/x-java-applet;
→ version=1.3" code="HelloWorld.class"
→ width="200" height="50" scriptable="false"
→ pluginspage="http://java.sun.com/products/
→ plugin/1.3/plugin-install.html">
 </embed>
</object>
</body>
</html>
```

Using Object and Embed Tags on Your Pages

Some browsers support the applet tag. Some browsers support the object tag. Others support the embed tag. **Listing 3.3** shows an example of the object and embed tags used together to support the largest number of browsers, and **Table 3.4** shows the attributes of the embed tag.

To place a Java applet on your Web page with the Object and Embed tags:

1. `<embed type="application/x-java-`
`→ applet;version=1.3" code=`
`→ "HelloWorld.class" width="200"`
`→ height="50" scriptable="false"`
`→ pluginspage="http://java.sun.com/`
`→ products/plugin/1.3/plugin-install.`
`→ html">`

Here, the embed tag is placed after the param tags and before the closing object tag. Browsers (such as some versions of Netscape) that don't understand the object tag won't just skip it. Instead, they'll look inside it, hoping that they'll find something that they can handle. The information in the embed tag is for them.

The attributes used here have similar values to those used in the previous examples, but they're all grouped together in the embed tag itself instead of using associated param tags.

2. `</embed>`

The embed tag is closed here.

Table 3.4

Attributes of the Embed Tag	
ATTRIBUTE	**DESCRIPTION**
align	The applet's alignment on the Web page (see **Table 3.5**).
alt	Alternate text that should display (but doesn't in most browsers) if the browser doesn't support Java.
code	The name of the applet's class file.
codebase	The directory containing the file referenced in the code attribute. It's unneeded if the applet is in the same directory as the HTML file calling it.
height	The amount of vertical room, in pixels, that the browser will set aside for the applet.
hspace	The amount of horizontal empty space, in pixels, that the browser will put around the applet.
name	The name is a way of identifying the applet for either CSS or JavaScript.
pluginspage	Per Sun, should be set to a page where the user can download the latest and greatest version of Java. You can get up to the minute info at http://java.sun.com/products/plugin/.
scriptable	Set to true or false to set whether the applet is scriptable from the HTML page.
type	Should be "application/x-java-applet;version=1.3" or "application/x-java-applet". The former specifies a version number and the latter doesn't; choose a version number only if your code requires that the browser support this version of Java.
vspace	The amount of vertical empty space, in pixels, that the browser will put around the applet.
width	The amount of horizontal room, in pixels, that the browser will set aside for the applet.

Listing 3.4 Always be sure to display a message for non-Java-enabled browsers.

```
<html>
<head>
 <title>Listing 3.4</title>
</head>
<body bgcolor="white">
<object classid="clsid:8AD9C840-044E-11D1-
→ B3E9-00805F499D93" width="200" height="50"
→ codetype="application/java">
 <param name="code" value="HelloWorld.class">
 <param name="type" value="application/x-java-
→ applet;version=1.3">
 <param name="scriptable" value="false">
 <embed type="application/x-java-applet;
→ version=1.3" code="HelloWorld.class"
→ width="200" height="50" scriptable="false"
→ pluginspage="http://java.sun.com/
→ products/plugin/1.3/plugin-install.html">
  <h1>If you had Java, you'd be seeing a cool
→ applet now</h1>
 </embed>
</object>
</body>
</html>
```

Figure 3.4 Let people know that they should upgrade and find out what they're missing.

Displaying a Message for Non-Java Browsers

While most browsers these days have Java, some people use old browsers, and some surf the Web with Java turned off. In these cases, you should display a message letting people know the cool things they're missing, as demonstrated in **Listing 3.4**.

To display a message for browsers without Java:

◆ `<h1>If you had Java, you'd be seeing a cool applet now</h1>`

You might think that this looks just like normal HTML, and you'd be correct—it is. However, because it's within the `object` and `embed` tags, it's only shown when the user can't display the Java applet. **Figure 3.4** shows how this displays on the screen.

✔ Tips

■ In **Figure 3.4**, you might notice that the "no Java" message isn't in the same area that's set aside for the Java applet. Because the browser doesn't understand Java, it doesn't know about the `height` and `width` attributes in the surrounding tags. Be sure to keep this in mind when laying out your pages.

■ Any HTML tags can go into this area. Be creative, but also be careful about closing any tags you open.

To Enable Java in Your Browser

Some browsers allow Java to be disabled. If Java has been disabled in your browser, you'll want to enable it so you can see Java in action. **Figure 3.5** shows Netscape 6 for

Windows Advanced preferences, which include a checkbox to enable or disable Java, and **Figure 3.6** shows Internet Explorer 5 for Mac Java preferences.

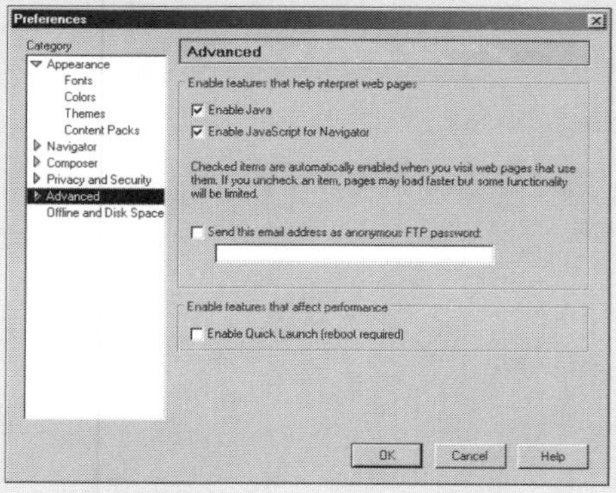

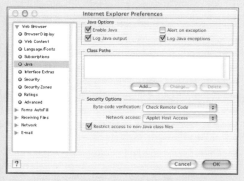

Figure 3.5 If you don't have Java enabled, you can't see the cool Java effects.

Figure 3.6 Internet Explorer/Mac allows Java to be turned off, unlike Internet Explorer/Windows.

Listing 3.5 Here's a way to move an applet from its default position.

```
                    Listing
<html>
<head>
 <title>Listing 3.5</title>
</head>
<body bgcolor="white">
<object classid="clsid:8AD9C840-044E-11D1-
→ B3E9-00805F499D93" width="200" height="50"
→ align="right" codetype="application/java">
 <param name="code" value="HelloWorld.class">
 <param name="type" value="application/x-java-
→ applet;version=1.3">
 <param name="scriptable" value="false">
 <embed type="application/x-java-applet;
→ version=1.3" code="HelloWorld.class"
→ width="200" height="50" align="right"
→ scriptable="false" pluginspage="http://java.
→ sun.com/products/plugin/1.3/plugin-
→ install.html">
 </embed>
</object>
</body>
</html>
```

Listing 3.6 Here's another way to move an applet around.

```
                    Listing
<html>
<head>
 <title>Listing 3.6</title>
</head>
<body bgcolor="white">
<object classid="clsid:8AD9C840-044E-11D1-
→ B3E9-00805F499D93" width="200" height=
→ "50" vspace="100" hspace="100" codetype=
→ "application/java">
 <param name="code" value="HelloWorld.class">
 <param name="type" value="application/x-java-
→ applet;version=1.3">
 <param name="scriptable" value="false">
 <embed type="application/x-java-applet;
→ version=1.3" code="HelloWorld.class"
→ width="200" height="50" vspace="100"
→ hspace="100" scriptable="false" pluginspage=
→ "http://java.sun.com/products/plugin/1.3/
→ plugin-install.html">
 </embed>
</object>
</body>
</html>
```

Positioning Java Applets on the Page

Applets can be positioned on a Web page much like any other object, such as images. **Listings 3.5** and **3.6** show how an applet can be moved from the default alignment.

To position a Java applet:

1. `<object classid="clsid:8AD9C840-044E-` `→ 11D1-B3E9-00805F499D93" width=` `→ "200" height="50" align="right"` `→ codetype="application/java">`

   In **Figure 3.7**, the HelloWorld applet is on the right side of the window. This is because the align attribute has been set to right.

2. `<embed type="application/x-java-` `→ applet; version=1.3" code=` `→ "HelloWorld.class" width="200"` `→ height="50" align="right"` `→ scriptable="false" pluginspage=` `→ "http://java.sun.com/products/` `→ plugin/1.3/plugin-install.html">`

   Setting the align attribute of the embed tag to right puts it into place for all Java-enabled browsers.

   continued

POSITIONING JAVA APPLETS ON THE PAGE

To put padding around a Java applet:

1. `<object classid="clsid:8AD9C840-044E-` → `11D1-B3E9-00805F499D93" width="200"` → `height="50" vspace="100" hspace=` → `"100" codetype="application/java">`

   In **Figure 3.8**, the HelloWorld applet is surrounded by 100 pixels of white space on all sides, due to the settings of the hspace and vspace attributes.

2. `<embed type="application/x-java-` → `applet;version=1.3" code=` → `"HelloWorld.class" width="200"` → `height="50" vspace="100" hspace=` → `"100" scriptable="false"` → `pluginspage="http://java.sun.com/` → `products/plugin/1.3/plugin-` → `install.html">`

   Once again, the hspace and vspace attributes are set in the EMBED tag.

✔ Tip

■ Other valid values for align are described in **Table 3.5**.

Figure 3.7 Here the applet is aligned on the right-hand side of the window.

Figure 3.8 The applet now has a 100-pixel-wide border on every side.

Table 3.5

Alignment Values	
ALIGNMENT	DESCRIPTION
left	Aligns the applet area flush left.
right	Aligns the applet area flush right.
top	Displays the applet area at the top of the available area.
texttop	Aligns the applet area with the highest text displayed adjacent to the applet area.
middle	Aligns the middle of the applet area with the baseline of adjacent text.
absmiddle	Aligns the middle of the applet area with the middle of the largest adjacent item.
baseline	Aligns the bottom of the applet area with the baseline of adjacent text.
bottom	Aligns the bottom of the applet area with the bottom of adjacent text.
absbottom	Aligns the bottom of the applet area with the bottom of largest adjacent item.

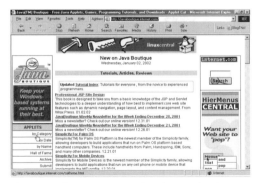

Figure 3.9 The Java Boutique has thousands of different Java applets.

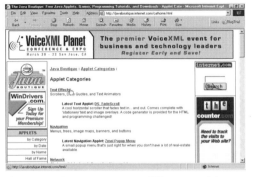

Figure 3.10 There are over 1000 different special-effects applets...

Figure 3.11 ...including hundreds of different text effects.

Finding Applets on the Web

There are a number of resources on the Web that can provide you with free or inexpensive applets. Before you go to the trouble of writing your own applet, it doesn't hurt to see if someone has already invented that particular wheel.

In this case, we're going to look for a news scroller applet, similar to the ones used by many news sites. We'll start at the Java Boutique home page at http://javaboutique.
→ internet.com (**Figure 3.9**).

To get an applet off the Web:

1. At the Java Boutique home page, click the link for Applets by Category, on the left. **Figure 3.10** shows a number of different categories.

2. Click "Text Effects," which is at the top. The "Text Effects" area has a large variety of effects, as shown in **Figure 3.11.**

continued

3. Click Vertical Scrollers. There are lots of applets here, so we look for one that's small, free, and includes the source code. Of the applets on the list (as shown in **Figure 3.12**) one that meets the criteria is tinyScroller.

4. Click tinyScroller to go to the description and download page, as shown in **Figure 3.13.** Here we find the two things we need: the class file and documentation of how the applet works.

✔ Tips

■ There are numerous other places on the Web where you can find applets, some of which are listed in Appendix A.

■ If you want the most current version of tinyScroller, or you want to see other applets by the same author (Chris Ricci), you can visit the One Wolf WebArt Java collection at http://www.chiamonkey.
→ com/scoobysnacks.

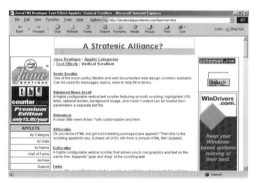

Figure 3.12 There are dozens of different applets just for scrolling text.

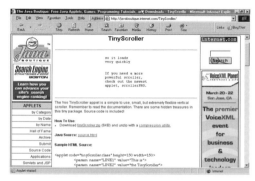

Figure 3.13 This is the Java Boutique's page for the tinyScroller applet.

Listing 3.7 This example shows how to refer to an applet with multiple parameters.

```
                      Listing
<html>
<head>
 <title>Tiny Scroller</title>
</head>
<body bgcolor="white">
<object classid="clsid:8AD9C840-044E-11D1-
→ B3E9-00805F499D93" width="200" height="150"
→ codetype="application/java">
 <param name="code" value="tinyScroller.
 → class">
 <param name="type" value="application/x-java-
 → applet;version=1.3">
 <param name="scriptable" value="false">
 <param name="line1" value="In today's top
 → story:">
 <param name="line2" value=" Java 2: Visual
 → QuickStart Guide">
 <param name="line3" value=" breaks all
 → previous sales">
 <param name="line4" value=" records, as rumor
 → spreads">
 <param name="line5" value=" that book contains">
 <param name="line6" value=" hard-hitting
 → information,">
 <param name="line7" value=" sparkling prose,">
 <param name="line8" value=" live nude girls,">
 <param name="line9" value=" and free beer">
 <param name="bgred" value="255">
 <param name="bggreen" value="255">
 <param name="bgblue" value="255">
 <param name="fgred" value="0">
 <param name="fggreen" value="0">
 <param name="fgblue" value="0">
 <param name="maxline" value="9">
 <embed type="application/x-java-applet;
 → version=1.3" code="tinyScroller.class"
 → width="200" height="150" line1="In today\'s
 → top story:" line2=" Java 2: Visual QuickStart
 → Guide" line3=" breaks all previous sales"
 → line4=" records, as rumor spreads" line5="
 → that book contains" line6=" hard-hitting
 → information," line7=" sparkling prose,"
 → line8=" live nude girls," line9=" and free
 → beer" bgred="255" bggreen="255" bgblue=
 → "255" fgred="0" fggreen="0" fgblue="0"
 → maxline="9" scriptable="false" pluginspage=
 → "http://java.sun.com/products/plugin/1.3/
 → plugin-install.html">
  <h1>You should use a Java-enabled
  → browser!</h1>
 </embed>
</object>
</body>
</html>
```

Passing Parameters to an Applet

In order to use a canned applet, you need a way to pass parameters from HTML to Java. In other words, someone who knows only HTML should be able to get the applet to display something different by making changes to the page in HTML. This is accomplished by means of the param tag used as shown in **Listing 3.7**.

A well-documented applet will include a list of all the possible parameters, showing all the possible values including default values. The documentation for the tinyScroller applet (as downloaded in the previous section) is shown in the sidebar.

If a canned applet doesn't accept parameters, you can still use it on your page, but it means that what you're displaying isn't personalized in any way—anyone else with the same applet will have identical results. Here, we pass parameters to the tinyScroller applet to display a unique page.

To pass parameters to an applet:

1. `<param name="line1" value="In today's`
   `→ top story:">`
   `<param name="line2" value=" Java 2:`
   `→ Visual QuickStart Guide">`

   A param tag consists of two attributes, name and value, both of which are required. For each name, there must be an associated value. For this use of the tinyScroller applet, we'll set line1 through line9 to get the results that we see scrolled in **Figures 3.14** and **3.15**.

   continued

2. `<param name="bgred" value="255">`
`<param name="bggreen" value="255">`
`<param name="bgblue" value="255">`
`<param name="fgred" value="0">`
`<param name="fggreen" value="0">`
`<param name="fgblue" value="0">`

Here we set the background color to white (red, green, and blue all set to 255) and the foreground color to black (red, green, and blue all set to 0). These are the defaults, so the Web page display would be the same even if these values were missing.

3. `<param name="maxline" value="9">`

If there are fewer than 12 lines to scroll, `maxline` needs to be set to the correct number, which in this case is 9.

4. `<embed type="application/x-java-`
  → `applet;version=1.3" code=`
  → `"tinyScroller.class" width="200"`
  → `height="150" line1="In today\'s`
  → `top story:" line2=" Java 2: Visual`
  → `QuickStart Guide" line3=" breaks`
  → `all previous sales" line4="`
  → `records, as rumor spreads" line5="`
  → `that book contains" line6=" hard-`
  → `hitting information," line7="`
  → `sparkling prose," line8=" live nude`
  → `girls," line9=" and free beer"`
  → `bgred="255" bggreen="255" bgblue=`
  → `"255" fgred="0" fggreen="0" fgblue=`
  → `"0" maxline="9" scriptable="false"`
  → `pluginspage="http://java.sun.com/`
  → `products/plugin/1.3/plugin-`
  → `install.html">`

Instead of using separate `param` tags, the `embed` tag passes all the information the applet needs as attributes.

✔ Tip

- In the above example, some parameters were not set, as the defaults were acceptable. The background and foreground colors could have been left off as well, as they're just using the defaults.

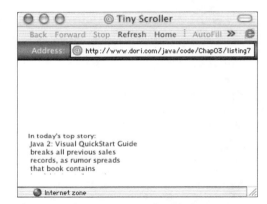

Figure 3.14 The text comes up from the bottom…

Figure 3.15 and scrolls off at the top.

The tinyScroller Applet

The documentation for the `tinyScroller` applet reads:

Title: tinyScroller
Author: Christian Ricci, One Wolf WebArt
Email: chris@onewolf.com

Notice: This applet and the rest of the tinyApplet series are free for both commercial and personal use. You may not, however, redistribute this applet or its associated material as part of a CD or book without the express written permission of the author.

Parameters

`line1–line100` (Some Required): `line1` through `line100` make up the content to be displayed. If you're not using all 100 lines you don't have to define them all but the applet will stop reading lines at the first NULL line it encounters.

`bgred`, `bggreen`, `bgblue` (Optional): You may set the background color of the applet by passing the one byte (0–255) RGB (Red, Green and Blue) component values. The background color defaults to white.

`fgred`, `fggreen`, `fgblue` (Optional): You may set the foreground (font) color for the applet by passing the one byte (0–255) RGB (Red, Green and Blue) component values. The foreground color defaults to white.

`fontname` and `fontsize` (Optional): You may force the font type and size by passing these values. If you pass one, you'll need to pass both.

`spacing` (Optional): You may define the line spacing by passing it as a parameter. Spacing defaults to twelve.

`delay` (Optional): `Delay` controls the time interval between shifts in the line positions. Delay defaults to 100 milliseconds.

`xpos` (Optional): `xpos` stands for X position. It controls the horizontal position of the lines within the applet. `xpos` defaults to five.

`direction` (Optional): `direction` allows you to specify whether you want the applet to scroll up (`direction=0`) or to scroll down (`direction=1`). `direction` defaults to zero.

`background` (Optional): If you wish to use a graphic for the background of the applet, pass the filename here. You may pass a JPG or GIF.

Displaying a graphic does, however, impact the speed of the screen update. As a result, you may notice a flicker. Also, bear in mind that the graphic will move with the text. I don't wrap the graphic so it should be large enough (larger than the applet) to display continuously.

`fixedbg` (Optional): If you're utilizing a background graphic but you don't want it to scroll with the text, pass a Y with this parameter.

This is useful when you're trying to incorporate the applet into a page with a textured background or when you're framing the applet inside a border.

PASSING PARAMETERS TO AN APPLET

YOUR FIRST APPLETS

By now you may be saying, "Hey, when do we get to start writing our own applets, already? This is supposed to be a book on writing Java, not just how to use existing programs!"

In this chapter, we'll start getting into the code—we'll start off slow, then add pieces one at a time.

"Hello, world!"

It's a tradition that the first program you write in a language always prints out the phrase "Hello, world!" I don't know why, but it's required. In **Applet 4.1**, you see how it's done; **Listing 4.1** shows the HTML file; and **Figure 4.1** shows your message to the world in a Web browser.

To write your first applet:

1. `public class HelloWorld extends`
   `→ java.applet.Applet`

   This starts off your applet. What you're writing is a new class, one that extends the standard `Applet` class. The name of this new class is `HelloWorld`.

   `Public`, here and everywhere else, means that we're not worried about who's accessing this applet.

2. `{`

   The left curly brace is used to show that the statements that follow are within the class we've just started.

3. `public void paint(java.awt.Graphics g)`

   `Paint()` is a method of `HelloWorld`. We want to display something on the screen, so we're going to have `paint()` do the work for us.

   The `paint()` method is declared `void`, because it doesn't return anything. Later we'll see methods that return a value.

   `Paint()` is passed a `Graphics` object—that's the value inside the parentheses, which is then available to be used inside this method. Within `paint()`, we want to give that object a shorter name than `java.awt.Graphics`, so we'll call it `g`. Putting a space in between these values means that they aren't two different parameters being passed; instead, it's a single parameter (the first value) that's called inside the method by the name passed as the second value.

Listing 4.1 This HTML file calls the `HelloWorld.class` file.

```
<html>
<head>
 <title>My First Applet</title>
</head>
<body bgcolor="white">
<object classid="clsid:8AD9C840-044E-11D1-
→ B3E9-00805F499D93" width="400" height="50"
→ codetype="application/java">
<param name="code" value="HelloWorld.class">
<param name="type" value="application/x-java-
→ applet;version=1.3">
<param name="scriptable" value="false">
<embed type="application/x-java-applet;
→ version=1.3" code="HelloWorld.class" width=
→ "400" height="50" scriptable="false"
→ pluginspage="http://java.sun.com/products/
→ plugin/1.3/plugin-install.html">
</embed>
</object>
</body>
</html>
```

Applet 4.1 This applet displays the (in)famous "Hello, world" message that tradition requires all new programmers to write.

```
public class HelloWorld extends
→ java.applet.Applet {

  public void paint(java.awt.Graphics g) {
    g.drawString("Hello, world!", 100, 25);
  }
}
```

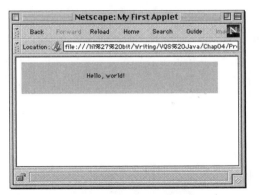

Figure 4.1 Congratulations, you've passed your initiation and written your first Java applet!

4. {

The left curly brace shows that any following statements are a part of this method.

5. g.drawString("Hello, world!", 100 , → 25);

Now, we use g (that graphics object we named in the previous step) to draw a string in the browser window. We're going to draw it at 100 pixels over and 25 pixels down, and the text we're drawing (i.e., printing) is "Hello, world!"

6. }

The right curly brace signifies the end of the paint method.

7. }

This finishes off the HelloWorld class.

✔ Tip

■ If you're used to JavaScript, you might be wondering whether the semicolon at the end of step 5 is necessary. This is another of the many differences between Java and JavaScript—in JavaScript, they're optional, but in Java, they're required.

"HELLO, WORLD!"

Using Fonts

Being able to write out "Hello, World" is pretty cool, as a first step, but it's pretty blah to look at. **Applet 4.2** shows the same applet, but this time with the phrase written in 36-point bold Times Roman (as shown in **Figure 4.2**).

To specify fonts in an applet:

1. `import java.awt.Graphics;`
`import java.awt.Font;`

Rather than always refer to `java.awt.Graphics` by its full name (which is rather long, isn't it?), we can tell Java to just `import` the entire class. Once that's done, a simple reference to `Graphics` is sufficient. In these two lines, both `Graphics` and `Font` are imported.

2. `Font f = new Font("TimesRoman",`
`→ Font.BOLD,36);`

This line creates a new font object named f, and sets it to be initialized to 36-point bold Times Roman.

3. `g.setFont(f);`

Within the `paint` method, we set the graphic object g to use the value of the font object f we set in the previous step.

✔ Tip

■ Java fonts aren't what you'd expect to find on your system, as Java has its own fonts, which have only some relationship to the ones that you're used to using on your computer. In Java, you can expect to find Courier, Dialog, Helvetica, TimesRoman, and Symbol. **Table 4.1** shows how each of these will display on your system. If you're using Java 2, you should use `monospaced` instead of Courier, `sanserif` instead of Helvetica, and `serif` instead of TimesRoman.

Applet 4.2 Now, we say it big and bold.

```
import java.awt.Graphics;
import java.awt.Font;

    public class HelloWorld extends java.applet.
    → Applet {

    Font f = new Font("TimesRoman",Font.BOLD,36);

    public void paint(Graphics g) {
    g.setFont(f);
    g.drawString("Hello, world!", 100 , 25);
    }

}
```

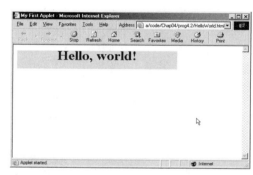

Figure 4.2 That's a little more friendly!

Table 4.1

Java Font Mapping		
JAVA FONTS	MAC FONTS	WINDOWS FONTS
Courier	Courier	Courier New
Dialog	Geneva	MS Sans Serif
Helvetica	Helvetica	Arial
Symbol	Symbol	WingDings
TimesRoman	Times Roman	Times New Roman

Applet 4.3 Use the init method to set the applet's background.

```
import java.awt.*;

public class HelloWorld extends java.applet.
→ Applet {

 Font f = new Font("TimesRoman",Font.BOLD,36);

   public void init() {
   setBackground(Color.white);
 }

   public void paint(Graphics g) {
     g.setFont(f);
     g.drawString("Hello, world!", 100 , 25);
   }

}
```

Figure 4.3 Now we look less like newbie applet writers.

Setting the Background Color

Even though we now have our text just the way we want it, it's still being displayed on whatever background color the user has set as their default. It might be white, it might be gray—it could even be magenta or puce. There's a way to change that, too, to make the applet blend in with the rest of the HTML page. **Figure 4.3** shows the much more pleasant appearance of **Applet 4.3**.

To change the background color:

1. `public void init() {`

   This is a new method, `init()`. Use this method for things that you want to set the first time and never again.

2. `setBackground(Color.white);`

   The `setBackground` command sets the background for the applet on the HTML page. In this case, we're setting the background color to white.

3. `}`

   The right curly bracket ends the `init()` method.

✔ Tips

- The colors that can be used by name (such as white, above) are black, blue, cyan, darkGray, gray, green, lightGray, magenta, orange, pink, red, white, and yellow.

- Other colors can be used by calculating the RGB values of the color. In this case, you would say `setBackground(new` → `Color(42,42,42))`.

- We've changed the beginning import value again, this time to `java.awt.*`. This says that, instead of importing just one or two parts of `java.awt`, we'll just import everything at once.

Passing Parameters from HTML to Java

In Chapter 3, we saw how to pass information from HTML to Java. **Applet 4.4** shows how you can write an applet so that it reads information from the HTML file. **Figure 4.4** shows the results of this applet when run with the HTML file shown in **Listing 4.2**.

To read parameters from HTML:

1. `String whatToSay;`

This line declares a new `string` variable, `whatToSay`. This will contain the text that you want to print in the browser window.

2. `this.whatToSay = getParameter`
   `→ ("whatToSay");`

The HTML file contains a `param` tag within the `object` tag. This `param` tag has two attributes: `name` and `value`, where the former is set to "whatToSay" and the latter to "Hello, readers!" In addition, the `embed` tag has an attribute, `whatToSay`,

Listing 4.2 We use HTML to pass the phrase "Hello, readers!" to our Java applet.

```
<html>
<head>
 <title>My First Applet</title>
</head>
<body bgcolor="white">
<object classid="clsid:8AD9C840-044E-11D1-
→ B3E9-00805F499D93" width="400" height="50"
→ codetype="application/java">
 <param name="code" value="HelloWorld.class">
 <param name="type" value="application/x-java-
 → applet;version=1.3">
 <param name="scriptable" value="false">
 <param name="whatToSay" value="Hello,
 → readers!">
 <embed type="application/x-java-applet;
 → version=1.3" code="HelloWorld.class"
 → width="400" height="50" whatToSay="Hello,
 → readers!" scriptable="false" pluginspage=
 → "http://java.sun.com/products/plugin/1.3/
 → plugin-install.html">
 </embed>
</object>
</body>
</html>
```

The Seven Common Methods

There are seven methods that are commonly used in applets. This is referred to as "overriding," because they already exist for applets—if you use them, you're overriding the default. If you use one of these methods, that method is said to be "overridden." The seven are:

`init()`: Use this when you want something to happen when the applet is initialized.

`start()`: This is called when the applet becomes visible, after `init` has completed or when the user (after having gone somewhere else) returns to the Web page containing the applet.

`stop()`: Called when the applet is no longer displayed, such as when the page is closed, or hidden.

`destroy()`: The last step before an applet is closed; this is the cleaning-up step.

The previous four are all part of `java.applet.Applet`. The next three are part of `java.awt.Component`.

`paint()`: Displays the applet.

`repaint()`: Tells Java to call update as soon as possible.

`update()`: Redraws the applet by calling `paint`.

Applet 4.4 We grab the passed parameter from HTML in the init method.

```
                      Applet
import java.awt.*;

public class HelloWorld extendsjava.applet.
→ Applet {
 Font f = new Font("TimesRoman",Font.BOLD,36);
 String whatToSay;

 public void init() {
  setBackground(Color.white);
  this.whatToSay = getParameter("whatToSay");
  if (this.whatToSay == null) {
   this.whatToSay = "Hello, world!";
  }
 }

 public void paint(Graphics g) {
  g.setFont(f);
  g.drawString(this.whatToSay, 100 , 25);
 }

}
```

Figure 4.4 And then, the applet shows the result.

which is set to "Hello, readers!" In the applet, getParameter() reads whichever tag the browser understands, looking for the value of whatever's been passed as a parameter. In this case, the name of the parameter is whatToSay, and so the value of the string is set to "Hello, readers!"

3. `if (this.whatToSay == null) {`

Just in case we didn't find a valid parameter, we should set the string value to something. To check its status, we compare it to null. If they're equal, we need to give it a value.

4. `this.whatToSay = "Hello, world!";`

How about the traditional "Hello, world!" just to let us know that we didn't pass in something more edifying?

5. `}`

The right curly brace closes off the if statement.

✔ Tip

- Where did that this come from, and what does it mean? The variable whatToSay has been defined as part of the class. When the method inside that same class refers to whatToSay, the method needs to know that it's a local variable. The Java keyword this is used to make that clear. You can think of this as meaning, "Which whatToSay are we referring to here? Oh, the one that's part of this class; this one." Whenever this is used, it means we're referring to a variable that the method should know about from within the class.

Adding Comments

All good programmers add comments to their programs. The sooner you get into the habit, the easier you'll find learning Java, especially when you need to refer back to your code later. **Applet 4.5** shows the same applet as in the previous example, with the addition of two comments.

To add comments:

1. /*

This is my first applet

*/

There are two kinds of comments in Java, single-line and multi-line. This is a multi-line comment. It starts with the /* (slash and asterisk) characters, and Java ignores everything up until it finds a following */ (asterisk then slash). It's an excellent idea to get in the habit of always starting your program with a comment that states what the code does (or at least, what you're expecting it to do).

2. // whatToSay is passed from HTML

This is a single-line comment. It can be anywhere in a line, either at the beginning of the line or following some code. In either case, everything to the right of the two slashes is a comment. The comment area ends at the line break.

Applet 4.5 Always comment your code—you'll be happy you did later!

```
/*
  This is my first applet
*/
import java.awt.*;

public class HelloWorld extends java.applet.
→ Applet {
  Font f = new Font("TimesRoman",Font.BOLD,36);
  String whatToSay;

  public void init() {
    setBackground(Color.white);
    this.whatToSay = getParameter("whatToSay");
    → // whatToSay is passed from HTML
    if (this.whatToSay == null) {
      this.whatToSay = "Hello, world!";
    }
  }

  public void paint(Graphics g) {
    g.setFont(f);
    g.drawString(this.whatToSay, 100 , 25);
  }
}
```

Applet 4.6 An example of using other font styles.

```
/*
 This is my first applet
 Here we show how to change the font style
*/
import java.applet.*;
import java.awt.*;

public class HelloWorld extends Applet {
 Font f = new Font("TimesRoman",Font.ITALIC,36);

 public void init() {
  setBackground(Color.white);
 }

 public void paint(Graphics g) {
  g.setFont(f);
  g.drawString("Now in Italics", 100 , 25);
 }

}
```

Figure 4.5 And here's what it looks like in your browser.

Changing the Font Style

Bold text is OK, but you don't want it all the time. **Applet 4.6** changes the font style, as shown in **Figure 4.5**.

To change font styles:

◆ Font f = new Font("TimesRoman",
→ Font.ITALIC,36);

Instead of Font.BOLD, use Font.ITALIC to display the text in 36-point Times Roman italic.

✔ Tip

■ The font styles understood by Java are Font.PLAIN, Font.BOLD, and Font.ITALIC. Each of these styles is really just stored internally as a number. So when you want a string to be both bold and italic, simply add the two together: Font.BOLD + Font.ITALIC.

Changing Colors

Along with font faces, sizes, and styles, Java gives you control over colors. **Figure 4.6** shows the result of **Applet 4.7**, which changes the font color to red.

To change colors:

◆ g.setColor(Color.red);

Just before we call g.drawString() to display the message, we call g.setColor() to change the color of the graphics object g. In this case, we set the color of the message to red.

✔ Tip

■ The colors available here are the same colors listed in *Setting the Background Color*, earlier in this chapter.

Applet 4.7 You can use Java to display colored text.

```
/*
 This is my first applet
 Here we show how to change the font color
*/
import java.applet.*;
import java.awt.*;

public class HelloWorld extends Applet {
  Font f = new Font("TimesRoman",Font.BOLD,36);

  public void init() {
    setBackground(Color.white);
  }

  public void paint(Graphics g) {
    g.setFont(f);
    g.setColor(Color.red);
    g.drawString("Wow-Red!", 100 , 25);
  }

}
```

Figure 4.6 Here's an example of bright red text.

STRINGS AND THINGS

In Chapter 4, we used some variables without really understanding what they were. Here, we'll cover the concept in greater depth.

Java and other programming languages use variables to store information so you can refer to that information again later in your program. For example, we can set the variable myName to "Dori". In Java, this is written as myName = "Dori". The equal sign means "is set to." Afterwards, the variable myName can be used any time we need the value "Dori".

If someone else uses this applet later, they can set myName to "Sean" simply by replacing the previous statement with myName = "Sean" in the applet. Anywhere the code later references the myName variable, it will automatically see the name "Sean" instead of the name "Dori" from then on, keeping you from having to change each reference individually.

String Variables

One of the basic types of variable you'll need is the string variable. A *string* is any piece of text between two quote symbols. **Listing 5.1** and **Applet 5.1** show our first example of a string variable.

To declare and use a string variable:

1. String stringVarWithValue = "Hey, I'm
→ a string!";

This line creates a new string variable, called stringVarWithValue. At the same time we create it, we give it a value of "Hey, I'm a string!"

2. g.drawString(this.stringVarWithValue,
→ 50 , 150);

This line draws the string this.string VarWithValue at the position 50 pixels over and 150 pixels down as shown in **Figure 5.1**.

Listing 5.1 This HTML file calls Applet 5.1.

```
Listing
<html>
<head>
 <title>Listing 5.1</title>
</head>
<body bgcolor="white">
<object classid="clsid:8AD9C840-044E-11D1-
→ B3E9-00805F499D93" width="400" height="500"
→ codetype="application/java">
 <param name="code" value="Applet1.class">
 <param name="type" value="application/x-java-
 → applet;version=1.3">
 <param name="scriptable" value="false">
 <embed type="application/x-java-applet;
 → version=1.3" code="Applet1.class"
 → width="400" height="500" scriptable="false"
 → pluginspage="http://java.sun.com/products/
 → plugin/1.3/plugin-install.html">
 </embed>
</object>
</body>
</html>
```

Applet 5.1 Declaring, initializing, and using a string.

```
Applet
import java.awt.*;
import java.applet.Applet;

public class Applet1 extends Applet{
 String stringVarWithValue = "Hey, I'm a
 → string!";
 Font f = new Font("TimesRoman",Font.BOLD,36);

 public void init() {
   setBackground(Color.white);
 }

 public void paint(Graphics g) {
   g.setFont(f);
   g.drawString(this.stringVarWithValue, 50 ,
   → 150);
 }

}
```

STRING VARIABLES

Figure 5.1 There's our string, big as life!

✔ Tips

- Note that when we want to display something in the applet area, we put the code in the paint() method.

- A variable can be named almost anything, with just a few limitations. The name must start with a letter, dollar sign ($), or underscore (_), and after that may contain any number or letter. This means, for example, that variable names cannot contain spaces or dashes.

STRING VARIABLES

More about Strings

You don't always have to initialize (give
a value to) a string when you declare it.
Sometimes, you know that you'll need it
later, but you don't yet know what value it
will have. **Listing 5.2** and **Applet 5.2** show
an example of a string that's declared as part
of the class, but not initialized until we use
the paint() method.

To declare a string variable without initialization:

1. String stringVar;

This line creates a new string variable,
which we'll call stringVar.

2. this.stringVar = "Now I have a
→ value.";

Now, down in the paint() method, we've
finally decided what value we want this
string to have.

Listing 5.2 This HTML file calls Applet 5.2.

```
<html>
<head>
 <title>Listing 5.2</title>
</head>
<body bgcolor="white">
<object classid="clsid:8AD9C840-044E-11D1-
→ B3E9-00805F499D93" width="400" height="500"
→ codetype="application/java">
 <param name="code" value="Applet2.class">
 <param name="type" value="application/x-java-
→ applet;version=1.3">
 <param name="scriptable" value="false">
 <embed type="application/x-java-applet;
→ version=1.3" code="Applet2.class" width=
→ "400" height="500" scriptable="false"
→ pluginspage="http://java.sun.com/
→ products/plugin/1.3/plugin-install.html">
 </embed>
</object>
</body>
</html>
```

Applet 5.2 We add a little complexity by declaring the
variable and setting it in two different places.

```
import java.awt.*;
import java.applet.Applet;

public class Applet2 extends Applet{
 String stringVar;
 String stringVarWithValue = "Hey, I'm a
→ string!";
 Font f = new Font("TimesRoman",Font.BOLD,36);

 public void init() {
   setBackground(Color.white);
 }

 public void paint(Graphics g) {
   this.stringVar = "Now I have a value.";

   g.setFont(f);
   g.drawString(this.stringVar, 50 , 50);
   g.drawString(this.stringVarWithValue, 50 ,
→ 100);
 }

}
```

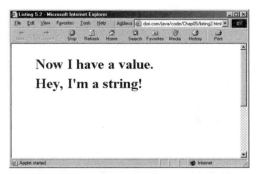

Figure 5.2 But when they're both displayed on the screen, both string variables appear the same.

3. `g.drawString(this.stringVar, 50 , 50);`

Now that `stringVar` has been both declared and initialized, there's no difference between it and our other string variable, as shown in **Figure 5.2**.

✔ Tip

- If you declare a variable without setting it, it will be equal to null (nothing) until you do set it. Null is not the same as `""`; that's an empty string, but it does have a value. Null means that no value has been set for this variable at all. To check to see if `stringVar` hasn't been set, your code should, if necessary, check `if (stringVar == null)`.

Variable Scope

No, this doesn't mean that we have variables that need to use mouthwash, although errors with variable scope have been known to make programmers get their mouths washed out with soap.

In this example, as shown in **Listing 5.3** and **Applet 5.3**, a variable with the same name can be declared both at the class level and at the method level. You and your code can then become very confused as to which variable you mean.

To demonstrate scope:

1. `String stringVar = "";`

This line declares the variable for the `Applet3` class.

2. `String stringVar = "I'm a local`
`→ variable";`

This line, within the `paint()` method, creates and initializes an entirely new variable with no relation to the other, even though they have the same name.

3. `g.drawString(stringVar, 50 , 50);`

This line displays the local variable, which has a value, as shown in **Figure 5.3**.

4. `g.drawString(this.stringVar, 50 , 100);`

Because of the `this.` before the `stringVar`, this variable gets its value from outside the method. Because this particular variable hasn't been set, nothing prints on this line.

Listing 5.3 This HTML file calls Applet 5.3.

```
Listing
<html>
<head>
 <title>Listing 5.3</title>
</head>
<body bgcolor="white">
<object classid="clsid:8AD9C840-044E-11D1-
→ B3E9-00805F499D93" width="400" height="500"
→ codetype="application/java">
 <param name="code" value="Applet3.class">
 <param name="type" value="application/x-java-
→ applet;version=1.3">
 <param name="scriptable" value="false">
 <embed type="application/x-javaapplet;version=
→ 1.3" code="Applet3.class" width="400" height=
→ "500" scriptable="false" pluginspage=
→ "http://java.sun.com/products/plugin/1.3/
→ plugin-install.html">
 </embed>
</object>
</body>
</html>
```

Applet 5.3 This applet demonstrates a type of problem that can cause you hours of frustration: variable scope.

```
Applet
import java.awt.*;
import java.applet.Applet;

public class Applet3 extends Applet{
 String stringVar ="";
 String stringVarWithValue = "Hey, I'm
→ a string!";
 Font f = new Font("TimesRoman",Font.BOLD,36);

 public void init() {
  setBackground(Color.white);
 }

 public void paint(Graphics g) {
  String stringVar = "I'm a local variable";

  g.setFont(f);
  g.drawString(stringVar, 50 , 50);
  g.drawString(this.stringVar, 50 , 100);
  g.drawString(this.stringVarWithValue, 50 ,
→ 150);
 }

}
```

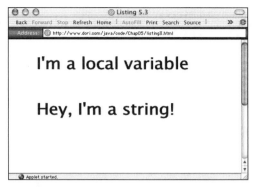

Figure 5.3 Which stringVar variable has which value?

✔ Tips

- In this example, the "this." in the last g.drawstring() call isn't required. Java would still be able to find the correct variable to display without it. However, including it lets you keep better track of what you're doing, so examples in this book will always use this style.

- The best way to avoid problems with scope is to be very careful with variable names. A simple mistake here can lead to hours of debugging headaches.

What is Scope?

In most of the world, when you talk about "Broadway," people know that you're referring to a street in New York City. While the street itself is in New York, people globally understand your reference. You can think of Broadway as a global.

However, if you're in San Diego, California, and you refer to "Broadway," people will think that you're referring to a major street in their downtown area. This is a local value. In San Diego, not being clear about whether you're referring to the locally known "Broadway" or the globally known "Broadway" can lead to confusion.

If you're in San Diego, the default is the local version, and you have to explicitly state "New York City's Broadway" in order to refer to the other. Outside of San Diego, people will think of New York's Broadway first, unless they have some other local version of Broadway.

The "scope" of each of these streets is where each is the default, that is, the one that will be automatically thought of if no other identifying information is given. The scope of San Diego's Broadway is local—inside the city and a few outlying suburbs. The scope of New York's Broadway is global, that is, people anywhere in the world will know to where you're referring.

With software, the easiest way to avoid questions about a variable's scope is to avoid using two variables with the same name in two different places doing two different things. If you must go down this slippery slope, be clear about your variable's scope!

String Methods

A variety of string methods (that is, methods that apply to strings) are built into Java. **Listing 5.4** and **Applet 5.4** show what a few of them can do.

To use string methods:

1. `g.drawString("The string is:`
   `→ \""+this.stringVar+"\"", 50 , 75);`

   If we want to display quotes in Java, they must be **escaped**. That is, if the code just is `"""`, Java won't understand that we want to display the center quote. Putting the backslash in front of a character tells Java to just pass it right on through; don't interpret it. We can't just say The string is: " " and expect Java to know that the second quote is something we want to print, but the first and third are the beginning and end of a string. So, we *escape* the quote character—we tell Java to pretend that it doesn't see the next character—by putting a "\" (backslash) before it.

Listing 5.4 This HTML file calls Applet 5.4.

```
<html>
<head>
 <title>Listing 5.4</title>
</head>
<body bgcolor="white">
<object classid="clsid:8AD9C840-044E-11D1-
→ B3E9-00805F499D93" width="400" height="500"
→ codetype="application/java">
 <param name="code" value="Applet4.class">
 <param name="type" value="application/x-java-
 → applet;version=1.3">
 <param name="scriptable" value="false">
 <embed type="application/x-javaapplet;
 → version=1.3" code="Applet4.class" width="400"
 → height="500" scriptable="false" pluginspage=
 → "http://java.sun.com/products/plugin/1.3/
 → plugin-install.html">
 </embed>
</object>
</body>
</html>
```

Applet 5.4 This applet displays some of the most common string methods.

```
import java.awt.*;
import java.applet.Applet;

public class Applet4 extends Applet{
 String stringVar = "Hey, I'm a string!";
 Font f = new Font("TimesRoman",Font.BOLD,20);

 public void init() {
   setBackground(Color.white);
 }

 public void paint(Graphics g) {
   g.setFont(f);
   g.drawString("The string is: "+this.stringVar, 50 , 50);
   g.drawString("The string is: \""+this.stringVar+"\"", 50 , 75);
   g.drawString("The string's length is: "+this.stringVar.length(), 50 , 100);
   g.drawString("Lowercase: "+this.stringVar.toLowerCase(), 50 , 125);
   g.drawString("Uppercase: "+this.stringVar.toUpperCase(), 50 , 150);
 }

}
```

Figure 5.4 Here's the string, its length, and how it looks in all lowercase and all uppercase.

2. g.drawString("The string's length is:
→ "+this.stringVar.length(), 50 , 100);

Once we have declared a string in Java, we automatically inherit some methods. One of these is length(), which we can use to get the length of a string; in this case, the result is 18, as shown in **Figure 5.4**.

3. g.drawString("Lower case:
→ "+this.stringVar.toLowerCase(),
→ 50 , 125);

Another string method we've inherited is toLowerCase(), which does just what it sounds like it does: causes every character in the string, whether upper- or lower-case, to be displayed in lowercase letters.

4. g.drawString("Upper case:
→ "+this.stringVar.toUpperCase(),
→ 50 , 150);

And of course, if there's a toLowerCase(), there must be a toUpperCase(), which displays the string in all uppercase letters.

✔ Tip

- Using these methods does not change the value of the string! For example, the toLowerCase() method simply displays the string in all lowercase letters; it does not change the value of the string itself.

All Types of Numbers

Java has six different types of numeric variables. (Those readers who are familiar with JavaScript will find this a little odd, as JavaScript only has one numeric variable type.) **Listing 5.5** and **Applet 5.5** show the maximum value of each type.

To declare numeric variables:

1. byte myByte = Byte.MAX_VALUE;
short myShort = Short.MAX_VALUE;
int myInt = Integer.MAX_VALUE;
long myLong = Long.MAX_VALUE;
float myFloat = Float.MAX_VALUE;
double myDouble = Double.MAX_VALUE;

In this step, we declare one of each of the six types of numeric variable, and simultaneously initialize it to the maximum value for its type.

2. g.drawString("The maximum value of a
→ byte is: "+this.myByte, 10 , 20);
g.drawString("The maximum value of a
→ short is: "+this.myShort, 10 , 40);
g.drawString("The maximum value of an
→ integer is: "+this.myInt, 10 , 60);
g.drawString("The maximum value of a
→ long is: "+this.myLong, 10 , 80);
g.drawString("The maximum value of a
→ float is: "+this.myFloat, 10 , 100);
g.drawString("The maximum value of a
→ double is: "+this.myDouble, 10 , 120);

These lines display the maximum value for each of the numeric variable types, as shown in **Figure 5.5**. Which you use depends on what range of values you think that variable will need to hold.

The range of values for each numeric type is shown in **Table 5.1**. For the most part, you'll be using integers, with the occasional switch to float (also known as floating point) variables when decimal values are required.

Listing 5.5 This HTML file calls for Applet 5.5.

```
<html>
<head>
 <title>Listing 5.5</title>
</head>
<body bgcolor="white">
<object classid="clsid:8AD9C840-044E-11D1-
→ B3E9-00805F499D93" width="500" height="500"
→ codetype="application/java">
 <param name="code" value="Applet5.class">
 <param name="type" value="application/x-java-
→ applet;version=1.3">
 <param name="scriptable" value="false">
 <embed type="application/x-java-applet;
→ version=1.3" code="Applet5.class" width="500"
→ height="500" scriptable="false" pluginspage=
→ "http://java.sun.com/products/plugin/1.3/
→ plugin-install.html">
 </embed>
</object>
</body>
</html>
```

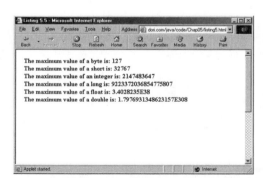

Figure 5.5 Bytes are small, doubles are huge, and here's everything in between.

Applet 5.5 This applet declares and initializes an example of each of the six numeric types, and also displays their largest values.

```
                               Applet
import java.awt.*;
import java.applet.Applet;

public class Applet5 extends Applet{
 byte myByte = Byte.MAX_VALUE;
 short myShort = Short.MAX_VALUE;
 int myInt = Integer.MAX_VALUE;
 long myLong = Long.MAX_VALUE;
 float myFloat = Float.MAX_VALUE;
 double myDouble = Double.MAX_VALUE;

 Font f = new Font("TimesRoman",Font.BOLD,16);

 public void init() {
   setBackground(Color.white);
 }

 public void paint(Graphics g) {
   g.setFont(f);
   g.drawString("The maximum value of a byte is: " + this.myByte, 10 , 20);
   g.drawString("The maximum value of a short is: " + this.myShort, 10 , 40);
   g.drawString("The maximum value of an integer is: " + this.myInt, 10 , 60);
   g.drawString("The maximum value of a long is: " + this.myLong, 10 , 80);
   g.drawString("The maximum value of a float is: " + this.myFloat, 10 , 100);
   g.drawString("The maximum value of a double is: " + this.myDouble, 10 , 120);
 }

}
```

ALL TYPES OF NUMBERS

✔ Tips

- No, your eyes aren't deceiving you. There is a difference between byte and Byte, between short and Short, and so on. The first of each pair (in all lowercase) is what Java refers to as a "primitive." Primitives, while they can be passed in and out of methods and assigned to variables, are not actually objects with methods of their own. In order to use the MAX_VALUE constant for each numeric object, we have to refer instead to the class associated with that primitive. **Table 5.1** shows which class is associated with each primitive.

- Up until now, everything we've seen has been part of Java 1.0. While the byte and short primitives are also part of Java 1.0, the Byte and Short classes were not added until Java 1.1.

- For a number to be displayed using g.drawString(), the number must be converted to a string. Handily enough, concatenating a number to a string (via the "+" operator) is enough to do the job.

Table 5.1

Range of Numeric Types

PRIMITIVE	CLASS	RANGE
byte	Byte	−128 to 127
short	Short	−32768 to 32767
int	Integer	−2147483648 to 2147483647
long	Long	−9223372036854775808 to 9223372036854775807
float	Float	−1.40239846E-45 to 3.4028235E38
double	Double	4.94065645841246544E-324 to 1.79769313486231E308

Listing 5.6. This HTML file calls Applet 5.6.

```
                    Listing
<html>
<head>
 <title>Listing 5.6</title>
</head>
<body bgcolor="white">
<object classid="clsid:8AD9C840-044E-11D1-
→ B3E9-00805F499D93" width="500" height="500"
→ codetype="application/java">
 <param name="code" value="Applet6.class">
 <param name="type" value="application/x-java-
→ applet;version=1.3">
 <param name="scriptable" value="false">
 <embed type="application/x-java-applet;
→ version=1.3" code="Applet6.class" width="500"
→ height="500" scriptable="false" pluginspage=
→ "http://java.sun.com/products/plugin/1.3/
→ plugin-install.html">
 </embed>
</object>
</body>
</html>
```

Applet 5.6 Here's how we go from numbers to strings
and back again.

```
                    Applet
import java.awt.*;
import java.applet.Applet;

public class Applet6 extends Applet{
 Integer myInt = new Integer(Integer.MAX_VALUE);
→ String myString;
 Font f = new Font("TimesRoman",Font.BOLD,16);

 public void init() {
   setBackground(Color.white);
 }

 public void paint(Graphics g) {
   g.setFont(f);
   g.drawString("The maximum value of an
→ integer is: "+this.myInt, 10 , 40);
   g.drawString("And it can be displayed as a
→ string like this: ", 10, 60);
   this.myString = this.myInt.toString();
   g.drawString(this.myString,10, 80);
   g.drawString("And converted back like
→ this: "+Integer.valueOf(this.myString),
→ 10, 100);
 }

}
```

Converting between Strings and Numbers

Often, you'll need to convert a number to a string (to display it using a string method, for instance), or a string to a number (to apply a math calculation, perhaps). Java makes this simple and straightforward, as shown in **Listing 5.6** and **Applet 5.6**.

To convert between strings and numbers:

1. `this.myString = this.myInt.toString();`

   Converting a number to a string is as simple as calling the `toString()` method. This does not change the number itself to a string, it just returns the numeric value in string form.

2. `g.drawString("And converted back like`
   `→ this:" + Integer.valueOf(this.`
   `→ myString), 10, 100);`

   The String class doesn't contain a method to turn itself into a number, so we have to use the Integer method `valueOf()`. This returns the integer value of the string if it contains a valid number, or an error otherwise. Once converted, the now-numeric String is displayed, as shown in **Figure 5.6**.

✔ Tip

■ Note the difference between the previous task and this example in the way we declare myInt. In the previous example, we were declaring myInt to be an instance of the primitive type int, and in this case, myInt is an instance of the class Integer. The value of the variable is the same, but making it an instance of the Integer class allows us to use that class's methods.

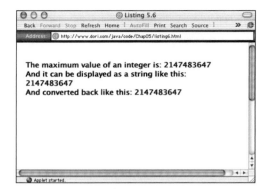

Figure 5.6 The largest integer value, converted to a string and then back to an integer.

Listing 5.7. This HTML file calls Applet 5.7.

```
┌─────────────── Listing ───────────────┐
<html>
<head>
 <title>Listing 5.7</title>
</head>
<body bgcolor="white">
<object classid="clsid:8AD9C840-044E-11D1-
→ B3E9-00805F499D93" width="500" height="500"
→ codetype="application/java">
<param name="code" value="Applet7.class">
<param name="type" value="application/x-java-
→ applet;version=1.3">
<param name="scriptable" value="false">
<embed type="application/x-java-applet;
→ version=1.3" code="Applet7.class" width="500"
→ height="500" scriptable="false" pluginspage=
→ "http://java.sun.com/products/plugin/1.3/
→ plugin-install.html">
</embed>
</object>
</body>
</html>
```

Converting between Types of Numbers

Given that Java has six different ways of storing numbers, you'll occasionally need to convert numbers from one form to another. **Listing 5.7** and **Applet 5.7** show you how to do this using the methods inherited from the Double object.

To convert numbers from one type to another:

1. Double myDouble = new Double(Math.PI);

This line declares a new object, myDouble, of type Double, and initializes it to the value of pi.

continued

Applet 5.7 Java provides straightforward ways of converting between types of numbers.

```
┌─────────────── Applet ───────────────┐
import java.awt.*;
import java.applet.Applet;

public class Applet7 extends Applet{
 Double myDouble = new Double(Math.PI);
 Byte myByte = new Byte(myDouble.byteValue());
 Short myShort = new Short(myDouble.shortValue());
 Integer myInt = new Integer(myDouble.intValue());
 Long myLong = new Long(myDouble.longValue());
 Float myFloat = new Float(myDouble.floatValue());

 Font f = new Font("TimesRoman",Font.BOLD,16);

 public void init() {
   setBackground(Color.white);
 }

 public void paint(Graphics g) {
   g.setFont(f);
   g.drawString("The value of pi as a byte is: " + this.myByte, 10 , 20);
   g.drawString("The value of pi as a short is: " + this.myShort, 10 , 40);
   g.drawString("The value of pi as an integer is: " + this.myInt, 10 , 60);
   g.drawString("The value of pi as a long is: " + this.myLong, 10 , 80);
   g.drawString("The value of pi as a float is: " + this.myFloat, 10 , 100);
   g.drawString("The value of pi as a double is: " + this.myDouble, 10 , 120);
 }

}
```

2.
```
Byte myByte = new Byte
    → (myDouble.byteValue());
Short myShort = new Short
    → (myDouble.shortValue());
Integer myInt = new Integer
    → (myDouble.intValue());
Long myLong = new Long
    → (myDouble.longValue());
Float myFloat = new Float
    → (myDouble.floatValue());
```

These five lines declare five numeric objects, one of each of the six types (when you include Double). Each is initialized to the value of myDouble, modified by the appropriate method for its type.

✔ Tip

■ Converting a number from float or double to any of the other types simply truncates the decimal portion of the number, as shown in **Figure 5.7**.

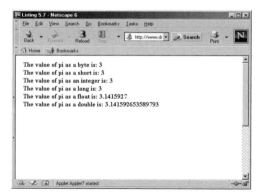

Figure 5.7 All of our pieces of pi.

Listing 5.8 This HTML file calls Applet 5.8.

```
                    Listing
<html>
<head>
 <title>Listing 5.8</title>
</head>
<body bgcolor="white">
<object classid="clsid:8AD9C840-044E-11D1-
→ B3E9-00805F499D93" width="500" height="500"
→ codetype="application/java">
 <param name="code" value="Applet8.class">
 <param name="type" value="application/x-java-
→ applet;version=1.3">
 <param name="scriptable" value="false">
 <embed type="application/x-java-applet;
→ version=1.3" code="Applet8.class" width="500"
→ height="500" scriptable="false" pluginspage=
→ "http://java.sun.com/products/plugin/1.3/
→ plugin-install.html">
 </embed>
</object>
</body>
</html>
```

Applet 5.8 Using casting to convert a number from one type to another.

```
                    Applet
import java.awt.*;
import java.applet.Applet;

public class Applet8 extends Applet{
  double myDouble = Math.PI;
  Font f = new Font("TimesRoman",Font.BOLD,16);

  public void init() {
    setBackground(Color.white);
  }

  public void paint(Graphics g) {
    g.setFont(f);
    g.drawString("The value of pi as a byte is:
→ "+(byte)this.myDouble, 10 , 20);
    g.drawString("The value of pi as a short
→ is: "+(short)this.myDouble, 10 , 40);
    g.drawString("The value of pi as an
→ integer is: "+(int)this.myDouble, 10 ,
→ 60);
    g.drawString("The value of pi as a long is:
→ "+(long)this.myDouble, 10 , 80);
    g.drawString("The value of pi as a float
→ is: " +(float)this.myDouble, 10 , 100);
    g.drawString("The value of pi as a double
→ is: "+this.myDouble, 10 , 120);
  }

}
```

Converting by Casting

Another technique for converting between variable types is called *casting*. This style of conversion enables you to get the value in a different format without actually creating a new object or converting the old object. **Listing 5.8** and **Applet 5.8** demonstrate casting.

To cast one type to another:

◆ g.drawString("The value of pi as a
→ byte is: "+(byte)this.myDouble, 10 ,
→ 20);
g.drawString("The value of pi as a
→ short is: "+(short)this.myDouble,
→ 10 , 40);
g.drawString("The value of pi as an
→ integer is: "+(int)this.myDouble,
→ 10 , 60);
g.drawString("The value of pi as a
→ long is: "+(long)this.myDouble,
→ 10 , 80);
g.drawString("The value of pi as a
→ float is: "+(float)this.myDouble,
→ 10 , 100);

This applet starts off much like the previous example (**Applet 5.7**) but only declares and initializes the double primitive myDouble.

continued

When it comes time to print the value of each, `this.myDouble` is printed each time, but cast to the type that we're looking for, as shown in **Figure 5.8**. To cast a variable as another type, you put the type desired within parentheses just before the value that you have. For instance, `(short)this.myDouble` returns a short.

✔ Tips

■ Java allows you to cast objects into other objects, but requires that they be related by inheritance—one must be either a subclass or a superclass of the other.

■ Note that in this example `myDouble` is declared as the primitive `double`, not the object `Double`. Also, the type that we're casting each object into is the primitive version, not the object version, of the type. This is required because Java will not allow you to cast primitive types to objects, or vice versa.

Figure 5.8 More pieces of pi.

CONVERTING BY CASTING

Listing 5.9 This HTML file calls Applet 5.9.

```
                        Listing
<html>
<head>
 <title>Listing 5.9</title>
</head>
<body bgcolor="white">
<object classid="clsid:8AD9C840-044E-11D1-
→ B3E9-00805F499D93" width="500" height="500"
→ codetype="application/java">
 <param name="code" value="Applet9.class">
 <param name="type" value="application/x-java-
→ applet;version=1.3">
 <param name="scriptable" value="false">
 <embed type="application/x-java-applet;
→ version=1.3" code="Applet9.class" → width=
→ "500" height="500" scriptable="false"
→ pluginspage="http://java.sun.com/products/
→ plugin/1.3/plugin-install.html">
 </embed>
</object>
</body>
</html>
```

Arrays of Objects

Often, you'll want to use several related objects of the same type. Instead of declaring different variables for each, you can declare one variable as an array, which then contains multiple values. In **Listing 5.9** and **Applet 5.9**, we use an array to contain the days of the week.

To use arrays:

1. String[] dayOfTheWeek = {"Sunday",
  → "Monday", "Tuesday", "Wednesday",
  → "Thursday", "Friday", "Saturday"};
  This line declares and initializes an array of type String, with the name dayOfTheWeek. The square brackets after String signify that what follows is an array. Each of the values within the curly brackets is assigned to the array.

continued

ARRAYS OF OBJECTS

Applet 5.9 Using arrays to avoid having to create multiple identical objects.

```
                                              Applet
import java.awt.*;
import java.applet.Applet;

public class Applet9 extends Applet{
 String[] dayOfTheWeek = {"Sunday","Monday","Tuesday","Wednesday","Thursday","Friday","Saturday"};
 String[] ordinalNumber = {"first","second","third","fourth","fifth","sixth","seventh"};
 Font f = new Font("TimesRoman",Font.BOLD,16);

 public void init() {
  setBackground(Color.white);
 }

 public void paint(Graphics g) {
  g.setFont(f);

  g.drawString(""The "+ordinalNumber[0]+" day of the week is "+dayOfTheWeek[0], 10 , 20);
  g.drawString("The "+ordinalNumber[1]+" day of the week is "+dayOfTheWeek[1], 10 , 40);
  g.drawString("The "+ordinalNumber[2]+" day of the week is "+dayOfTheWeek[2], 10 , 60);
  g.drawString("The "+ordinalNumber[3]+" day of the week is "+dayOfTheWeek[3], 10 , 80);
  g.drawString("The "+ordinalNumber[4]+" day of the week is "+dayOfTheWeek[4], 10 ,100);
  g.drawString("The "+ordinalNumber[5]+" day of the week is "+dayOfTheWeek[5], 10 ,120);
  g.drawString("The "+ordinalNumber[6]+" day of the week is "+dayOfTheWeek[6], 10 ,140);
 }

}
```

In this case, there are seven elements in the array, which are referred to as elements 0 through 6.

2. `String[] ordinalNumber = {"first",`
   `→ "second", "third", "fourth",`
   `→ "fifth", "sixth", "seventh"};`
   Here we declare and initialize another string array, this one named `ordinalNumber`.

3. `g.drawString("The " + ordinalNumber[0]+"`
   `→ day of the week is "+dayOfTheWeek[0],`
   `→ 10 , 20);`
   This line prints out that the "first" day of the week is "Sunday". Remember, the first element of the array is at position 0.

4. `g.drawString("The " + ordinalNumber[1]+"`
   `→ day of the week is "+dayOfTheWeek[1],`
   `→ 10 , 40);`
   `g.drawString("The " + ordinalNumber[2]+"`
   `→ day of the week is "+dayOfTheWeek[2],`
   `→ 10 , 60);`
   `g.drawString("The " + ordinalNumber[3]+"`
   `→ day of the week is "+dayOfTheWeek[3],`
   `→ 10 , 80);`
   `g.drawString("The " + ordinalNumber[4]+"`
   `→ day of the week is "+dayOfTheWeek[4],`
   `→ 10 ,100);`
   `g.drawString("The " + ordinalNumber[5]+"`
   `→ day of the week is "+dayOfTheWeek[5],`
   `→ 10 ,120); g.drawString("The " +`
   `→ ordinalNumber[6]+" day of the week`
   `→ is "+dayOfTheWeek[6], 10 ,140);`
   These lines print out the rest of the days of the week (array elements 1 through 6), as shown in **Figure 5.9**.

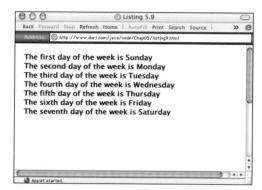

Figure 5.9 Here are the days of the week.

✔ Tips

- Looking at this example, you might think that because all of the `g.drawString()` lines are virtually identical, there ought to be a way to write this code with less repetition. You'll learn how to do so in Chapter 6, where you'll revisit this example as you learn about loops.

- Each element of an array is still a variable of its own, and can be modified independently of the others.

DECISIONS, DECISIONS

Java applets don't always flow straight through from beginning to end. Sometimes, it's necessary to skip a segment of code, or to execute the same segment more than once. This is called *flow control*—controlling the way the applet flows through your code. In this chapter, you'll see how to make your code follow your directions.

Conditionals: The if Statement

The simplest way to control the code that is executed in your applet is with the `if` statement. This command simply says, "if some value is true, then execute the commands within the following braces. Otherwise, skip this code." **Listing 6.1** and **Applet 6.1** show you how to use a conditional to get Java to display some text that you just entered.

To use an "if" statement:

1. `import java.awt.event.*;`

   For the first time, we're going to be handling user-generated events here, so, we have to import the `java.awt.event` classes so that we can use them later.

2. `public class Applet1 extends Applet`
   `→ implements ActionListener {`

   Our new applet is called **Applet1**, and is defined as extending the **Applet** class. There's a new concept here, where our applet `implements actionListener`. This means that we're setting up our applet to respond to user input (an *event*), and so, our applet needs to *listen* for any user interaction. **Table 6.1** shows which `listeners` you need to set up for which events.

3. `TextField inField = new`
   `→ TextField(12);`
   `Font f = new Font("TimesRoman",`
   `→ Font.BOLD,24);`
   `String enteredText = "";`

   Here we create three new variables: the text field `inField`, which will contain whatever the user enters; a font variable `f`, which is set to 24-point bold Times Roman, and a string `enteredText`, which will store what the user entered and will later be displayed in the applet. To start with, we'll set it to the empty string.

Listing 6.1 Call the applet inside the browser window.

```
<html>
<head>
 <title>Listing 6.1</title>
</head>
<body bgcolor="white">
<object classid="clsid:8AD9C840-044E-11D1-
→ B3E9-00805F499D93" width="500" height="100"
→ codetype="application/java">
 <param name="code" value="Applet1.class">
 <param name="type" value="application/x-java-
→ applet;version=1.3">
 <param name="scriptable" value="false">
 <embed type="application/x-java-
→ applet;version=1.3" code="Applet1.class"
→ width="500" height="100" scriptable="false"
→ pluginspage="http://java.sun.com/
→ products/plugin/1.3/plugin-install.html">
 </embed>
</object>
</body>
</html>
```

Applet 6.1 If you enter text into inField, Java will redisplay what you typed.

```
import java.awt.*;
import java.applet.Applet;
import java.awt.event.*;

public class Applet1 extends Applet implements
→ ActionListener {
 TextField inField = new TextField(12);
 Font f = new Font("TimesRoman",Font.BOLD,24);
 String enteredText = "";

 public void init() {
   setBackground(Color.white);
   inField.addActionListener(this);
   add(inField);
 }

 public void paint(Graphics g) {
   g.setFont(f);
   if (enteredText != "") {
     g.drawString("You entered: " +
→ enteredText , 20, 60);
   }
 }

 public void actionPerformed(ActionEvent e) {
   enteredText = inField.getText();
   repaint();
 }
}
```

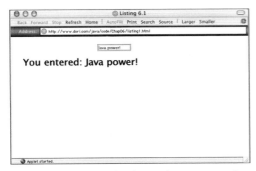

Figure 6.1 Here the applet shows what you entered.

✔ Tips

■ If you've ever programmed in another language, you might be expecting to see a "then" after the "if." In Java, the "then" is just assumed to be there.

■ It's common in Java to see an if statement followed by a single indented line with no curly braces. This is valid Java syntax, and means that the one line following the if is the sole statement to be executed when the if check is true. However, this book will use curly braces for clarity's sake.

4. `inField.addActionListener(this);`
   `add(inField);`

Here are two new lines in our `init()` method. The first tells Java that we want to use that `ActionListener` discussed in step 2 on our new `inField` text field. That way, the applet is now *registered* to listen for events happening to this field, so Java knows that it should listen and respond when the user enters text (i.e., does an action) in that entry field area. The second line tells Java to actually display that entry field area in the applet window.

5. `if (enteredText != "") {`
       `g.drawString("You entered: " +`
       → `enteredText , 20, 60);`
   `}`

If, and only if, `enteredText` has some value other than a zero-length string, we display what the user entered. If nothing has been entered, nothing will happen here.

6. `public void actionPerformed`
   → `(ActionEvent e) {`
       `enteredText = inField.getText();`
       → `repaint();`
   `}`

Because we added the `ActionListener` up above, the `actionPerformed()` method will handle any events triggered by the user. The only event that can happen in this applet is text being entered. When that happens, we set `enteredText` to be that data. Then we call the `repaint()` method, and the result is shown in **Figure 6.1**.

continued

Table 6.1

Java Events		
INTERFACE	COMPONENTS	METHODS
ActionListener	Button List TextField MenuItem	actionPerformed()
AdjustmentListener	Scrollbar	adjustmentValueChanged()
ComponentListener	All components	componentHidden() componentMoved() componentResized() componentShown()
ContainerListener	All containers	componentAdded() componentRemoved()
FocusListener	All components	focusGained() focusLost()
ItemListener	Checkbox CheckBoxMenuItem Choice ItemSelectable List	itemStateChanged()
KeyListener	All components	keyPressed() keyReleased() keyTyped()
Mouse Listener	All components	mouseClicked() mouseEntered() mouseExited() mousePressed() mouseReleased()
MouseMotionListener	All components	mouseDragged() mouseMoved()
TextListener	TextComponent	textValueChanged()
WindowListener	Window	windowActivated() windowClosed() windowClosing() windowDeactivated() windowDeiconified() windowIconified() windowOpened()

Listing 6.2 Let's play a game of "guess the number."

```
                    Listing
<html>
<head>
 <title>Listing 6.2</title>
</head>
<body bgcolor="white">
<object classid="clsid:8AD9C840-044E-11D1-
→ B3E9-00805F499D93" width="500" height="100"
→ codetype="application/java">
<param name="code" value="Applet2.class">
<param name="type" value="application/x-java-
→ applet;version=1.3">
<param name="scriptable" value="false">
<embed type="application/x-java-applet;
→ version=1.3" code="Applet2.class"
→ width="500" height="100" scriptable="false"
→ pluginspage="http://java.sun.com/products/
→ plugin/1.3/plugin-install.html">
</embed>
</object>
</body>
</html>
```

Catching Errors

When you allow users to enter data, sometimes the data they enter won't be quite what you want. **Listing 6.2** and **Applet 6.2** show you how to *catch* the errors before they can hurt your code.

To catch errors:

1. `TextField guessField = new`
   `→ TextField(5);`
   `int nextGuess = -1;`

   The variable `guessField` is defined as type `TextField`, with a length of 5. This is the text entry box where users will enter their guesses. The variable `nextGuess` is where we'll be storing the values that the user enters, so we'll start it off as -1. That number isn't a valid guess, so we'll use it as a flag to show we're just starting out and no numbers have been entered yet.

2. `int targetNum = (int)(java.lang.Math.`
   `→ random() * 100)+1;`

   The Java method `java.lang.Math.` `random()` generates a random number between 0 and 1 (for example, .722 or .111). We then multiply this number by 100 (resulting in 72.2 or 11.1). Finally, we take its integer value (that is, we strip off everything to the right of the decimal point) to produce a result between 0 and 99. Adding 1 to that number produces a result between 1 and 100, and then we store it in the variable `targetNum`. Both `nextGuess` and `targetNum` are of type `int`.

   continued

3. `String numberStatus = nextGuess + "`
   `→ is correct";`
   `g.setFont(f);`

Inside the `paint()` method we define a new String, `numberStatus`. It's initialized to a value of `nextGuess` followed by a message that assumes that `nextGuess` was correct, as shown in **Figure 6.2**. Then we set the window's font to `f`.

4. `if (nextGuess != targetNum) {`
   `   numberStatus = nextGuess + " is`
   `   → not correct";`
   `}`

Here's our first `if` statement. This code checks to see if `nextGuess` is not equal to `targetNum`, i.e., if the number the user entered doesn't match the number that we're looking for. If this is true—that is, if the numbers don't match—then we execute the code within the curly braces. Otherwise, we do nothing. In this case, if the two are different, `numberStatus` is reset to say that the user entered a number that was not correct, as seen in **Figure 6.3**.

Applet 6.2 Call the applet inside the browser window.

```
import java.awt.*;
import java.applet.Applet;
import java.awt.event.*;

public class Applet2 extends Applet implements
→ ActionListener {
 TextField guessField = new TextField(5);
 int nextGuess = -1;
 int targetNum = (int)(java.lang.Math.random()
 → * 100)+1;
 Font f = new Font("TimesRoman",Font.BOLD,24);

 public void init() {
   setBackground(Color.white);
   guessField.addActionListener(this);
   add(guessField);
 }

 public void paint(Graphics g) {
   String numberStatus = nextGuess + " is
   → correct";

   g.setFont(f);
   if (nextGuess != targetNum) {
     numberStatus = nextGuess + " is not
     → correct";
   }
     if (nextGuess < 1) {
       numberStatus = "Guess a number
     → between 1 and 100";
   }
   g.drawString(numberStatus, 20, 60);
 }

 public void actionPerformed(ActionEvent e) {
  if (e.getSource() instanceof TextField) {
   try {
     nextGuess = Integer.parseInt(guessField.
     → getText());
   }
   catch (NumberFormatException x) {
     nextGuess = -1;
   }
   repaint();
  }
 }
}
```

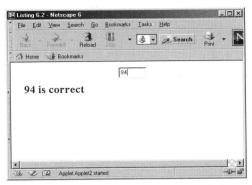

Figure 6.2 Here's the hoped for result of our applet.

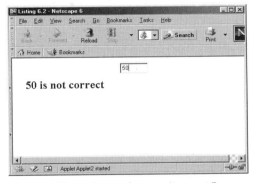

Figure 6.3 "Sorry, that number wasn't correct."

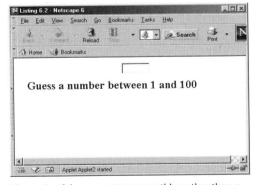

Figure 6.4 If the user enters something other than a number, they'll get these instructions.

5.
```
if (nextGuess < 1) {
    numberStatus = "Guess a number
    → between 1 and 100";
}
```

Here's another `if` statement. In this one, we check to see if `nextGuess` is less than 1, which is our flag that an invalid value was entered. In this case, we remind the user what it is we're expecting to see. **Figure 6.4** shows this in action.

6. `g.drawString(numberStatus, 20, 60);`

This code displays whatever value `numberStatus` was set to (reflecting whether the user-entered value was correct, incorrect, or invalid).

7.
```
public void actionPerformed
→ (ActionEvent e) {
    if (e.getSource() instanceof
    → TextField) {
```

Here's where some action finally occurs: in the `actionPerformed()` method. This method is invoked when the user enters something into the text field. First, we check to see if the event that caused the `actionPerformed()` method to run is one that the method knows how to handle. The only event we're going to handle here is a change to the text field, so we check if the source of the event is an instance of `TextField`.

continued

8.
```
try {
  nextGuess = Integer.parseInt
  → (guessField.getText());
}
catch (NumberFormatException x) {
  nextGuess = -1;
}
repaint();
```

A `try` is a special kind of `if` statement. In this situation, we're going to attempt to execute a statement where there's a chance an error might occur. So we just `try` the statement. If it's valid, everything's fine. If it's invalid, we throw an exception. Well, if an exception is thrown, it needs to be caught, which takes place in the `catch` statement. In this case, we're going to take what the user entered and try to turn it into a number. Since the user could have entered anything, we put the attempt to convert the entered value to a number in a `try` statement. If the input can be turned into an integer, `nextGuess` is set to that number. If not, a `NumberFormatException` exception is thrown and then caught, which causes `nextGuess` to be set to -1. Either way, we call the `repaint()` method to redraw the window.

✔ Tip

- Yes, this is a very convoluted way to write this applet. On the average, a user would have to guess 50 or more numbers before they would pick the right one. The next example will show a better approach.

Java Throws a Tantrum

Think about a little kid throwing a tantrum: "I'm not going to eat my spinach, I'm not, I'm not, and you can't make me."

Java doesn't throw tantrums, but it can throw exceptions, which can be very similar. In both cases, you have a "do this or else!" situation, caused by an unexpected or unwanted event. The kid doesn't want to eat spinach, and in this example, Java doesn't want to turn letters into numbers.

With a small child, the "or else" depends on the kid. When Java throws an exception, you, the programmer, need to catch it (unlike that kid, who's going to catch it if he doesn't eat his veggies). The `catch` keyword tells Java what to do when possible exceptions have been thrown.

Listing 6.3. Call Applet 6.3 inside the browser window.

```
Listing
<html>
<head>
 <title>Listing 6.3</title>
</head>
<body bgcolor="white">
<object classid="clsid:8AD9C840-044E-11D1-
➜ B3E9-00805F499D93" width="500" height="100"
➜ codetype="application/java">
 <param name="code" value="Applet3.class">
 <param name="type" value="application/x-java-
 ➜ applet;version=1.3">
 <param name="scriptable" value="false">
 <embed type="application/x-java-applet;
 ➜ version=1.3" code="Applet3.class" width="500"
 ➜ height="100" scriptable="false" pluginspage=
 ➜ "http://java.sun.com/products/plugin/1.3/
 ➜ plugin-install.html">
 </embed>
</object>
</body>
</html>
```

More Conditionals: if/else Statements

It makes sense that if you sometimes want code to be executed only if some value is true, at other times you'll want code to be executed only if a value is false. In this case, you use an `else` statement, which allows you to define a block of code that's executed only when the check in the `if` statement fails. **Listing 6.3** and **Applet 6.3** show an improved "guess a number" game where the user is given some feedback about how close their guess is to the correct answer.

To use an if/else construct:

1. `if (nextGuess != targetNum) {`

   We start off by checking to see if the user's guess matches what the computer is expecting. The following block of code is only executed if the guess was incorrect.

2. `if (nextGuess < 1) {`
   `    numberStatus = "Guess a number`
   `    ➜ between 1 and 100";`
   `}`

   First, we check to see if `nextGuess` has a value of -1, which occurs on the first pass through this code and when an invalid value was entered. If so, the message "Guess a number between 1 and 100" is displayed.

   continued

3. `else {`

Otherwise, if `nextGuess` is not equal to `targetNum`, and `nextGuess` is a valid number, then we want to execute the statements in the `else` clause. In this case, the `else` clause consists of another if/else construct.

4.
```
if (nextGuess < targetNum) {
  numberStatus = nextGuess + " is
→ too low";
}
else {
  numberStatus = nextGuess + " is
→ too high";
}
```

Here, we check if `nextGuess` is less than `targetNum`. If so, `nextGuess` is displayed, along with the message that it was too low, otherwise, the `nextGuess` is displayed with a message that says that the entry was too high. **Figure 6.5** shows the result when the guess was too high, and **Figures 6.6** and **6.7** show the result when the guess was too low. If the entry matched `targetNum`, the message in **Figure 6.8** is shown.

Applet 6.3 A better game of "guess the number."

```
import java.awt.*;
import java.applet.Applet;
import java.awt.event.*;

public class Applet3 extends Applet implements
→ ActionListener {
 TextField guessField = new TextField(5);
 int nextGuess = -1;
 int targetNum = (int)(java.lang.Math.random()
→ * 100)+1;
 Font f = new Font("TimesRoman",Font.BOLD,24);

 public void init() {
   setBackground(Color.white);
   guessField.addActionListener(this);
   add(guessField);
 }

 public void paint(Graphics g) {
   StringnumberStatus = nextGuess + " is
→ correct";

   g.setFont(f);
   if (nextGuess != targetNum) {
     if (nextGuess < 1) {
       numberStatus = "Guess a number between
→ 1 and 100";
   }
   else {
    if (nextGuess < targetNum) {
       numberStatus = nextGuess + " is too low";
    }
    else {
     numberStatus = nextGuess + " is too high";
    }
   }
  }
  g.drawString(numberStatus, 20, 60);
 }

 public void actionPerformed(ActionEvent e) {
   if (e.getSource() instanceof TextField) {
     try {
       nextGuess = Integer.parseInt
→ (guessField.getText());
     }
     catch (NumberFormatException x) {
       nextGuess = -1;
     }
    repaint();
   }
  }
 }
```

Figure 6.5 We'll start by guessing 50, and see whether we're high or low. In this case, 50 was too high.

Figure 6.6 Split the difference between 1 and 50, and try 25—in this case, too low.

Figure 6.7 Split the difference between 25 and 50, and try 37—still too low.

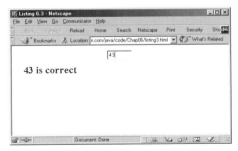

Figure 6.8 We split the difference between 37 and 50, and 43 was correct!

✔ Tip

- In the previous example, the user would have had to make 50 guesses to have a 50% chance of getting the right answer. In this example, the user should always be able to get the right answer within seven guesses.

Around and Around with Loops

With an if/else structure, you have code that you execute either once or not at all. Sometimes, though, you'll have code that you want to execute over and over again. This is called a "loop." **Listing 6.4** and **Applet 6.4** demonstrate one type of loop: the for loop. Here, we're going to let the user enter a number, and then print that many asterisks in the window.

Looping the Loop

A for loop has three parts, as shown in **Figure 6.10**:

1. The initialization step. The first time through the loop, this is what the loop variable is initialized to.

2. The limiting step. This is where we say when to stop looping. While normal people count from one to ten, it's common in programming languages to count from zero to nine. In both cases, the code inside the loop is run ten times, but the latter method works better with languages (like Java) where arrays start with a zero-th position. That's why you'll see loops have a limitation of "less than userNum" instead of "less than or equal to userNum."

3. The increment step. This is where we say by how much to increase the loop counter on each pass through the loop. In this case, we add one each time through using ++ to add one to i's value.

i=0;	i<userNum;	i++
Intialization	Limiting	Increment

Figure 6.10: The three parts of a loop.

Listing 6.4 This listing calls Applet 6.4.

```
<html>
<head>
 <title>Listing 6.4</title>
</head>
<body bgcolor="white">
<object classid="clsid:8AD9C840-044E-11D1-
→ B3E9-00805F499D93" width="500" height="100"
→ codetype="application/java">
 <param name="code" value="Applet4.class">
 <param name="type" value="application/x-java-
→ applet;version=1.3">
 <param name="scriptable" value="false">
 <embed type="application/x-java-applet;
→ version=1.3" code="Applet4.class" width=
→ "500" height="100" scriptable="false"
→ pluginspage="http://java.sun.com/products/
→ plugin/1.3/plugin-install.html">
 </embed>
</object>
</body>
</html>
```

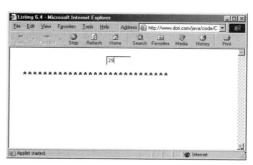

Figure 6.9 The user asked for 29 asterisks, and that's what they got.

Applet 6.4: This applet asks the user for a number and then loops through that many times.

```
                    Applet
import java.awt.*;
import java.applet.Applet;
import java.awt.event.*;

public class Applet4 extends Applet implements
→ ActionListener {
 TextField userField = new TextField(5);
 int userNum = -1;
 Font f = new Font("TimesRoman",Font.BOLD,24);

 public void init() {
   setBackground(Color.white);
   userField.addActionListener(this);
   add(userField);
 }

 public void paint(Graphics g) {
   String outStr = "";
   int i;

   g.setFont(f);
   if (userNum < 1 || userNum > 50) {
     outStr = "Enter a number between 1 and 50";
   }
   else {
    for (i=0; i<userNum; i++) {
     outStr = outStr + "*";
    }
   }
  g.drawString(outStr, 20, 60);
 }

 public void actionPerformed(ActionEvent e) {
   if (e.getSource() instanceof TextField) {
     try {
       userNum = Integer.
        → parseInt(userField.getText());
     }
     catch (NumberFormatException x) {
       userNum = -1;
     }
     repaint();
   }
 }
}
```

To use a for loop:

1.
```
if (userNum < 1 || userNum > 50) {
  outStr = "Enter a number between
  → 1 and 50";
}
```
First, we make sure that the user entered a valid number: it must be between 1 and 50.

2.
```
else {
   for (i=0; i<userNum; i++) {
   outStr = outStr + "*";
  }
}
```
Otherwise, we execute the for loop. The first part of the for loop initializes the loop counter, i, to 0. The second part says to continue looping so long as i is less than the value the user entered. The third part says to add one to i every time the loop goes around. **Figure 6.9** shows the result after the user has entered "29." The variable outStr starts off empty and adds an asterisk to itself with each pass through the loop.

✔ Tip

■ The || characters between the check for userNum less than 1 and userNum greater than 50 are read as "or," which means that the following lines are executed if either part is true. If we wanted it to only happen if both were true, we'd use an "and" instead, which uses the && syntax instead of the ||.

Another Loop through Loops: The while Loop

Java has three different ways of doing loops. The first is the `for` loop, and the other two are variations on the `while` loop. With a `while` loop, as shown in **Listing 6.5** and **Applet 6.5**, the loop continues to execute so long as the condition you're checking for is true. Once it's no longer true, the loop terminates. If the first time you check the condition the result is false, the loop is never executed at all.

Listing 6.5. Set up Applet 6.5 to be executed.

```
<html>
<head>
 <title>Listing 6.5</title>
</head>
<body bgcolor="white">
<object classid="clsid:8AD9C840-044E-11D1-
→ B3E9-00805F499D93" width="500" height="100"
→ codetype="application/java">
 <param name="code" value="Applet5.class">
 <param name="type" value="application/x-java-
→ applet;version=1.3">
 <param name="scriptable" value="false">
 <embed type="application/x-java-applet;
→ version=1.3" code="Applet5.class" width="500"
→ height="100" scriptable="false" pluginspage=
→ "http://java.sun.com/products/plugin/1.3/
→ plugin-install.html">
 </embed>
</object>
</body>
</html>
```

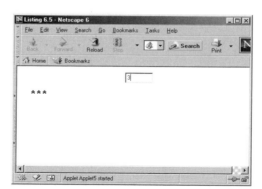

Figure 6.11. In this case, the user only wanted three.

Applet 6.5. How many asterisks does the user want to display?

```
Applet
import java.awt.*;
import java.applet.Applet;
import java.awt.event.*;

public class Applet5 extends Applet implements
→ ActionListener {
 TextField userField = new TextField(5);
 int userNum = -1;
 Font f = new Font("TimesRoman",Font.BOLD,24);

 public void init() {
  setBackground(Color.white);
  userField.addActionListener(this);
  add(userField);
 }

 public void paint(Graphics g) {
   String outStr = "";
   int i = 0;

   g.setFont(f);
   if (userNum > 50) {
     userNum = -1;
   }
   if (userNum < 1) {
   outStr = "Enter a number between 1 and 50";
   }
   while (i < userNum) {
    outStr = outStr + "*";
    i++;
   }
   g.drawString(outStr, 20, 60);
 }

  public void actionPerformed(ActionEvent e)
  {
    if (e.getSource() instanceof TextField) {
      try {
    userNum = Integer.
    → parseInt(userField.getText());
   }
   catch (NumberFormatException x) {
    userNum = -1;
   }
    repaint();
  }
 }
}
```

To use a while loop:

◆
```
while (i < userNum) {
 outStr = outStr + "*";
 i++;
}
```

The variable userNum is either a number between 1 and 50 (all valid values), or it's −1 (when an invalid entry was made). With i initialized to be 0, this loop will never be executed when userNum is invalid, because 0 is never less than −1. If userNum is valid, the loop will be executed that many times, as shown in **Figure 6.11**. Each time through the loop, i is incremented by one. For instance, if userNum is 25, this loop will be run 25 times. If userNum is −1, the while loop will initially check if 0 is less than -1. Since it isn't, the loop will never be entered.

✔ Tip

■ Make sure that you have some way of ending a while loop! For instance, if you left off the i++; line in the above example, you'd create what's called an "infinite loop": one that has no way of ending itself (at least not until it crashes your machine).

The Last Loop: The do/while Loop

The last kind of Java loop is the do/while loop. In this format, the check for continuing the loop is at the end of the loop instead of at the beginning. This means that the loop will always execute at least once. **Listing 6.6** and **Applet 6.6** demonstrate the do/while loop.

To use a do/while loop:

◆ do {
        outStr = outStr + "*";
        i++;
    } while (i < userNum);

With this construct, outStr will always have at least one asterisk, so we want to be careful about how we get to this area of the code. In other words, you'll want to check if userNum is -1 before you start this loop.

As long as i is less than userNum, this loop will continue to execute, as shown in **Figure 6.12**.

Listing 6.6 This listing calls Applet 6.6.

```
                      Listing
<html>
<head>
 <title>Listing 6.6</title>
</head>
<body bgcolor="white">
<object classid="clsid:8AD9C840-044E-11D1-
→ B3E9-00805F499D93" width="500" height="100"
→ codetype="application/java">
 <param name="code" value="Applet6.class">
 <param name="type" value="application/x-java-
 → applet;version=1.3">
 <param name="scriptable" value="false">
 <embed type="application/x-java-applet;
 → version=1.3" code="Applet6.class" width="500"
 → height="100" scriptable="false" pluginspage=
 → "http://java.sun.com/products/plugin/1.3/
 → plugin-install.html">
 </embed>
</object>
</body>
</html>
```

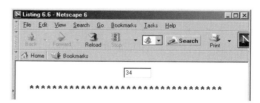

Figure 6.12 The user requested 34 asterisks.

Applet 6.6 Using a do/while loop to process the
user's request.

```
                    Applet

 import java.awt.*;
 import java.applet.Applet;
 import java.awt.event.*;

 public class Applet6 extends Applet implements
 ActionListener {
  TextField userField = new TextField(5);
  int userNum = -1;
  Font f = new Font("TimesRoman",Font.BOLD,24);

  public void init() {
    setBackground(Color.white);
    userField.addActionListener(this);
    add(userField);
  }

  public void paint(Graphics g) {
    String outStr = "";
    int i = 0;

    g.setFont(f);
    if (userNum < 1 || userNum > 50) {
      outStr = "Enter a number between 1 and
      → 50";
    }
    else {
      do {
        outStr = outStr + "*";
        i++;
      } while (i < userNum);
    }
    g.drawString(outStr, 20, 60);
  }

  public void actionPerformed(ActionEvent e) {
    if (e.getSource() instanceof TextField) {
      try {
        userNum = Integer.parseInt(userField.
        getText());
      }
      catch (NumberFormatException x) {
        userNum = -1;
      }
      repaint();
    }
  }
 }
```

Take a Break from Loops

It's possible to be inside a loop, but encounter a condition under which you want to leave the loop immediately. This is called a break.

In **Listing 6.7** and **Applet 6.7**, the user is allowed to enter any number they like. However, no matter how large the number, the loop is limited to 20 times around.

To break from a loop:

◆ ```
for (i=0; i<userNum; i++) {
  if (i >= 20) break;
  outStr = outStr + "*";
}
```

This is a standard for loop, which would normally loop around until i was equal to userNum. The addition of the break in the middle, however, causes the loop to always exit when i reaches 20.

The break command causes execution to jump to the first line after the loop, as shown in **Figure 6.13**.

**Listing 6.7.** Set up Applet 6.7.

```
<html>
<head>
 <title>Listing 6.7</title>
</head>
<body bgcolor="white">
<object classid="clsid:8AD9C840-044E-11D1-
→ B3E9-00805F499D93" width="500" height="100"
→ codetype="application/java">
 <param name="code" value="Applet7.class">
 <param name="type" value="application/x-java-
→ applet;version=1.3">
 <param name="scriptable" value="false">
 <embed type="application/x-java-applet;
→ version=1.3" code="Applet7.class" width="500"
→ height="100" scriptable="false" pluginspage=
→ "http://java.sun.com/products/plugin/1.3/
→ plugin-install.html">
 </embed>
</object>
</body>
</html>
```

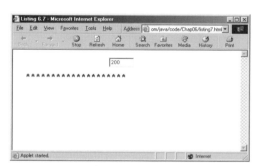

Figure 6.13 No matter what number we put in, the maximum is really 20.
```

Applet 6.7 This applet demonstrates the use of a break to exit a loop.

```
                     Applet
import java.awt.*;
import java.applet.Applet;
import java.awt.event.*;

public class Applet7 extends Applet implements
→ ActionListener {
 TextField userField = new TextField(5);
 int userNum = -1;
 Font f = new Font("TimesRoman",Font.BOLD,24);

 public void init() {
  setBackground(Color.white);
  userField.addActionListener(this);
  add(userField);
 }

 public void paint(Graphics g) {
  String outStr = "";
  int i;

  g.setFont(f);
  if (userNum < 1) {
   outStr = "Enter a number between 1 and 20";
  }
  else {
    for (i=0; i<userNum; i++) {
     if (i >= 20) break;
     outStr = outStr + "*";
    }
  }
  g.drawString(outStr, 20, 60);
 }

  public void actionPerformed(ActionEvent e) {
    if (e.getSource() instanceof TextField) {
      try {
        userNum = Integer.parseInt
        → (userField.getText());
      }
      catch (NumberFormatException x) {
        userNum = -1;
      }
        repaint();
    }
  }
}
```

✔ Tip

■ Java also has a `continue` command. When you use `continue`, the remaining lines in the loop are skipped and execution resumes at the start of the loop. If, in this example, we substituted `continue` for `break`, the code would skip setting `outStr` once i was greater or equal to 20, but would continue to go around the loop `userNum` times, instead of quitting early as `break` does.

The Case with case

Java provides one more way for you to control the flow of your code: the switch/case statement. The easiest way to understand the switch/case statement is to think of it as a shorthand way of combining a whole bunch of if/else statements. Instead of saying "if today is Monday do this, else if today is Tuesday do some other thing, else if today is Wednesday do something else entirely," we can just use a switch/case statement on the task and look at each possible value individually.

Listing 6.8 and **Applet 6.8** use the venerable rock, scissors, paper game to demonstrate the switch/case statement.

To use switch/case:

1. public class Applet8 extends Applet
→ implements ItemListener {

Because our new applet is going to use a set of radio buttons instead of the text field that we've used in all the other examples, we need a new type of listener, itemListener. This will allow us to use the itemStateChanged() method, which will be triggered by a user clicking on a radio button.

2. CheckboxGroup userCheckbox;
Checkbox rockCheckBox,
→ scissorsCheckBox, paperCheckBox;

Each radio button is an individual Checkbox at this point. In step 4, they'll all be added to the same CheckboxGroup, which will tell Java that they're related

3. userCheckbox = new CheckboxGroup();
This creates the new CheckboxGroup, which we're calling userCheckbox.

Listing 6.8 This sets up the game in Applet 6.8.

```
                        Listing
<html>
<head>
 <title>Listing 6.8</title>
</head>
<body bgcolor="white">
<object classid="clsid:8AD9C840-044E-11D1-
→ B3E9-00805F499D93" width="500" height="100"
→ codetype="application/java">
 <param name="code" value="Applet8.class">
 <param name="type" value="application/x-java-
→ applet;version=1.3">
 <param name="scriptable" value="false">
 <embed type="application/x-java-applet;
→ version=1.3" code="Applet8.class" width="500"
→ height="100" scriptable="false" pluginspage=
→ "http://java.sun.com/products/plugin/1.3/
→ plugin-install.html">
 </embed>
</object>
</body>
</html>
```

Applet 6.8 Let's see if we can beat the applet.

```
                     Applet

import java.awt.*;
import java.applet.Applet;
import java.awt.event.*;

public class Applet8 extends Applet implements
→ ItemListener {
 int appNum = (int)(java.lang.Math.random() *
 → 3)+1;
 Font f = new Font("TimesRoman",Font.BOLD,16);
 CheckboxGroup userCheckbox;
 Checkbox rockCheckBox, scissorsCheckBox,
 → paperCheckBox;
 boolean firstTime = true;
 String userChoice;

 public void init() {
  setBackground(Color.white);

  userCheckbox = new CheckboxGroup();
  rockCheckBox = new Checkbox("Rock",
  → userCheckbox,false);
  rockCheckBox.addItemListener(this);
  add(rockCheckBox);

  scissorsCheckBox = new Checkbox("Scissors",
  → userCheckbox,false);
  scissorsCheckBox.addItemListener(this);
  add(scissorsCheckBox);

  paperCheckBox = new Checkbox("Paper",
  → userCheckbox,false);
  paperCheckBox.addItemListener(this);
  add(paperCheckBox);
 }

 public void paint(Graphics g) {
  int userNum;
    String appChoice;

  g.setFont(f);

  if (firstTime) {
   g.drawString("Play Rock, Scissors, Paper
   → with me!",20,60);
   firstTime = false;
  }
  else {
   switch(appNum) {
   case 1:
    appChoice = "Rock";
    break;
   case 2:
    appChoice = "Scissors";
    break;
```

Applet continues on next page

4.
```
rockCheckBox = new Checkbox("Rock",
→ userCheckbox,false);
rockCheckBox.addItemListener(this);
→ add(rockCheckBox);
```

These lines create a new radio button called **rockCheckBox**, which is part of the **userCheckbox** group. Clicking on any radio button in this group will cause all the other radio buttons in this group to turn off. The first parameter of the **Checkbox()** method is the *label* (how it will be identified onscreen), the second its group, and the last its state: whether or not we want it to be clicked when first displayed. We then set up **addItemListener(this)** for this new radio button, so that future events involving this button will trigger the **itemStateChanged()** method. We finish up this code by adding the radio button to the applet window.

5.
```
switch(appNum) {
  case 1:
   appChoice = "Rock";
   break;
  case 2:
   appChoice = "Scissors";
   break;
  case 3:
   appChoice = "Paper";
   break;
  default:
   appChoice = "Error";
}
```

As in previous examples, we use Java's random-number generator to pick whether rock, scissors, or paper is the applet's choice. That results in appNum, a random number between 1 and 3. The applet now has to set a new variable, appChoice. Here, switch() chooses between case statements based on the value of appNum. The above code can be read as "if (appNum == 1) {appChoice="Rock"} else if (appNum==2) {appChoice="Scissors"} else if..." and so on.

continued

THE CASE WITH CASE

8.
```
switch (userChoice.charAt(0)) {
  case 'R':
   userNum = 1;
   break;
  case 'S':
   userNum = 2;
   break;
  case 'P':
   userNum = 3;
   break;
  default:
   userNum = 0;
}
```

In this segment, a char (a special type of string that contains only a single character) is being checked instead of a number. The user entered a choice by clicking on a radio button, which triggered an event. Java knows which radio button was pressed, and the applet here uses the first letter of the user's choice to convert that choice into a number to be compared to the applet's choice. **Figure 6.14** shows how the game begins, and **Figures 6.15**, **6.16**, and **6.17** show some of the possible outcomes.

7.
```
public void itemStateChanged
→ (ItemEvent e) {
 if (e.getSource() instanceof
 → Checkbox) {
  userChoice =
  → userCheckbox.
  → getSelectedCheckbox().
  → getLabel();
```

Here's the code that's triggered by the user's mouse click. If a Checkbox was clicked on, userChoice is set to the label of that particular Checkbox.

Applet 6.8 *continued*

```
    case 3:
     appChoice = "Paper";
     break;
    default:
     appChoice = "Error";
 }

  switch (userChoice.charAt(0)) {
    case 'R':
     userNum = 1;
     break;
    case 'S':
     userNum = 2;
     break;
    case 'P':
     userNum = 3;
     break;
    default:
     userNum = 0;
 }

 if (appNum == userNum) {
  g.drawString("Tie game--let's play
  → again.", 20, 60);
 }
 else {
  if ((userNum==1 && appNum==3) ||
  → (userNum==2 && appNum==1) ||
  → (userNum==3 && appNum==2)) {
   g.drawString("I win! I picked
   → "+appChoice+".", 20, 60);
  }
  else {
   g.drawString("You win! I picked
   → "+appChoice+".", 20, 60);
  }
 }
 g.drawString("Reload the page to play
 → another game",20,80);
 }
}

public void itemStateChanged(ItemEvent e) {
 if (e.getSource() instanceof Checkbox) {
  userChoice = userCheckbox.
  → getSelectedCheckbox().getLabel();
  repaint();
 }
 }
}
```

Figure 6.14 Ready to start the game...

Figure 6.15 The user wins the first game...

Figure 6.16 ...then a tie game...

Figure 6.17 ...and then the computer wins one.

✔ Tips

- A `switch`/`case` statement can only be used on four primitive types: `byte`, `char`, `int`, and `short`. This is why in the sixth step, above, we're checking just the first character of `userChoice` instead of the entire string.

- If the `break` is left out of any of the above `case` blocks, the code will fall through to the next block and execute that also. This can be a useful feature, but is also a major source of bugs. Remember to put a `break` at the end of each `case` statement!

- If none of the values in the `case` statements match, the default block is executed. No matter how sure you are that your code will never execute the default, you should always include it just in case.

THE CASE WITH CASE

WORKING
WITH THE USER

One of the main goals of using Java applets is to increase how much users interact with your pages. In this chapter, we'll cover ways to let users control the actions of applets, using both the mouse and the keyboard.

Drawing with the Mouse

This example combines the user's mouse movements with Java's event handlers to draw a line in the applet window. Because the applet is completely driven by the user, it does nothing at all until the user takes an action. Consequently, everything takes place within event handlers, where the Java applet, using the `MouseListener` interface (see "What is an Interface?" sidebar), handles the events that are triggered when the user presses and releases the mouse button. **Listing 7.1** and **Applet 7.1** allow the user to draw the line.

Listing 7.1 Putting a table with a border of 1 around an applet helps to show the applet's boundaries.

```
<html>
<head>
  <title>Listing 7.1</title>
</head>
<body bgcolor="white">
<table border="1">
  <tr>
    <td>
      <object classid="clsid:8AD9C840-044E-11D1-B3E9-00805F499D93" width="500" height="100"
      → codetype="application/java">
        <param name="code" value="Applet1.class">
        <param name="type" value="application/x-java-applet;version=1.3">
        <param name="scriptable" value="false">
        <embed type="application/x-java-applet;version=1.3" code="Applet1.class" width="500"
        → height="100" scriptable="false" pluginspage="http://java.sun.com/products/plugin/1.3/
        → plugin-install.html">
        </embed>
      </object>
    </td>
  </tr>
</table>
</body>
</html>
```

Applet 7.1 This applet handles and responds to the user's mouse movements.

```
import java.awt.*;
import java.applet.*;
import java.awt.event.*;

public class Applet1 extends Applet
→ implements MouseListener {
  Point startPt, endPt;

  public void init() {
    setBackground(Color.white);
    addMouseListener(this);
  }

  public void mousePressed(MouseEvent evt) {
    startPt = evt.getPoint();
  }

  public void mouseReleased(MouseEvent evt) {
    endPt = evt.getPoint();
    repaint();
  }

  public void paint(Graphics g) {
    if (endPt != null) {
      g.drawLine(startPt.x, startPt.y,
      → endPt.x, endPt.y);
    }
  }

  public void mouseClicked(MouseEvent evt) {
  }

  public void mouseEntered(MouseEvent evt) {
  }

  public void mouseExited(MouseEvent evt) {
  }
}
```

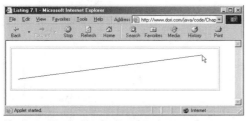

Figure 7.1 Displaying the line that the user drew.

To draw lines using the mouse:

1. ```
   public void mousePressed
   → (MouseEvent evt) {
       startPt = evt.getPoint();
   }
   ```

   The first event we need to handle is the `mousePressed()` event. This is triggered whenever the user clicks the mouse within the applet's boundaries.

   When this happens, the `mousePressed()` method is called and passed the event, which contains information about the mouse click. We then set the variable `startPt` to save the point where the user clicked the mouse.

2. ```
   public void mouseReleased
   → (MouseEvent evt) {
       endPt = evt.getPoint();
       repaint();
   }
   ```

   The `mouseReleased()` method is triggered when the user lets go of the mouse button. In contrast to the previous step, we now set `endPt` to the ending point of our line, and then call `repaint()` to force the applet to actually draw the line inside our window.

3. ```
   public void paint(Graphics g) {
       if (endPt != null) {
           g.drawLine(startPt.x, startPt.y,
           → endPt.x, endPt.y);
       }
   }
   ```

   In our `paint()` method, we actually do the line drawing, as shown in **Figure 7.1**. Once an end point has been set (by the `mouseReleased()` method), we're ready to draw a line.

   The `drawLine()` method takes four parameters: the x and y coordinates of the starting point and the x and y coordinates of the ending point.

   continued
   ```

4.
```
public void mouseClicked
→ (MouseEvent evt) {
}
public void mouseEntered
→ (MouseEvent evt) {
}
public void mouseExited
→ (MouseEvent evt) {
}
```

MouseListener requires that each of the methods it handles be defined within our applet. In this case, these three methods aren't required to achieve our goal, but we need to define them anyway.

✔ Tips

■ You might be wondering what would happen if we simply moved the drawLine() method into the mouseReleased() method, and skipped the paint() method altogether. Unfortunately, we can't do that, because behind the scenes, the paint() method is clearing the applet area before the new line is drawn. This lets you create new lines without seeing all your previous lines.

■ There's one big drawback to this applet: you can't see anything happen until you release the mouse button. To work properly, we ought to have some way of drawing the line on the screen while we're drawing it (not just after), but MouseListener doesn't have a way to track that event. The next task will show a solution to this dilemma.

What is an Interface?

While we've been using interfaces since Chapter 6, they haven't been specifically described yet.

The simplest way to describe an interface is as a collection of promises that your applet is agreeing to fulfill. If you look at **Table 6.1**, each interface corresponds to one or more methods. Implementing an interface in an applet says that you're promising to implement each of its required methods. In return, you'll get all the power of the interface; for instance, in these examples, they provide listeners for all the possible events that might be generated by the user.

While all applets extend the standard applet class and get the benefits that that provides, implementing an interface allows the applet to handle more complex interaction. In addition, unlike the way the applets extend only the applet class, an applet can implement more than one interface (as you'll see in later examples), getting the benefits of all of them simultaneously.

Drawing in Two Dimensions

You can draw many shapes in Java besides one-dimensional lines. **Listing 7.2** and **Applet 7.2** take the user's mouse movements and translate them into a two-dimensional object, using both the MouseListener and the MouseMotionListener interfaces.

To draw an object:

1. public class Applet2 extends Applet
  → implements MouseListener,
  → MouseMotionListener {

We want this applet to handle events provided by both MouseListener and MouseMotionListener, so we add both to our applet declaration.

continued

Listing 7.2 Placing an applet on a Web page.

```
                                    Listing
<html>
<head>
  <title>Listing 7.2</title>
</head>
<body bgcolor="white">
<table border="1">
  <tr>
    <td>
      <object classid="clsid:8AD9C840-044E-11D1-B3E9-00805F499D93" width="500" height="100"
      → codetype="application/java">
        <param name="code" value="Applet2.class">
        <param name="type" value="application/x-java-applet;version=1.3">
        <param name="scriptable" value="false">
        <embed type="application/x-java-applet;version=1.3" code="Applet2.class" width="500"
        → height="100" scriptable="false" pluginspage="http://java.sun.com/products/plugin/1.3/
        → plugin-install.html">
        </embed>
      </object>
    </td>
  </tr>
</table>
</body>
</html>
```

2. `int rectWidth, rectHeight, startX,` → `startY;`

The only difference between drawing a line (as in **Applet 7.1**) and drawing a rectangle is within the `paint()` method, where we handle the actual drawing. This method starts by declaring four local variables: `rectWidth` (the width of the rectangle), `rectHeight` (the height of the rectangle), and `startX` and `startY` (the x and y coordinates of the top-left corner of the rectangle).

3. `startX = Math.min(startPt.x,endPt.x);` `startY = Math.min(startPt.y,endPt.y);`

We start off by setting `startX` and `startY`. While a line can go in any direction, a rectangle needs to start drawing in the top-left corner. Because the user may have clicked in the lower-right corner (or upper-right or lower-left), we need to figure out where we want to start drawing. The `startX` and `startY` variables are calculated by finding the lesser of the two positions, using the `java.lang.Math.min()` method.

4. `rectWidth = Math.abs(endPt.x -` → `startPt.x);` `rectHeight = Math.abs(endPt.y -` → `startPt.y);`

Unlike a line, which just needs a beginning and ending point, a rectangle wants a beginning point, a width, and a height. Because where we start drawing may not be the same as `startPt` or `endPt`, the width and height need to be calculated. We do this by finding the absolute value (i.e., the positive value) of `startPt`'s x and y coordinates subtracted from `endPt`'s x and y coordinates. The result gives the correct width and height.

Applet 7.2 Here's how to draw a rectangle on that Web page, with the user setting the dimensions using the mouse.

```
import java.awt.*;
import java.applet.*;
import java.awt.event.*;

public class Applet2 extends Applet implements
→ MouseListener, MouseMotionListener {
  Point startPt, endPt;

  public void init() {
    setBackground(Color.white);
    addMouseListener(this);
    addMouseMotionListener(this);
  }

  public void paint(Graphics g) {
    int rectWidth, rectHeight, startX, startY;

    if (endPt != null) {
      startX = Math.min(startPt.x,endPt.x);
      startY = Math.min(startPt.y,endPt.y);
      rectWidth = Math.abs(endPt.x -
      → startPt.x);
      rectHeight = Math.abs(endPt.y -
      → startPt.y);

      g.fillRect(startX, startY, rectWidth,
      → rectHeight);
    }
  }

  public void mousePressed(MouseEvent evt) {
    startPt = evt.getPoint();
  }

  public void mouseDragged(MouseEvent evt) {
    endPt = evt.getPoint();
    repaint();
  }

  public void mouseReleased(MouseEvent evt) {
    endPt = evt.getPoint();
    repaint();
  }

  public void mouseClicked(MouseEvent evt) {
  }

  public void mouseEntered(MouseEvent evt) {
  }

  public void mouseExited(MouseEvent evt) {
  }

  public void mouseMoved(MouseEvent evt) {
  }
}
```

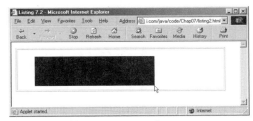

Figure 7.2 And here's our rectangle.

Table 7.1

Drawing Methods		
METHOD	DESCRIPTION	PARAMETERS
drawRect	Draw the outline of a rectangle	startX, startY, width, height
fillRect	Draw a filled-in rectangle	startX, startY, width, height
drawRoundRect	Draw a rectangle with rounded corners	startX, startY, width, height, curveX, curveY
drawOval	Draw the outline of an oval	startX, startY, width, height
fillOval	Draw a filled-in oval	startX, startY, width, height

5. `g.fillRect(startX, startY,`
   `→ rectWidth, rectHeight);`

   The fillRect() method draws a solid rectangle with the previously calculated dimensions, as shown in **Figure 7.2**. **Table 7.1** shows some of Java's other drawing methods.

6. `public void mouseDragged`
   `→ (MouseEvent evt) {`
      `endPt = evt.getPoint();`
      `repaint();`
   `}`

   Adding the mouseDragged() method (via MouseMotionListener) to our applet allows the user to see the rectangle being drawn as the mouse moves across the window. The code is identical to that in the mouseReleased() method, but both are needed to handle the rectangle while it's being drawn, and when it's completed.

7. `public void mouseMoved`
   `→ (MouseEvent evt) {`
   `}`

   In a similar fashion to the way the previous task required MouseClicked() MouseEntered() and MouseExited(), MouseMotionListener requires that our applet also include the mouseMoved() method.

✔ Tips

- Forcing the width and height to be the same will cause the rectangle methods to produce a square, and cause the oval methods to draw a circle.

- If you're not sure which methods are required by which interfaces, refer back to **Table 6.1**.

DRAWING IN TWO DIMENSIONS

Freehand Drawing

While drawing lines and boxes is interesting at first, you'll soon be looking for something a little more creative. **Listing 7.3** and **Applet 7.3** demonstrate how you can allow unlimited artistry within the boundaries of your applet.

To draw in your applet:

1. `Graphics g = getGraphics();`

Because we're going to be handling the drawing inside the `mouseDrag()` method, we need to create a graphics region. Here, we're declaring `g` and initializing it for later use.

2. `g.drawLine(startPt.x, startPt.y,`
→ `endPt.x, endPt.y);`

As in **Applet 7.1**, we draw a line from our starting point to our current point.

Listing 7.3 This listing places Applet 7.3 on the Web page.

```
<html>
<head>
  <title>Listing 7.3</title>
</head>
<body bgcolor="white">
<table border="1">
  <tr>
    <td>
      <object classid="clsid:8AD9C840-044E-11D1-B3E9-00805F499D93" width="500" height="100"
      → codetype="application/java">
        <param name="code" value="Applet3.class">
        <param name="type" value="application/x-java-applet;version=1.3">
        <param name="scriptable" value="false">
        <embed type="application/x-java-applet;version=1.3" code="Applet3.class" width="500"
        → height="100" scriptable="false" pluginspage="http://java.sun.com/products/plugin/1.3/
        → plugin-install.html">
        </embed>
      </object>
    </td>
  </tr>
</table>
</body>
</html>
```

Figure 7.3 Hey, this was fun!

3. startPt = endPt;

In order for this routine to work properly, startPt now needs to be reset to what we just used as endPt. In this way, our current point is now the beginning of the next line we're about to draw, and so on.

Because we're just drawing little connected line segments, the drawing appears to follow the path of the cursor, as shown in **Figure 7.3**.

Applet 7.3 You can allow the user to draw anything they want within the applet's boundaries (and within the boundaries of the user's artistic talent).

```
import java.awt.*;
import java.applet.*;
import java.awt.event.*;

public class Applet3 extends Applet implements MouseListener, MouseMotionListener {
  Point startPt, endPt;

  public void init() {
    setBackground(Color.white);
    addMouseListener(this);
    addMouseMotionListener(this);
  }

  public void mousePressed(MouseEvent evt) {
    startPt = new Point(evt.getX(), evt.getY());
  }

  public void mouseDragged(MouseEvent evt) {
    Graphics g = getGraphics();

    endPt = new Point(evt.getX(), evt.getY());
    g.drawLine(startPt.x, startPt.y, endPt.x, endPt.y);
    startPt = endPt;
  }

  public void mouseClicked(MouseEvent evt) {
  }

  public void mouseReleased(MouseEvent evt) {
  }

  public void mouseExited(MouseEvent evt) {
  }

  public void mouseEntered(MouseEvent evt) {
  }

  public void mouseMoved(MouseEvent evt) {
  }

}
```

FREEHAND DRAWING

Capturing Keystrokes

Working with the mouse is fun, but there's an entire keyboard to work with, too. **Listing 7.4** and **Applet 7.4** capture a keystroke entered by the user and display it on the Web page.

To capture keystrokes:

1. addKeyListener(this);
requestFocus();

Here's an addition to the interfaces we've used before, KeyListener. This enables us to catch the events triggered by pressing keys. We also call the requestFocus() method, which tells the applet that, even though we may not ever click inside the applet area in the browser window, we want the applet to have *focus*, i.e., to be the active item in the browser window. If the applet doesn't have focus, it won't be able to receive any of the keystrokes entered by the user.

Listing 7.4 This HTML displays Applet 7.4.

```
Listing
<html>
<head>
  <title>Listing 7.4</title>
</head>
<body bgcolor="white">
<table border="1"
  <tr>
    <td>
      <object classid="clsid:8AD9C840-044E-11D1-B3E9-00805F499D93" width="500" height="100"
      → codetype="application/java">
        <param name="code" value="Applet4.class">
        <param name="type" value="application/x-java-applet;version=1.3">
        <param name="scriptable" value="false">
        <embed type="application/x-java-applet;version=1.3" code="Applet4.class" width="500"
        → height="100" scriptable="false" pluginspage="http://java.sun.com/products/plugin/1.3/
        → plugin-install.html">
        </embed>
      </object>
    </td>
  </tr>
</table>
</body>
</html>
```

Applet 7.4 Here's where we grab the pressed key and display it on the Web page...

```
Applet
import java.awt.*;
import java.applet.*;
import java.awt.event.*;

public class Applet4 extends Applet
→ implements KeyListener {
  char currentChar = ' ';

  public void init() {
    setBackground(Color.white);
    setFont(new Font("Times Roman",
    → Font.BOLD,36));
    addKeyListener(this);
    requestFocus();
  }

  public void paint(Graphics g) {
    g.drawString(String.valueOf
    → (currentChar),200,50);
  }

  public void keyPressed(KeyEvent evt) {
    currentChar = evt.getKeyChar();
    repaint();
  }

  public void keyReleased(KeyEvent evt) {
  }

  public void keyTyped(KeyEvent evt) {
  }
}
```

2.
```
public void paint(Graphics g) {
    g.drawString(String.valueOf
    → (currentChar), 200, 50);
}
```

The paint() method takes the value of currentChar, turns it into a string, and uses the drawString() method to display the pressed key at position (200,50). The result is shown in **Figure 7.4**.

3.
```
public void keyPressed
→ (KeyEvent evt) {
    currentChar = evt.getKeyChar();
    repaint();
}
```

Whenever a key is pressed on the keyboard, the keyPressed() method is triggered. In this method, we're setting currentChar to the key pressed, which is stored in the event. The method then calls repaint() to redraw the applet.

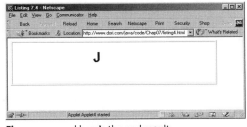

Figure 7.4 ...and here's the end result.

Moving Images Around

Okay, you've seen how to show the user what key they just pressed. But then again, the user knows what key they pressed—they're the one who pressed it, right?

In this example, we'll let the user press the arrow keys to move an image around the page. The butterfly will move in any direction that the user tells it to fly, as shown in **Listing 7.5** and **Applet 7.5**.

Figure 7.5 Our butterfly in motion (use your imagination).

To move an image using the arrow keys:

1.
```
public void paint(Graphics g) {
    g.drawImage(butterfly,xPos,
    ➝ yPos,this);
}
```
Whenever the `paint()` method is called, this code will display the butterfly gliding around the window, as shown in **Figure 7.5**.

Listing 7.5 Setting up the butterfly applet.

```
                              Listing
<html>
<head>
  <title>Listing 7.5</title>
</head>
<body bgcolor="white">
<table border="1">
  <tr>
    <td>
      <object classid="clsid:8AD9C840-044E-11D1-B3E9-00805F499D93" width="500" height="100"
      ➝ codetype="application/java">
        <param name="code" value="Applet5.class">
        <param name="type" value="application/x-java-applet;version=1.3">
        <param name="scriptable" value="false">
        <embed type="application/x-java-applet;version=1.3" code="Applet5.class" width="500"
        ➝ height="100" scriptable="false" pluginspage="http://java.sun.com/products/plugin/1.3/
        ➝ plugin-install.html">
        </embed>
      </object>
    </td>
  </tr>
</table>
</body>
</html>
```

Applet 7.5 Use the arrow keys to control the butterfly's direction.

```
                    Applet
import java.awt.*;
import java.applet.*;
import java.awt.event.*;

public class Applet5 extends Applet
→ implements KeyListener {
  int xPos, yPos;
  Image butterfly;

  public void init() {
    setBackground(Color.white);
    xPos = 100;
    yPos = 50;
    butterfly = getImage(getCodeBase(),
    → "butterfly.gif");
    addKeyListener(this);
    requestFocus();
  }

  public void paint(Graphics g) {
    g.drawImage(butterfly,xPos,yPos,this);
  }

  public void keyPressed(KeyEvent evt) {
    int x = evt.getKeyCode();

    switch (x) {
      case (KeyEvent.VK_UP):
        yPos -= 10;
        break;
      case (KeyEvent.VK_DOWN):
        yPos += 10;
        break;
      case (KeyEvent.VK_LEFT):
        xPos -= 10;
        break;
      case (KeyEvent.VK_RIGHT):
        xPos += 10;
        break;
    }
    repaint();
  }

  public void keyReleased(KeyEvent evt) {
  }

  public void keyTyped(KeyEvent evt) {
  }
}
```

2.
```
public void keyPressed
→ (KeyEvent evt) {
    int x = evt.getKeyCode();
```
The keyPressed() method is passed the event triggered by the pressed key. That event contains the pressed key, which we'll store in x.

3.
```
switch (x) {
    case (KeyEvent.VK_UP):
        yPos -= 10;
        break;
    case (KeyEvent.VK_DOWN):
        yPos += 10;
        break;
    case (KeyEvent.VK_LEFT):
        xPos -= 10;
        break;
    case (KeyEvent.VK_RIGHT):
        xPos += 10;
        break;
}
```
Given x (set in the previous step), we can use it in a switch statement (as defined in Chapter 6) to choose how to handle each arrow key. Each arrow key corresponds to one of the four Event directions: KeyEvent.VK_UP, KeyEvent.VK_DOWN, KeyEvent.VK_LEFT, and KeyEvent.VK_RIGHT. If the Up Arrow is pressed, the applet subtracts 10 from the butterfly's y coordinate. If the Down Arrow is pressed, 10 is added to the y coordinate. The Left and Right Arrows subtract and add 10 (respectively) to the x coordinate.

✔ Tip

■ If you move the butterfly both horizontally and vertically (for example, left and up) almost simultaneously, its movement appears almost realistic.

Using Modifier Keys

To make the butterfly's motion truly realistic, we need to be able to move it at different speeds. In this example, holding down the Shift key doubles the speed (in any direction) that the butterfly travels. **Listing 7.6** and **Applet 7.6** show how this is accomplished.

To use modifier keys to change an action:

◆
```
if (evt.isShiftDown()) {
    offset = 20;
}
else {
    offset = 10;
}
```
Within the keyPressed() method, we can check to see if a modifier key (or keys) was held down. In this case, we're checking to see if the Shift key was held down when the arrow key was pressed.

Figure 7.6 And here's the version 2 butterfly, happily winging around the Web.

Listing 7.6 This HTML places Applet 7.6 on the page.

```
Listing
<html>
<head>
  <title>Listing 7.6</title>
</head>
<body bgcolor="white">
<table border="1">
  <tr>
    <td>
      <object classid="clsid:8AD9C840-044E-11D1-B3E9-00805F499D93" width="500" height="100"
      → codetype="application/java">
        <param name="code" value="Applet6.class">
        <param name="type" value="application/x-java-applet;version=1.3">
        <param name="scriptable" value="false">
        <embed type="application/x-java-applet;version=1.3" code="Applet6.class" width="500"
        → height="100" scriptable="false" pluginspage="http://java.sun.com/products/plugin/1.3/
        → plugin-install.html">
        </embed>
      </object>
    </td>
  </tr>
</table>
</body>
</html>
```

Applet 7.6 The new and improved butterfly applet.

```
                    Applet
import java.awt.*;
import java.applet.*;
import java.awt.event.*;

public class Applet6 extends Applet
→ implements KeyListener {
  int xPos, yPos;
  Image butterfly;

  public void init() {
    setBackground(Color.white);
    xPos = this.getSize().width/2;
    yPos = this.getSize().height/2;
    butterfly = getImage(getCodeBase(),
    → "butterfly.gif");
    addKeyListener(this);
    requestFocus();
  }

  public void paint(Graphics g) {
    g.drawImage(butterfly,xPos,yPos,this);
  }

  public void keyPressed(KeyEvent evt) {
    int offset;
    int x = evt.getKeyCode();

    if (evt.isShiftDown()) {
      offset = 20;
    }
    else {
      offset = 10;
    }

    switch (x) {
      case (KeyEvent.VK_UP):
        yPos -= offset;
        break;
      case (KeyEvent.VK_DOWN):
        yPos += offset;
        break;
      case (KeyEvent.VK_LEFT):
        xPos -= offset;
        break;
      case (KeyEvent.VK_RIGHT):
        xPos += offset;
        break;
    }
    repaint();
  }

  public void keyTyped(KeyEvent evt) {
  }

  public void keyReleased(KeyEvent evt) {
  }
}
```

If so, we set the variable `offset` to 20; if not, it's set to 10. This variable is then used to change the x and y coordinates of the image. Obviously, if the variable is set to 20, the butterfly moves twice as fast. **Figure 7.6** shows the applet in action.

✔ Tip

- In the previous example, the initial values of xPos and yPos were hard-coded, that is, set once and never changed. There's no way to know if those would be valid values, so it's better to calculate the placement on the fly (so to speak). In this example, `this.getSize().width` and `this.getSize().height` are the dimensions of the applet boundary. Dividing each of these numbers by two puts the image in the direct center of the applet.

BUILDING A
USER INTERFACE

One of the main reasons for adding a Java applet to your page is to interact with the user. In order to interact with a user, you'll need to have a *user interface*: fields into which the user can enter data, checkboxes, and radio buttons for them to click, and so on.

This chapter covers the most common user-interface elements and how to add each to your applet.

Password Protecting a Page

It's very common to want to protect one page or one area of your Web site from the eyes of random surfers. **Listing 8.1** and **Applet 8.1** show a simple Java applet that requests a password. If the correct password is entered, the protected page is then loaded.

To password protect a page:

1. ```
   try {
       passwordURL = new URL
       → ("http://www.dori.com/java/");
   }
   catch (MalformedURLException err) {
       passwordURL = this.
       → getDocumentBase();
   }
   ```

   First, we create a new URL variable, and assign it the URL that we want to load if the correct password is entered. Here, the URL we want to go to is http://www.dori.com/java/. The try/catch is required, just in case the URL we're using isn't in a valid format, which would then trigger the MalformedURLException error (for more about try/catch, see Chapter 6). In that case, we would set the URL to be that of the current page.

Listing 8.1 This HTML file calls Applet 8.1.

```
Listing
<html>
<head>
 <title>Listing 8.1</title>
</head>
<body bgcolor="white">
<object classid="clsid:8AD9C840-044E-11D1-
→ 'B3E9-00805F499D93" width="500" height="300"
→ 'codetype="application/java">
 <param name="code" value="Applet1.class">
 <param name="type" value="application/x-java-
 → applet;version=1.3">
 <param name="scriptable" value="false">
 <embed type="application/x-java-applet;
 → version=1.3" code="Applet1.class" width="500"
 → height="300" scriptable="false" pluginspage=
 → "http://java.sun.com/products/plugin/1.3/
 → plugin-install.html">
 </embed>
</object>
</body>
</html>
```
```

Applet 8.1 This applet protects the following page by requiring the correct password.

```
                    Applet
import java.awt.*;
import java.applet.Applet;
import java.net.*;
import java.awt.event.*;

public class Applet1 extends Applet implements
→ ActionListener {
 TextField passwordField;
 boolean badPass = false;
 URL passwordURL;

 public void init() {
   setBackground(Color.white);

   try {
     passwordURL = new URL("http://www.dori.
     → com/java/");
   }
   catch (MalformedURLException err) {
     passwordURL = this.getDocumentBase();
   }

   add(new Label("Password"));
   passwordField = new TextField(10);
   passwordField.setEchoChar('*');
   passwordField.addActionListener(this);
   add(passwordField);
 }

 public void paint(Graphics g) {
   if (badPass) {
     g.drawString("Incorrect Password-try
     → again",200,40);
   }
 }

 public void actionPerformed(ActionEvent e) {
   if (passwordField.getText().equals
   → ("peachpit")) {
     getAppletContext().showDocument
     → (passwordURL);
   }
   else {
     badPass = true;
     repaint();
   }
 }
}
```

2.
```
add(new Label("Password"));
passwordField = new TextField(10);
passwordField.setEchoCharacter('*');
passwordField.addActionListener
→ (this);
add(passwordField);
```
The first line adds the label "Password" to the screen. Then, we create a text-entry field with a length of 10 characters named passwordField, which will echo asterisks (*) when text is typed into the field, add the ActionListener to catch when the user enters data into the field, and finally, add it to the screen as shown in **Figure 8.1**.

3.
```
if (badPass) {
    g.drawString("Incorrect
    → Password-try again",200,40);
}
```
If the bad password flag has been set (it is set in step 5), the line "Incorrect Password—try again" is displayed, as shown in **Figure 8.2**.

4. `if (passwordField.getText().equals`
→ `("peachpit")) {`
   `getAppletContext().showDocument`
   → `(passwordURL);`
`}`

When the user has finished entering data into the text field `passwordField`, the applet gets the entered data by calling `getText()` and then compares it to the password we're checking against, in this case "peachpit". If the values are equal, `showDocument()` is called to load the new URL into the browser window.

5. `else {`
   `badPass = true;`
   `repaint();`
`}`

If the password attempt failed, we set the bad password flag to `true` and repaint the applet.

✔ Tip

■ It's theoretically possible to guess the password or the destination URL by looking at the applet's `.class` file. To protect against this, you can either add a bunch of dummy strings to your applet or piece together the target password or the target URL by concatenating several strings.

Figure 8.1 Enter the password here.

Figure 8.2 If the correct password isn't entered, the error message is displayed.

Listing 8.2 This calls Applet 8.2.

```
                     Applet
<html>
<head>
<title>Listing 8.2</title>
</head>
<body bgcolor="white">
<object classid="clsid:8AD9C840-044E-11D1-
→ B3E9-00805F499D93" width="500" height="300"
→ codetype="application/java">
 <param name="code" value="Applet2.class">
 <param name="type" value="application/x-java-
 → applet;version=1.3">
 <param name="scriptable" value="false">
 <embed type="application/x-java-applet;
 → version=1.3" code="Applet2.class"
 → width="500" height="300" scriptable="false"
 → pluginspage="http://java.sun.com/
 → products/plugin/1.3/plugin-install.html">
 </embed>
</object>
</body>
</html>
```

Entering and Displaying Text

Java allows you to both enter text into a field and display text on the screen. In **Listing 8.2** and **Applet 8.2**, whatever you enter into the field is then displayed again by the applet.

To enter and display text:

1. `TextField inputField;`
   `String displayText = "Enter a string`
   `→ to display";`

   Two new variables are declared here, `inputField` (of type `TextField`) and `displayText` (of type `String`). The latter is initialized to the value "Enter a string to display." The first time the applet paints the screen, this is the text that will appear.

2. `add(new Label("Text String:"));`
   `inputField = new TextField(25);`
   `inputField.addTextListener(this);`
   `add(inputField);`

   These lines add the label "Text String:" to the screen, as well as a new text-entry field of 25 characters.

   continued

3. g.drawString(displayText,200,40);

This line within the paint() method uses drawString() to display the value of displayText on the screen. When it's first run, the value is "Enter a string to display," as shown in **Figure 8.3**. After that, whatever the user has entered is displayed, as shown in **Figure 8.4**.

4. displayText = inputField.getText(); repaint();

This code is executed when the event being handled is the user typing something into the text field. In this case, we get the value of inputField with the method getText() and repaint the screen.

✔ Tip

■ While **Applet 8.1** uses ActionListener to get the entered data from the text field, **Applet 8.2** uses TextListener. This is because in the former, we don't need to look at the text being entered until it's complete, while this applet is written to grab the user's keystrokes character by character and display them in the window.

Applet 8.2 This applet allows a user to enter a string, which will then be displayed on the screen.

```
import java.awt.*;
import java.applet.Applet;
import java.awt.event.*;

public class Applet2 extends Applet implements
→ TextListener {
  TextField inputField;
  String displayText = "Enter a string
  → to display";

  public void init() {
    setBackground(Color.white);

    add(new Label("Text String:"));
    inputField = new TextField(25);
    inputField.addTextListener(this);
    add(inputField);
  }

  public void paint(Graphics g) {
    g.drawString(displayText,200,40);
  }

  public void textValueChanged(TextEvent e) {
    displayText = inputField.getText();
    repaint();
  }
}
```

Figure 8.3 Here's what the applet looks like at the beginning...

Figure 8.4 ...and here's what it looks like after something's been entered.

Listing 8.3 Calls Applet 8.3.

```
                    Listing
<html>
<head>
 <title>Listing 8.3</title>
</head>
<body bgcolor="white">
<object classid="clsid:8AD9C840-044E-11D1-
→ B3E9-00805F499D93" width="550" height="300"
→ codetype="application/java">
 <param name="code" value="Applet3.class">
 <param name="type" value="application/x-java-
 → applet;version=1.3">
 <param name="scriptable" value="false">
 <embed type="application/x-java-applet;
 → version=1.3" code="Applet3.class" width=
 → "550"→ height="300" scriptable="false"
 → pluginspage="http://java.sun.com/products/
 → plugin/1.3/plugin-install.html">
 </embed>
</object>
</body>
</html>
```

Working with Checkboxes

One of the most common user-interface elements is the checkbox. This is an on/off field, where the box is either checked or not checked. In **Listing 8.3** and **Applet 8.3**, checkboxes are used to allow the user to pick the style of the displayed text.

To work with checkboxes:

1. Checkbox boldCheckbox=new
   → Checkbox("Bold",null,false);
   boldCheckbox.addItemListener(this);

   Checkbox italicCheckbox=new
   → Checkbox("Italic",null,false);
   italicCheckbox.addItemListener(this);

   This code creates two new checkboxes, one labeled "Bold" and the other labeled "Italic." The second parameter of Checkbox identifies whether a new checkbox is actually a radio button; in this case, it isn't, so the second parameter is null. The third parameter gives the initial value for each checkbox, which we've set to false so neither box starts off checked.

2. add(inputField);
   add(new Label(" FontStyle:"));
   add(boldCheckbox);
   add(italicCheckbox);

   This code adds four fields to our window: the text entry field, a label that says "Font Style:", and the two checkboxes.

3. Checkbox boxLabel = (Checkbox)
   → e.getSource();

   Here's where we start to handle checkbox events. The target of the event was a checkbox, so we cast the source of the event as a checkbox and call that variable boxLabel for later use.

   continued

WORKING WITH CHECKBOXES

Applet 8.3 A text-entry field and two checkboxes allow a string to be entered and displayed in four different styles.

```
                                          Applet

 import java.awt.*;
 import java.applet.Applet;
 import java.awt.event.*;

 public class Applet3 extends Applet implements TextListener, ItemListener  {
  TextField inputField;
  String displayText = "Enter a string to display";
  int fontStyle = Font.PLAIN;

  public void init() {
   setBackground(Color.white);

   add(new Label("Text String:"));
   inputField = new TextField(25);
   inputField.addTextListener(this);

   Checkbox boldCheckbox=new Checkbox("Bold",null,false);
   boldCheckbox.addItemListener(this);

   Checkbox italicCheckbox=new Checkbox("Italic",null,false);
   italicCheckbox.addItemListener(this);

   add(inputField);
   add(new Label("  Font Style:"));
   add(boldCheckbox);
   add(italicCheckbox);
  }

  public void paint(Graphics g) {
   g.setFont(new Font("TimesRoman",fontStyle,24));
   g.drawString(displayText,200,60);
  }

  public void textValueChanged(TextEvent e) {
   displayText = inputField.getText();
   repaint();
  }

  public void itemStateChanged(ItemEvent e) {
   Checkbox boxLabel = (Checkbox) e.getSource();

   if (boxLabel.getLabel() == "Bold") {
     if (boxLabel.getState()) {
      fontStyle += Font.BOLD;
     }
     else {
      fontStyle -= Font.BOLD;
     }
   }

   if (boxLabel.getLabel() == "Italic") {
    if (boxLabel.getState()) {
     fontStyle += Font.ITALIC;
    }
    else {
     fontStyle -= Font.ITALIC;
    }
   }
   repaint();
  }
 }
```

Figure 8.5 This is what is displayed when the applet is loaded.

Figure 8.6 When the "Bold" checkbox is checked, the string is displayed in bold text.

Figure 8.7 If "Italic" is then checked, the display is both bold and italic.

Figure 8.8 If "Bold" is subsequently unchecked, the string is displayed as italic only.

4.
```
if (boxLabel.getLabel() == "Bold") {
    if (boxLabel.getState()) {
        fontStyle += Font.BOLD;
    }
    else {
        fontStyle -= Font.BOLD;
    }
}
```
Here, we first check to see which checkbox the user clicked. In this case, the method getLabel() shows that we're working on "Bold." The method getState() returns the new value of the checkbox that the user has just toggled. If the value is true, the value of Font.BOLD is added to fontStyle; otherwise, Font.BOLD is subtracted.

5.
```
if (boxLabel.getLabel() == "Italic") {
    if (boxLabel.getState()) {
        fontStyle += Font.ITALIC;
    }
    else {
        fontStyle -= Font.ITALIC;
    }
}
```
In this case, we do the same thing, except that the user clicked "Italic." If the new value is true, Font.ITALIC is added to the current font; otherwise, Font.ITALIC is subtracted.

✔ Tip

■ How does Java change the font style just by adding and/or subtracting a variable? Internally, Java keeps three variables: Font.PLAIN (which has an internal value of 0), Font.BOLD (with a value of 1), and Font.ITALIC (with a value of 2). The variable fontStyle is therefore initialized above to be zero, as in **Figure 8.5**. If the user checks "Bold," fontStyle is set to 1, as in **Figure 8.6**. If the user then checks "Italic," fontStyle becomes 3, as in **Figure 8.7**. If the user then unchecks "Bold," fontStyle is 2, as in **Figure 8.8**.

WORKING WITH CHECKBOXES

Using Radio Buttons

Radio buttons are a special type of checkbox, where only one of the group may be selected at any one time. When a user clicks one of the buttons, Java handles turning all the others off. **Listing 8.4** and **Applet 8.4** use radio buttons to allow the user to pick a font size.

To use radio buttons:

1. fontSizeField = new CheckboxGroup();

```
Checkbox boxTwelve = new Checkbox
➝ ("12",fontSizeField,true);
Checkbox boxFourteen = new Checkbox
➝ ("14",fontSizeField,false);
Checkbox boxEighteen = new Checkbox
➝ ("18",fontSizeField,false);
Checkbox boxTwentyFour = new Checkbox
➝ ("24",fontSizeField,false);
```

This code, inside init(), creates the four radio buttons that control the font size of the displayed string. The variable fontSizeField is a CheckboxGroup, and using this as the second parameter to Checkbox identifies the new fields as part of the same radio button group. The radio button with the label "12" is initialized to be on by setting the third parameter to true.

2. boxTwelve.addItemListener(this);
boxFourteen.addItemListener(this);
boxEighteen.addItemListener(this);
boxTwentyFour.addItemListener(this);

Here, we add itemListener to each radio button to enable the applet to handle the event generated by a user clicking on a radio button.

continued

Listing 8.4 Calls Applet 8.4.

```
<html>
<head>
 <title>Listing 8.4</title>
</head>
<body bgcolor="white">
<object classid="clsid:8AD9C840-044E-11D1-
➝ B3E9-00805F499D93" width="550" height="300"
➝ codetype="application/java">
 <param name="code" value="Applet4.class">
 <param name="type" value="application/x-java-
 ➝ applet;version=1.3">
 <param name="scriptable" value="false">
 <embed type="application/x-java-applet;
 ➝ version=1.3" code="Applet4.class" width="550"
 ➝ height="300" scriptable="false" pluginspage=
 ➝ "http://java.sun.com/products/plugin/1.3/
 ➝ plugin-install.html">
 </embed>
</object>
</body>
</html>
```

Applet 8.4 This applet demonstrates how radio buttons are used; in this case, they let the user choose a font size.

```
                                        Applet
import java.awt.*;
import java.applet.Applet;
import java.awt.event.*;

public class Applet4 extends Applet implements TextListener, ItemListener {
 TextField inputField;
 String displayText = "Enter a string to display";
 int fontSize = 12;
 CheckboxGroup fontSizeField;

 public void init() {
   setBackground(Color.white);

   add(new Label("Text String:"));
   inputField = new TextField(20);
   inputField.addTextListener(this);
   add(inputField);

   add(new Label("Font Size:"));
   fontSizeField = new CheckboxGroup();

   Checkbox boxTwelve = new Checkbox("12",fontSizeField,true);
   Checkbox boxFourteen  = new Checkbox("14",fontSizeField,false);
   Checkbox boxEighteen = new Checkbox("18",fontSizeField,false);
   Checkbox boxTwentyFour = new Checkbox("24",fontSizeField,false);

   boxTwelve.addItemListener(this);
   boxFourteen.addItemListener(this);
   boxEighteen.addItemListener(this);
   boxTwentyFour.addItemListener(this);

   add(boxTwelve);
   add(boxFourteen);
   add(boxEighteen);
   add(boxTwentyFour);
 }

 public void paint(Graphics g) {
   g.setFont(new Font("TimesRoman",Font.PLAIN,fontSize));
   g.drawString(displayText,200,60);
 }

 public void textValueChanged(TextEvent e) {
   displayText=inputField.getText();
   repaint();
 }

 public void itemStateChanged(ItemEvent e) {
   fontSize=Integer.parseInt(fontSizeField.getSelectedCheckbox().getLabel());
   repaint();
  }
 }
}
```

3. add(boxTwelve);
   add(boxFourteen);
   add(boxEighteen);
   add(boxTwentyFour);

Here's where the four radio buttons are added to our applet window.

4. fontSize=Integer.parseInt(fontSize
   → Field.getSelectedCheckbox().
   → getLabel());

Inside the event handler, we can find out the new font size with one complex line of code. The easiest way to understand this line is by working from the inside out. Given that we know that we're working on the radio button group called `fontSizeField`, we can ask Java to return the radio button that's currently selected, using the method `getSelectedCheckbox()`. Given that, Java can return the label of that radio button, which returns the current font size as a string. `Integer.parseInt()` takes that resulting string and turns it into an integer, which is our new value for `fontSize` (**Figures 8.9**, **8.10**, and **8.11**).

Figure 8.9 Selecting 12 pt font size makes the text too small.

Figure 8.10 But 24 pt type is too large.

Figure 8.11 18 points is just right for this web page.

Listing 8.5 Calls Applet 8.5.

```
                    Listing
<html>
<head>
 <title>Listing 8.5</title>
</head>
<body bgcolor="white">
<object classid="clsid:8AD9C840-044E-11D1-
→ B3E9-00805F499D93" width="500" height="300"
→ codetype="application/java">
 <param name="code" value="Applet5.class">
 <param name="type" value="application/x-java-
→ applet;version=1.3">
 <param name="scriptable" value="false">
 <embed type="application/x-java-applet;
→ version=1.3" code="Applet5.class" width="500"
→ height="300" scriptable="false" pluginspage=
→ "http://java.sun.com/products/plugin/1.3/
→ plugin-install.html">
 </embed>
</object>
</body>
</html>
```

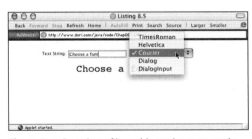

Figure 8.12 One view of how this applet appears, in this case using Internet Explorer on a Mac.

Figure 8.13 The same applet, but viewed using Netscape on a PC.

Selecting Menu Items

Pull-down menus give us another way to permit only one item from a group of items to be chosen. **Listing 8.5** and **Applet 8.5** use a pull-down menu to allow the user to choose which font a message is displayed in (**Figures 8.12** and **8.13**).

To use a pull-down menu:

1. fontMenu = new Choice();
   fontMenu.addItem("TimesRoman");
   fontMenu.addItem("Helvetica");
   fontMenu.addItem("Courier");
   fontMenu.addItem("Dialog");
   fontMenu.addItem("DialogInput");
   fontMenu.addItemListener(this);
   add(fontMenu);

   We start by declaring a new variable, fontMenu, of type Choice. Once we have this new variable, we can add menu items by calling addItem. The entire menu is then added to the screen by doing an add() of fontMenu after adding the ItemListener.

2. if (e.getSource() instanceof Choice) {
     fontFace=fontMenu.getSelectedItem();
     repaint();
   }

   If the event was an instance of Choice, we need to handle the new font face. Calling the getSelectedItem() method of fontMenu gives us the option that the user chose.

Applet 8.5 This applet sets up the new pull-down menu to allow the user to pick the font of their choice.

```
                                    Applet

import java.awt.*;
import java.applet.Applet;
import java.awt.event.*;

public class Applet5 extends Applet implements ItemListener, TextListener {
 TextField inputField;
 String displayText = "Enter a string to display";
 String fontFace = "TimesRoman";
 Choice fontMenu;

 public void init() {
   setBackground(Color.white);

   add(new Label("Text String:"));
   inputField = new TextField(20);
   inputField.addTextListener(this);

   add(inputField);

   fontMenu = new Choice();
   fontMenu.addItem("TimesRoman");
   fontMenu.addItem("Helvetica");
   fontMenu.addItem("Courier");
   fontMenu.addItem("Dialog");
   fontMenu.addItem("DialogInput");
   fontMenu.addItemListener(this);
   add(fontMenu);
 }

 public void paint(Graphics g) {
   g.setFont(new Font(fontFace,Font.PLAIN,24));
   g.drawString(displayText,150,60);
 }

 public void textValueChanged(TextEvent e) {
   displayText=inputField.getText();
   repaint();
 }

 public void itemStateChanged(ItemEvent e) {
  if (e.getSource() instanceof Choice) {
    fontFace=fontMenu.getSelectedItem();
    repaint();
  }
 }
}
```

Listing 8.6 Calls Applet 8.6.

```
<html>
<head>
 <title>Listing 8.6</title>
</head>
<body bgcolor="white">
<object classid="clsid:8AD9C840-044E-11D1-
→ B3E9-00805F499D93" width="800" height="300"
→ codetype="application/java">
 <param name="code" value="Applet6.class">
 <param name="type" value="application/x-java-
→ applet;version=1.3">
 <param name="scriptable" value="false">
 <embed type="application/x-java-applet;
→ version=1.3" code="Applet6.class" width="500"
→ height="300" scriptable="false" pluginspage=
→ "http://java.sun.com/products/plugin/1.3/
→ plugin-install.html">
 </embed>
</object>
</body>
</html>
```

Figure 8.14 The results of this applet on a Mac with Internet Explorer.

Figure 8.15 The results of this applet on a PC with Netscape 6.

Setting the Font Menu with Java

In the previous example, we set the list of fonts in the menu to be five hard-coded fonts that we expected Java to allow. Given that Java works on many different platforms with different setups, it makes much more sense to allow Java to query the user's system, calculate which fonts it supports, and then add them to a font menu. **Listing 8.6** and **Applet 8.6** demonstrate how this is done.

To display a font menu based on a user's system:

1. `String[] fontArray =`
   `→ GraphicsEnvironment.getLocalGraphics`
   `→ Environment().getAvailableFont`
   `→ FamilyNames();`

   First, we declare a string array called `fontArray`, which will be set to a list of fonts that Java supports. We then get the fonts by calling the built-in Java method `getAvailableFontFamilyNames()`.

2. `for (int i = 0; i < fontArray.length;`
   `→ i++) {`
   `  fontMenu.addItem(fontArray[i]);`
   `}`
   `fontMenu.addItemListener(this);`
   `add(fontMenu);`

   For each font name in `fontArray`, we add a menu item to `fontMenu`. **Figures 8.14** and **8.15** show the results of this on two different platforms.

3. `fontFace = fontArray[0];`

   The initial value of the `fontFace` variable can't be hard-coded (set to a fixed value), as we don't know what fonts Java might find available on the user's system. As a solution, here we initialize `fontFace` to be whatever font Java found first.

Applet 8.6 Use this applet to calculate and set up a personalized pull-down menu of fonts.

```
                              Applet
import java.awt.*;
import java.applet.Applet;
import java.awt.event.*;

public class Applet6 extends Applet implements TextListener, ItemListener {
 TextField inputField;
 String displayText = "Enter a string to display";
 String fontFace;
 Choice fontMenu;

 public void init() {
   setBackground(Color.white);

   add(new Label("Text String:"));
   inputField = new TextField(20);
   inputField.addTextListener(this);

   add(inputField);

   fontMenu = new Choice();
   String[] fontArray = GraphicsEnvironment.getLocalGraphicsEnvironment().
   → getAvailableFontFamilyNames();
   for (int i = 0; i < fontArray.length; i++) {
    fontMenu.addItem(fontArray[i]);
   }
   fontMenu.addItemListener(this);
   add(fontMenu);
   fontFace = fontArray[0];
 }

 public void paint(Graphics g) {
   g.setFont(new Font(fontFace,Font.PLAIN,24));
   g.drawString(displayText,150,60);
 }

 public void textValueChanged(TextEvent e) {
   displayText=inputField.getText();
   repaint();
 }

 public void itemStateChanged(ItemEvent e) {
  fontFace=fontMenu.getSelectedItem();
  repaint();
 }
}
```

Listing 8.7 Calls Applet 8.7.

```
==========  Listing  ==========
<html>
<head>
 <title>Listing 8.7</title>
</head>
<body bgcolor="white">
<object classid="clsid:8AD9C840-044E-11D1-
→ 1B3E9-00805F499D93" width="500" height="300"
→ 1codetype="application/java">
 <param name="code" value="Applet7.class">
 <param name="type" value="application/x-java-
→ applet;version=1.3">
 <param name="scriptable" value="false">
 <embed type="application/x-java-applet;
→ version=1.3" code="Applet7.class" width="500"
→ height="300" scriptable="false" pluginspage=
→ "http://java.sun.com/products/plugin/1.3/
→ plugin-install.html">
 </embed>
</object>
</body>
</html>
```

Using Text Areas

Two more common user-interface elements are text areas and buttons. Text areas are like text fields, but larger—they allow users to enter more than one line. Consequently, the way we've indicated in previous examples that we're done with text field data entry won't work with text areas. One solution to this is to use a button to tell the applet to check the text area for a changed value. **Listing 8.7** and **Applet 8.7** shows this at work.

To use text areas:

1. `inputField = new TextArea`
   `→ ("",4,20,TextArea.`
   `→ SCROLLBARS_VERTICAL_ONLY);`
   `add(inputField);`

   These lines create a new `TextArea` named `inputField`, 4 lines high by 20 characters wide, which is then added to the screen. The first parameter of the TextArea is the default that will be displayed when the screen is first drawn, the second and third are the height and width of the text box, and the last is an optional field that allows you to say if and where to draw scrollbars on this field.

2. `updateButton = new Button("Update`
   `→ Text");`
   `updateButton.addActionListener(this);`
   `add(updateButton);`

   This creates a new button named `updateButton`, containing the string "Update Text" and adds it to the screen.

   continued

Applet 8.7 We use a text area box and a button to allow the user to enter a long string to display.

```
                                      Applet
import java.awt.*;
import java.applet.Applet;
import java.awt.event.*;

public class Applet7 extends Applet implements ActionListener, ItemListener {
 TextArea inputField;
 String displayText = "Enter a string to display";
 int fontStyle = Font.PLAIN;
 Button updateButton;

 public void init() {
   setBackground(Color.white);

   add(new Label("Text Area:"));
   inputField = new TextArea("",4,20,TextArea.SCROLLBARS_VERTICAL_ONLY);
   add(inputField);

   add(new Label("Font Style:"));

   Checkbox BoldBox = new Checkbox("Bold",null,false);
   Checkbox ItalicBox = new Checkbox("Italic",null,false);
   BoldBox.addItemListener(this);
   ItalicBox.addItemListener(this);
   add(BoldBox);
   add(ItalicBox);

   updateButton = new Button("Update Text");
   updateButton.addActionListener(this);
   add(updateButton);
 }

 public void actionPerformed(ActionEvent e) {
   displayText=inputField.getText();
   repaint();
 }

 public void paint(Graphics g) {
   g.setFont(new Font("TimesRoman",fontStyle,24));
   g.drawString(displayText,10,150);
 }

 public void itemStateChanged(ItemEvent e) {
   Checkbox boxLabel = (Checkbox) e.getSource();

   if (boxLabel.getLabel() == "Bold") {
    if (boxLabel.getState()) {
      fontStyle += Font.BOLD;
    }
    else {
     fontStyle -= Font.BOLD;
    }
   }

   if (boxLabel.getLabel() == "Italic") {
     if (boxLabel.getState()) {
       fontStyle += Font.ITALIC;
     }
     else {
      fontStyle -= Font.ITALIC;
     }
   }
  repaint();
 }
}
```

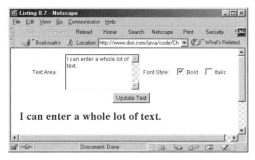

Figure 8.16 Here's how it looks in one browser...

Figure 8.17 ...and in another.

3. `public void actionPerformed`
   `→ (ActionEvent e) {`
   `displayText=inputField.getText();`
   `repaint();`
   `}`

Clicking on the button will trigger the `actionPerformed()` method. When that happens, these lines reset the displayed text to whatever is currently in `inputField` and redisplay the screen. The result of this is shown in **Figures 8.16** and **8.17**.

✔ Tip

■ The legal values for the 4th parameter to `TextArea` are `TextArea.SCROLLBARS_BOTH`, `TextArea.SCROLLBARS_HORIZONTAL_ONLY`, `TextArea.SCROLLBARS_VERTICAL_ONLY`, and `TextArea.SCROLLBARS_NEITHER`. Limiting where the scrollbars can be displayed allows the text to wrap within the text entry field.

USING TEXT AREAS

127

Using Scrolling Lists

The final type of user-interface element we'll look at is the scrolling list. With a scrolling list, a user can choose any number of options from a long list, as demonstrated in **Listing 8.8** and **Applet 8.8**.

To use a scrolling list:

1. `firstList = new List(3,true);`

   This line creates a new scrolling list named `firstList`. The first parameter says that the list will display three items on the screen, no matter how many items may actually be in the list. The second parameter says that it's acceptable for someone to choose more than one item from the list. If this was set to `false`, the list would act like a group of radio buttons, and choosing one item would turn all the others off.

2. ```
   firstList.add("London");
   firstList.add("Paris");
   firstList.add("Rome");
   firstList.add("Detroit");
   firstList.add("New York");
   firstList.addListener(this);
   add(firstList);
   ```

   Five cities are added to the list, and the list is then added to the screen.

3. ```
   secondList = new List(3,true);
   add(secondList);
   ```

   A new, empty list is now added, named `secondList`.

continued on page 130

Listing 8.8 Calls Applet 8.8.

```
Listing
<html>
<head>
 <title>Listing 8.8</title>
</head>
<body bgcolor="white">
<object classid="clsid:8AD9C840-044E-11D1-
→ B3E9-00805F499D93" width="500" height="300"
→ codetype="application/java">
 <param name="code" value="Applet8.class">
 <param name="type" value="application/x-java-
 → applet;version=1.3">
 <param name="scriptable" value="false">
 <embed type="application/x-java-applet;
 → version=1.3" code="Applet8.class" width="500"
 → height="300" scriptable="false" pluginspage=
 → "http://java.sun.com/products/plugin/1.3/
 → plugin-install.html">
 </embed>
</object>
</body>
</html>
```

Applet 8.8 How to handle two scrolling lists.

```
                                    Applet

import java.awt.*;
import java.applet.Applet;
import java.awt.event.*;

public class Applet8 extends Applet implements ItemListener {
 List firstList, secondList;

 public void init() {
   setBackground(Color.white);

   firstList = new List(3,true);
   add(new Label("Please choose from the following:"));
   firstList.add("London");
   firstList.add("Paris");
   firstList.add("Rome");
   firstList.add("Detroit");
   firstList.add("New York");
   firstList.addItemListener(this);
   add(firstList);

   secondList = new List(3,true);
   add(secondList);
 }

 public void itemStateChanged(ItemEvent e) {
   String[] addItems = firstList.getSelectedItems();

   secondList.removeAll();
   for (int i=0; i<addItems.length; i++) {
    secondList.add(addItems[i]);
   }
   repaint();
 }
}
```

4. `String[] addItems = firstList.`
`→ getSelectedItems();`

```
secondList.removeAll();
for (int i=0; i<addItems.length; i++) {
    secondList.addItem(addItems[i]);
}
repaint();
```

This applet takes the items that the user has chosen in the first list and displays them in the second list.

Whenever an item is selected or deselected in the first list, this code gets a list of all of firstList's selected items and stores it in the addItems string array. Next, secondList is emptied and then rebuilt with the list from addItems. **Figures 8.18** and **8.19** show the results of the author trying to decide on a destination for her next vacation.

Figure 8.18 Should I go to London, Paris, or New York?

Figure 8.19 Or should I go to London, Rome, or New York?

LOOKING AT LAYOUT

You may have noticed in the previous chapters that in Java, user-interface elements decide for themselves where they want to appear in the browser window. In this chapter, we'll see how you can take charge of your interface using Java's LayoutManagers.

No Layout is FlowLayout

If no LayoutManager is specified, Java assumes that you want to use the simplest Layout-Manager, called FlowLayout. **Listing 9.1** and **Applet 9.1** create a bunch of buttons that just "flow" where they want to.

To use FlowLayout implicitly:

◆ buttonText = spaces.substring(1,i) +
  → "Button #" + i + spaces.
  → substring(1,i);
  this.add(new Button(buttonText));

This code draws ten buttons on the screen, as shown in **Figures 9.1** and **9.2**. Because no LayoutManager has been set, the buttons are displayed centered in the applet area.

Listing 9.1 Display the applet in the browser window.

```
Listing

<html>
<head>
 <title>Listing 9.1</title>
</head>
<body bgcolor="white">
<object classid="clsid:8AD9C840-044E-11D1-
→ B3E9-00805F499D93" width="400" height="100"
→ codetype="application/java">
<param name="code" value="Applet1.class">
<param name="type" value="application/x-java-
→ applet;version=1.3">
<param name="scriptable" value="false">
<embed type="application/x-java-applet;
→ version=1.3" code="Applet1.class" width="400"
→ height="100" scriptable="false" pluginspage=
→ "http://java.sun.com/products/plugin/1.3/
→ plugin-install.html">
</embed>
</object>
</body>
</html>
```

Applet 9.1 This applet throws ten buttons of different sizes onto the window.

```
Applet

import java.awt.*;
import java.applet.*;

public class Applet1 extends Applet {

 public void init() {
   String spaces = "          ",buttonText;

   setBackground(Color.white);

   for (int i=1; i<=10; i++) {
    buttonText = spaces.substring(1,i)
    → + "Button #" + i + spaces.substring(1,i);
    this.add(new Button(buttonText));
   }
 }
}
```

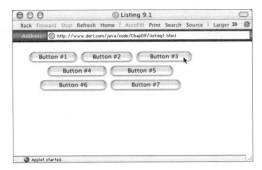

Figure 9.1 This is how this applet looks on a Macintosh...

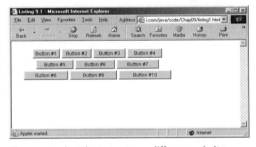

Figure 9.2 ...but there are some differences in its appearance on a PC.

✔ Tips

■ To make it more obvious how the example works, an increasing number of spaces is added to each button. This causes the buttons to be varying sizes.

■ You'll notice that the Mac example only managed to display seven of the ten buttons the applet was supposed to display. That's because buttons that use OS X's Aqua interface are considerably larger than buttons on other operating systems. The moral here: test everywhere to make sure your applet works on as many platforms as possible. To get around this issue in the rest of the applets in this chapter, we'll increase the height and width specified for those applets.

Using FlowLayout

Alternatively, the layout can be explicitly set to use FlowLayout, which gives the applet a little more control over how its components are displayed. **Listing 9.2** and **Applet 9.2** provide an example of an applet where the user-interface elements are left-aligned.

Listing 9.2. This HTML file calls the Java applet.

```
                        Applet
<html>
<head>
 <title>Listing 9.2</title>
</head>
<body bgcolor="white">
<object classid="clsid:8AD9C840-044E-11D1-
→ B3E9-00805F499D93" width="400" height="200"
→ codetype="application/java">
<param name="code" value="Applet2.class">
<param name="type" value="application/x-java-
→ applet;version=1.3">
<param name="scriptable" value="false">
<embed type="application/x-java-applet;
→ version=1.3" code="Applet2.class" width="400"
→ height="200" scriptable="false" pluginspage=
→ "http://java.sun.com/products/plugin/1.3/
→ plugin-install.html">
</embed>
</object>
</body>
</html>
```

Applet 9.2 Here's how to make the buttons align themselves on the left.

```
                        Applet
import java.awt.*;
import java.applet.*;

public class Applet2 extends Applet {

 public void init() {
   String spaces = "            ",buttonText;

   setBackground(Color.white);

   this.setLayout(new FlowLayout
   → (FlowLayout.LEFT));
   for (int i=1; i<=10; i++) {
    buttonText = spaces.substring(1,i)
    → + "Button #" + i + spaces.substring(1,i);
    this.add(new Button(buttonText));
   }
 }
}
```

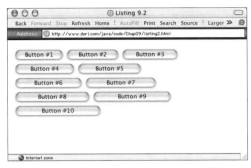

Figure 9.3 The same buttons on the Mac, now aligned on the left.

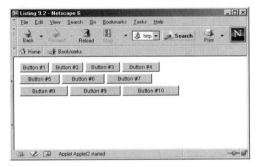

Figure 9.4 The same buttons, aligned on the left in Windows.

To use FlowLayout explicitly:

◆ `this.setLayout(new FlowLayout`
  `→ (FlowLayout.LEFT));`

The easiest way to understand this line is to start from the innermost parentheses and work our way out. `FlowLayout.LEFT` is a Java-defined constant that tells the applet to display the objects in the applet left-aligned. Alternatively, we could have used `FlowLayout.RIGHT` or `FlowLayout.CENTER`.

The alignment constant is passed to a class, `FlowLayout`. A new instance of this class is created (via the keyword `new`) and is passed to `this.setLayout`, which defines the LayoutManager for this applet. **Figures 9.3** and **9.4** show this applet, with the buttons now aligned on the left.

Giving Your Applet Some Space

Along with defining the alignment of your user-interface elements, you can also define how much space the applet puts between them. Like alignment, spacing is set once for the applet, and applies to every component. **Listing 9.3** and **Applet 9.3** demonstrate a right-aligned applet with expanded spacing.

Listing 9.3 This listing calls Applet 9.3.

```
<html>
<head>
<title>Listing 9.3</title>
</head>
<body bgcolor="white">
<object classid="clsid:8AD9C840-044E-11D1-
→ B3E9-00805F499D93" width="400" height="200"
→ codetype="application/java">
<param name="code" value="Applet3.class">
<param name="type" value="application/x-java-
→ applet;version=1.3">
<param name="scriptable" value="false">
<embed type="application/x-java-applet;
→ version=1.3" code="Applet3.class" width="400"
→ height="200" scriptable="false" pluginspage=
→ "http://java.sun.com/products/plugin/1.3/
→ plugin-install.html">
</embed>
</object>
</body>
</html>
```

Applet 9.3 This version of the applet displays the buttons right-aligned, with increased horizontal spacing.

```
import java.awt.*;
import java.applet.*;

public class Applet3 extends Applet {

  public void init() {
    String spaces = "          ",buttonText;

    setBackground(Color.white);

    this.setLayout(new FlowLayout(FlowLayout.
    → RIGHT,35,5));
    for (int i=1; i<=10; i++) {
      buttonText = spaces.substring(1,i)
      → + "Button #" + i + spaces.
      → substring(1,i);
      this.add(new Button(buttonText));
    }
  }
}
```

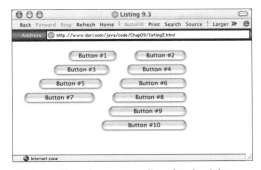

Figure 9.5 These buttons are aligned to the right...

Figure 9.6 ...and show the desired space in between.

To define spacing with FlowLayout:

◆ `this.setLayout(new FlowLayout` → `(FlowLayout.RIGHT,35,5));`

`FlowLayout` can be passed either one parameter (as in the previous example) or three. The second parameter is the horizontal spacing between components, and the third parameter is the vertical spacing. In this example, the horizontal spacing is 35 pixels and the vertical spacing is 5 pixels. **Figures 9.5** and **9.6** show how these applets look in different browsers.

✔ Tip

■ In this example, we're using the word "component" interchangeably with "user-interface element." That's because the two are equivalent here. Later, we'll see how a component can actually be much more than just a button.

Using BorderLayout

FlowLayout isn't the only LayoutManager, just the simplest. BorderLayout has a few more capabilities with only a little more complexity. An applet that uses BorderLayout can handle up to five components. Each component is assigned a direction: North, South, East, West, or Center.

The North and South components will be displayed with a width equal to the entire applet area and a height that's just big enough for the button name. The West and East components will take as much height as is necessary to fill up the entire applet area, with a width that's just big enough for the button name. The Center component gets whatever is left over. **Listing 9.4** and **Applet 9.4** show BorderLayout in use.

Listing 9.4 This HTML file displays the Java applet in the window.

```
<html>
<head>
<title>Listing 9.4</title>
</head>
<body bgcolor="white">
<object classid="clsid:8AD9C840-044E-11D1-
→ B3E9-00805F499D93" width="400" height="100"
→ codetype="application/java">
<param name="code" value="Applet4.class">
<param name="type" value="application/x-java-
→ applet;version=1.3">
<param name="scriptable" value="false">
<embed type="application/x-java-applet;
→ version=1.3" code="Applet4.class" width="400"
→ height="100" scriptable="false" pluginspage=
→ "http://java.sun.com/products/plugin/1.3/
→ plugin-install.html">
</embed>
</object>
</body>
</html>
```

Applet 9.4 A simple example of a BorderLayout.

```
import java.awt.*;
import java.applet.*;

public class Applet4 extends Applet {

  public void init() {
    String[] borders = {"North","West",
    → "Center","East","South"};

    setBackground(Color.white);

    this.setLayout(new BorderLayout(35,5));
    for (int i=0; i<5; i++) {
      this.add(borders[i], new Button
      → (borders[i] + " Button"));
    }
  }
}
```

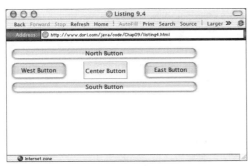

Figure 9.7 An applet that uses BorderLayout can specify in which of five directions each component can be placed.

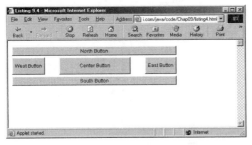

Figure 9.8 Although only one component can be placed in any given direction.

To use BorderLayout:

1. `this.setLayout(new BorderLayout`
   `→ (35,5));`

   This sets the applet's LayoutManager to BorderLayout, with horizontal spacing set to 35 pixels and vertical spacing to 5 pixels.

2. `this.add(borders[i], new Button`
   `→ (borders[i] + " Button"));`

   Here we add five buttons, each with a specific border direction (the first parameter), and a unique name (the second parameter) based on the button's direction. **Figures 9.7** and **9.8** show how the applet appears when complete.

Using GridLayout

Another LayoutManager is `GridLayout`. With `GridLayout`, an applet can display nicely aligned rows and columns of components. **Listing 9.5** and **Applet 9.5** demonstrate how to use `GridLayout`.

Listing 9.5 This calls Applet 9.5.

```
<html>
<head>
<title>Listing 9.5</title>
</head>
<body bgcolor="white">
<object classid="clsid:8AD9C840-044E-11D1-
→ B3E9-00805F499D93" width="400" height="100"
→ codetype="application/java">
<param name="code" value="Applet5.class">
<param name="type" value="application/x-java-
→ applet;version=1.3">
<param name="scriptable" value="false">
<embed type="application/x-java-applet;
→ version=1.3" code="Applet5.class" width="400"
→ height="100" scriptable="false" pluginspage=
→ "http://java.sun.com/products/plugin/1.3/
→ plugin-install.html">
</embed>
</object>
</body>
</html>
```

Applet 9.5 A 3 by 3 example of a GridLayout.

```
import java.awt.*;
import java.applet.*;

public class Applet5 extends Applet {

  public void init() {
    setBackground(Color.white);

    this.setLayout(new GridLayout(0,3,20,20));
    for (int i=1; i<10; i++) {
      this.add(new Button(" Button "+i));
    }
  }
}
```

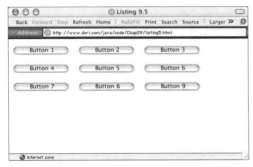

Figure 9.9 Three buttons across by three down...

Figure 9.10 ... all in perfectly aligned rows and columns.

To use GridLayout:

◆ `this.setLayout(new GridLayout`
   `→ (0,3,20,20));`

   `GridLayout` can take either two or four parameters. The first two parameters are always the number of rows and the number of columns that the applet should display. If four parameters are present, the third parameter is horizontal spacing and the fourth is vertical spacing. **Figure 9.9** and **Figure 9.10** show our nice, even grid of buttons.

✔ Tip

■ In this example, the number of rows being passed is zero, and the number of columns is set to three. When one of these two numbers is zero, the true value is calculated based on the other value and the number of components being displayed.

Standing Out With Insets

Java allows you to set the margins of a layout by specifying its *inset*. With `insets`, the top, bottom, left, and right-hand margins are all defined, and can help to align your user-interface elements in the window. **Listing 9.6** and **Applet 9.6** demonstrate usage of the `Insets` class with a `GridLayout`.

Listing 9.6 This listing displays Applet 9.6.

```
<html>
<head>
<title>Listing 9.6</title>
</head>
<body bgcolor="white">
<object classid="clsid:8AD9C840-044E-11D1-
→ B3E9-00805F499D93" width="400" height="100"
→ codetype="application/java">
<param name="code" value="Applet6.class">
<param name="type" value="application/x-java-
→ applet;version=1.3">
<param name="scriptable" value="false">
<embed type="application/x-java-applet;
→ version=1.3" code="Applet6.class" width=
→ "400" height="100" scriptable="false"
→ pluginspage="http://java.sun.com/products/
→ plugin/1.3/plugin-install.html">
</embed>
</object>
</body>
</html>
```

Applet 9.6 Here's how to make your applets stand out.

```java
import java.awt.*;
import java.applet.*;

public class Applet6 extends Applet {

  public void init() {
    setBackground(Color.white);

    this.setLayout(new GridLayout(0,3,5,5));
    for (int i=1; i<10; i++) {
      this.add(new Button(" Button "+i));
    }
  }

  public Insets getInsets() {
   return new Insets(10,10,10,10);
  }
}
```

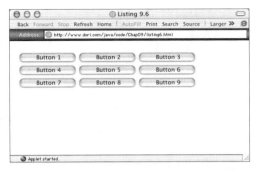

Figure 9.11 While the Mac and Windows versions do look different...

Figure 9.12 ...they both display away from the top-left corner.

To set the Insets:

1. `public Insets getInsets() {`

   In this statement, we say that the public method `getInsets()` will return a value of the class `Insets`.

2. `return new Insets(10,10,10,10);`

   In this example, each margin is set to ten pixels. The order of parameters is top, left, bottom, and right. **Figure 9.11** and **Figure 9.12** display a `GridLayout` surrounded by a ten-pixel margin.

Using Panels to Add Components

Previously, we mentioned that components and user-interface elements weren't necessarily the same thing. In this example, we'll see how several user-interface elements can be combined to make a single component using *panels*.

A *container* is an abstract Java class that contains components. A window is an example of a container. A *panel* is a special type of container, because it is contained within a container, and is itself a container. In other words, it can contain components, but it is also itself a component of a window. The elements are added to the panel, and then the panel is added to the window.

Listing 9.7 and **Applet 9.7** use a combination of panels and BorderLayout to show how more than five elements can be added to a BorderLayout.

To use a panel:

1. northPanel = new Panel();
   southPanel = new Panel();
   centerPanel = new Panel();
   eastPanel = new Panel();
   westPanel = new Panel();

   Where previously we added five buttons to a GridLayout to fill it up, we're now going to use five panels. Here, we create five new panels, each named with its future direction.

2. for (int i = 1; i<4; i++) {

   The simplest way to add three buttons to each panel is within a loop.

Listing 9.7 This HTML file displays Applet 9.7.

```
<html>
<head>
<title>Listing 9.7</title>
</head>
<body bgcolor="white">
<object classid="clsid:8AD9C840-044E-11D1-
 B3E9-00805F499D93" width="600" height="200"
 codetype="application/java">
<param name="code" value="Applet7.class">
<param name="type" value="application/x-java-
 applet;version=1.3">
<param name="scriptable" value="false">
<embed type="application/x-java-applet;
 version=1.3" code="Applet7.class" width="600"
 height="200" scriptable="false" pluginspage=
 "http://java.sun.com/products/plugin/1.3/
 plugin-install.html">
</embed>
</object>
</body>
</html>
```

Applet 9.7 Using a combination of Panels and BorderLayout to get a certain effect.

```
import java.awt.*;
import java.applet.*;

public class Applet7 extends Applet {
Panel northPanel, southPanel, centerPanel,
 eastPanel, westPanel;

 public void init() {
   setBackground(Color.white);

   northPanel = new Panel();
   southPanel = new Panel();
   centerPanel = new Panel();
   eastPanel = new Panel();
   westPanel = new Panel();

   for (int i = 1; i<4; i++) {
    northPanel.add(new Button("North #" + i));
    southPanel.add(new Button("South #" + i));
    centerPanel.add(new Button("C #" + i));
    eastPanel.add(new Button("E #" + i));
    westPanel.add(new Button("W #" + i));
   }

   this.setLayout(new BorderLayout(1,1));
   add("North", northPanel);
   add("South", southPanel);
   add("Center", centerPanel);
   add("East", eastPanel);
   add("West", westPanel);
 }
}
```

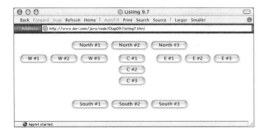

Figure 9.13 This is the effect on a Macintosh.

Figure 9.14 With Windows we get similar but not identical results.

3. `northPanel.add(new Button("North #" +`
`→ i));`
`southPanel.add(new Button("South #" +`
`→ i));`
`centerPanel.add(new Button("C #"+i));`
`eastPanel.add(new Button("E #" + i));`
`westPanel.add(new Button("W #" + i));`

In this block, three buttons are added to each panel. Using the loop variable i as part of the button name helps to keep them straight.

4. `this.setLayout(new BorderLayout`
`→ (1,1));`

The applet is set to use `BorderLayout`, with a height and width spacer of one pixel. This does not change the layout of the panels, just the applet. Unless explicitly defined otherwise, the layout for the panels is `FlowLayout`.

5. `add("North", northPanel);`
`add("South", southPanel);`
`add("Center", centerPanel);`
`add("East", eastPanel);`
`add("West", westPanel);`

Here, the panels are added to the applet window, each to its particular direction. **Figure 9.13** shows how this appears on a Macintosh. The groups of three buttons appear horizontally in the North, South, East, and West directions. Center gets whatever room is left over, which in this case leaves the three buttons in a column. **Figure 9.14** shows the same applet in Windows, where, due to the difference in button size between platforms, all three buttons fit in a single Center row.

USING PANELS TO ADD COMPONENTS

Using CardLayout

Another Java LayoutManager is CardLayout. CardLayout has one major difference from all the other LayoutManagers: it purposefully doesn't show every element that you put into the window. Instead, each element added to a CardLayout is a new *card*, which overlays the previously placed element. Think about dealing out a deck of cards one by one, with each card laid carefully over the previous card. Java allows the user to move forward and backward through that deck of cards, always showing just one card at any time.

Listing 9.8 and **Applet 9.8** show how to combine Panels with a CardLayout and a BorderLayout to describe the desired page.

To use CardLayout:

1.
```
direction = new Panel();
Button leftButton=new Button("<");
Button rightButton=new Button(">");
leftButton.addActionListener(this);
rightButton.addActionListener(this);
direction.add(leftButton);
direction.add(rightButton);
```

In order to be able to move backwards and forwards through the cards, the user needs some method of navigation. Here, we create a new Panel with two buttons, one with a forward arrow and one with a backward arrow. Clicking on each of these buttons will cause either the next or previous card to display.

Listing 9.8 This displays Applet 9.8 in the browser.

```
<html>
<head>
<title>Listing 9.8</title>
</head>
<body bgcolor="white">
<object classid="clsid:8AD9C840-044E-11D1-
→ B3E9-00805F499D93" width="400" height="100"
→ codetype="application/java">
<param name="code" value="Applet8.class">
<param name="type" value="application/x-java-
→ applet;version=1.3">
<param name="scriptable" value="false">
<embed type="application/x-java-applet;
→ version=1.3" code="Applet8.class" width="400"
→ height="100" scriptable="false" pluginspage=
→ "http://java.sun.com/products/plugin/1.3/
→ plugin-install.html">
</embed>
</object>
</body>
</html>
```

Applet 9.8 CardLayout only shows one card at a time.

```
                    Applet
import java.awt.*;
import java.applet.*;
import java.awt.event.*;

public class Applet8 extends Applet implements
→ ActionListener {
 Panel cards, direction;
 CardLayout layout;

 public void init() {
   setBackground(Color.white);

   direction = new Panel();
   Button leftButton=new Button("<");
   Button rightButton=new Button(">");
   leftButton.addActionListener(this);
   rightButton.addActionListener(this);
   direction.add(leftButton);
   direction.add(rightButton);

   cards = new Panel();
   layout = new CardLayout();
   cards.setLayout(layout);
   for (int i = 0; i<10; i++) {
    cards.add("Card # Button" + i,
    → new Button("Card #" + i));
   }

   this.setLayout(new BorderLayout(30,30));
   add("North", direction);
   add("Center", cards);
  }

 public void actionPerformed(ActionEvent e) {
   if (e.getActionCommand()=="<") {
    layout.previous(cards);
   }
   if (e.getActionCommand()==">") {
    layout.next(cards);
   }
  }
 }
}
```

2.
```
cards = new Panel();
layout = new CardLayout();
cards.setLayout(layout);
```
Here, we first create a new **Panel** named cards and a new **CardLayout** named layout. Then, we set the cards **Panel** to use the layout **LayoutManager**.

3.
```
for (int i = 0; i<10; i++) {
   cards.add("Card # Button" + i,
   → new Button("Card #"+i));
}
```
This loop adds ten buttons to the **cards Panel**, each of which lays on top of the previous button. The first parameter is the name of the card, and the second is the label of the button itself on the screen.

4.
```
this.setLayout(new
→ BorderLayout(30,30));
add("North", direction);
add("Center", cards);
```
Our overall window is set here to use the **BorderLayout LayoutManager**, with spacing of 30 pixels in both directions. The "direction" **Panel** is placed in the **North**, and the "cards" **Panel** is placed in the **Center**.

continued

USING CARDLAYOUT

5. `if (e.getActionCommand()=="<") {`
     `layout.previous(cards);`
`}`

This code handles the event that occurs when the user clicks on the "<" button. In this case, simply calling the `layout.previous()` method and passing the `cards` parameter causes, for example, Card #4 to be covered by Card #3, as shown in **Figure 9.15**.

6. `if (e.getActionCommand()==">") {`
   `layout.next(cards);`
`}`

In **Figure 9.16**, we see a user clicking the ">" button to go from Card#1 to Card #2. This action (clicking the button) triggers an event (the code being called). Here, the `layout.next()` method with the `cards` parameter, causes the next card in the deck to be displayed.

✔ Tip

■ Note that while we're using `BorderLayout`, only two of the five directions are in use. While `BorderLayout` is limited to five maximum directions, there's no limitation on the minimum.

Figure 9.15 Moving from Card #4 to Card #3.

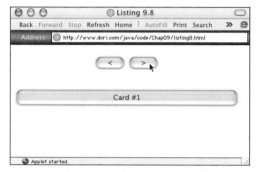

Figure 9.16 Moving from Card #1 to Card #2.

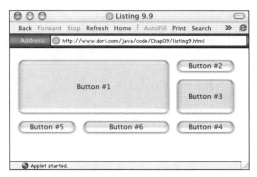

Figure 9.17 How the applet displays on a Mac.

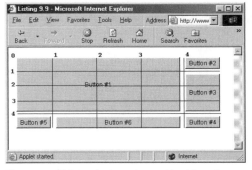

Figure 9.18 And how the applet displays in Windows.

Figure 9.19 This applet is a 5 by 5 grid, with each component taking up a specified amount of space.

Using GridBagLayout

Yes, that's really what it's called. GridBagLayout is simultaneously the most complicated and most versatile of all Java's Layout Managers. It supports as many elements as you wish to put in the window, with fairly precise positioning. However, the power does come at a price, that of complexity. Oh, and having to put up with a silly name, too.

Each GridBagLayout consists of one or more GridBagConstraints. Each element's attributes are added to the GridBag Constraint, and then the element itself is added to the GridBagLayout using the variables in GridBagConstraints. Because GridBagConstraints can be used over and over again, any element's variables that are the same as that of the previously added element do not need to be reinitialized.

The simplest way to understand how GridBagLayout works is to envision a grid with components that are able to cover more than one grid cell. **Listing 9.9** and **Applet 9.9** show an example of a simple GridBagLayout with six buttons in a 5 by 5 grid. Each component specifies how many cells it will take up in each direction, as well as whether or not to expand (and in which direction) if space is available. **Figures 9.17** and **9.18** show how this applet appears on different platforms, while **Figure 9.19** shows how this layout is based on a 5 by 5 grid.

To use GridBagLayout:

1. GridBagLayout thisLayout = new
   → GridBagLayout();
   GridBagConstraints c = new
   → GridBagConstraints();

   Here, we create two new variables: thisLayout, an instance of GridBag Layout, and c, an instance of GridBag Constraints().

continued

2. `c.fill = GridBagConstraints.BOTH;`

This line states that all components in this layout should grow in both directions when there is space available. **Table 9.1** shows other valid values for `fill`.

3. `c.insets = new Insets(5,5,5,5);`

Each component in this layout has a margin of 5 pixels on all sides.

4. `c.gridx = 0;`
`c.gridy = 0;`

The first component will start with its top-left corner in position (0,0).

5. `c.gridwidth = 4;`
`c.gridheight = 4;`

This component has a height of 4 grid cells, and a width of 4 grid cells.

6. `c.weightx = 1.0;`
`c.weighty = 1.0;`

If there is room in the layout for this component to expand, its growth will have higher priority than any component with a `weightx` or `weighty` less than 1, and a lower priority than any component with a `weightx` or `weighty` greater than 1.

7. `makeButton(1);`

This calls a local method with a parameter of 1, which creates a button called "Button #1" with the just-described attributes.

Listing 9.9 This listing displays Applet 9.9 in the browser window.

```
<html>
<head>
<title>Listing 9.9</title>
</head>
<body bgcolor="white">
<object classid="clsid:8AD9C840-044E-11D1-
→ B3E9-00805F499D93" width="400" height="150"
→ codetype="application/java">
<param name="code" value="Applet9.class">
<param name="type" value="application/x-java-
→ applet;version=1.3">
<param name="scriptable" value="false">
<embed type="application/x-java-applet;
→ version=1.3" code="Applet9.class" width="400"
→ height="150" scriptable="false" pluginspage=
→ "http://java.sun.com/
→ products/plugin/1.3/plugin-install.html">
</embed>
</object>
</body>
</html>
```

Applet 9.9 It's a silly sounding name for a very powerful LayoutManager.

```
                    Applet
import java.awt.*;
import java.applet.*;

public class Applet9 extends Applet {
  GridBagLayout thisLayout = new
  → GridBagLayout();
  GridBagConstraints c = new
  → GridBagConstraints();

  public void init() {
    setBackground(Color.white);
    this.setLayout(thisLayout);

    c.fill = GridBagConstraints.BOTH;
    c.insets = new Insets(5,5,5,5);

    c.gridx = 0;
    c.gridy = 0;
    c.gridwidth = 4;
    c.gridheight = 4;
    c.weightx = 1.0;
    c.weighty = 1.0;
    makeButton(1);

    c.gridx = 4;
    c.gridwidth = 1;
    c.gridheight = 1;
    c.weightx = 0.0;
    c.weighty = 0.0;
    makeButton(2);

    c.gridy = 1;
    c.gridheight = 3;
    makeButton(3);

    c.gridy = 4;
    c.gridheight = 1;
    makeButton(4);

    c.gridx = 0;
    makeButton(5);

    c.gridx = 1;
    c.weightx = 1.0;
    makeButton(6);
  }

  protected void makeButton(int buttonNo) {
    Button newButton = new Button("Button #" +
    → buttonNo);
    thisLayout.setConstraints(newButton,c);
    add(newButton);
  }
}
```

8.
```
c.gridx = 4;
c.gridwidth = 1;
c.gridheight = 1;
c.weightx = 0.0;
c.weighty = 0.0;
makeButton(2);
```
Here we describe and create a second button. This time the top-left corner is at (4,0)—there's no need to specify `gridy`, because it hasn't changed from the previous button. The width and height of this button is exactly 1 by 1 grid cell, and it has the lowest possible priority for growth in either axis.

9.
```
c.gridy = 1;
c.gridheight = 3;
makeButton(3);
```
The third button has a top-left corner at (4,1), a width of 1, and a height of 3 grid cells.

10.
```
c.gridy = 4;
c.gridheight = 1;
makeButton(4);
```
Button 4 has a top-left corner of (4,4), and takes up a 1 by 1 grid cell.

11.
```
c.gridx = 0;
makeButton(5);
```
Button 5 is identical to button 4, except that its top-left corner is at (0,4).

12.
```
c.gridx = 1;
c.weightx = 1.0;
makeButton(6);
```
The last button has a top-left corner at (1,4), and would normally have a size of a 1 by 1 grid cell. However, because `weightx` is set to 1, and because no other components exist, it stretches along the x-axis to fill the available area.

continued

USING GRIDBAGLAYOUT

13.
```
protected void makeButton(int
→buttonNo) {
    Button newButton = new Button
    →("Button #" + buttonNo);
    thisLayout.setConstraints
    →(newButton,c);
    add(newButton);
}
```

The makeButton() method creates a button, with a label that is built using the numeric parameter passed to it. The setConstraints() method takes a component and a GridBagConstraints object, and associates the GridBag Constraints object with that component. The new button, now associated with the specified GridBagConstraints, is then added to the layout.

Table 9.1

GridBagConstraints Variables

NAME	VALID CONSTANTS (DEFAULT IN ITALICS)	DESCRIPTION
anchor	*CENTER*, EAST, NORTH, NORTHEAST, NORTHWEST, SOUTH, SOUTHEAST, SOUTHWEST, WEST	Specifies where to display the component when the available cell area is larger than the component
fill	BOTH, HORIZONTAL, *NONE*, VERTICAL	Specifies in which direction a component should grow if there is room available
gridheight	REMAINDER	The height of the component, measured in grid cells; default is 1
gridwidth	REMAINDER	The width of the component, measured in grid cells; default is 1
gridx	*RELATIVE*	The x-axis position of the component, as seen on a grid
gridy	*RELATIVE*	The y-axis position of the component, as seen on a grid
insets		Specfies the margins for a component; default is (0,0,0,0)
ipadx		Specifies the amount of internal padding added to a component in the x-axis; default is 0
ipady		Specifies the amount of internal padding added to a component in the y-axis; default is 0
weightx		Specifies how this component should expand in the x-axis compared to other components; the higher the number, the higher the priority; default is 0.0
weighty		Specifies how this component should expand in the y-axis compared to other components; the higher the number, the higher the priority; default is 0.0

IMAGE MANIPULATION AND ANIMATION

One area where Java shines in comparison to HTML or JavaScript is in its handling of images and animation. You can use Java to display a simple image, or just a part of an image. Java can display a single image in a random location or a random image in a single location.

Animated GIFs are common on the Web to handle simple animation. But with Java, you can have animation that responds to the user or animation that follows a random sequence.

There are some pretty tricky concepts here, so follow along closely, keep your hands inside while the pages are moving, and please—no flash photography.

Displaying an Image

In the same way a journey starts with a single step, displaying moving pictures starts with just a single image. **Applet 10.1** puts an image into your Java window.

This example assumes that you have 52 images corresponding to a normal deck of playing cards. The cards are named *card1.gif* to *card52.gif*, and the goal is to display one in the browser window.

To display an image:

1. int randomCard = (int)
→ (java.lang.Math.random() * 52)+1;

First we create a new integer object named randomCard and initialize it to be a random number between 1 and 52, signifying which playing card will be displayed.

2. setBackground(Color.black);

Here the background is set to black. The HTML, as shown in **Listing 10.1**, gives the applet a very small area, so the black background puts a small frame around the displayed card.

Listing 10.1 Display the applet in the browser window.

```
                     Listing
<html>
<head>
<title>Listing 10.1</title>
</head>
<body bgcolor="white">
<object classid="clsid:8AD9C840-044E-11D1-
→ B3E9-00805F499D93" width="47" height="65"
→ codetype="application/java">
 <param name="code" value="Applet1.class">
 <param name="type" value="application/x-java-
 → applet;version=1.3">
 <param name="scriptable" value="false">
 <embed type="application/x-java-applet;
 → version=1.3" code="Applet1.class" width=
 → "47" height="65" scriptable="false"
 → pluginspage="http://java.sun.com/products/
 → plugin/1.3/plugin-install.html">
 </embed>
</object>
</body>
</html>
```

Applet 10.1 This applet displays a random image on a page.

```
                    Applet
import java.awt.*;
import java.applet.*;

public class Applet1 extends Applet {
  Image thisCard;

  public void init() {
    int randomCard =
    → (int)(java.lang.Math.random() * 52)+1;

    setBackground(Color.black);
    thisCard = getImage(getCodeBase(),
    → "card"+randomCard+".gif");
  }

  public void paint(Graphics g) {
    g.drawImage(thisCard,2,2,this);
  }
}
```

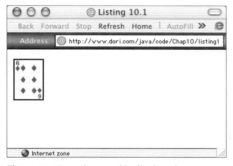

Figure 10.1 A random card is displayed.

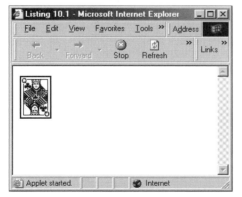

Figure 10.2 By reloading the page, another random card is displayed.

3. `thisCard = getImage(getCodeBase(),`
`→ "card"+randomCard+".gif");`

Here's where we load the card. The `getImage()` method has two parameters: the directory that contains the image and the name of the image. The `getCodeBase()` method says that the image is in the same directory as the `.class` file, and the image name is calculated and assembled based on the random number generated in step 1.

4. `public void paint(Graphics g) {`
`  g.drawImage(thisCard,2,2,this);`
`}`

The `paint()` method is where we call `drawImage()` to display the card in the browser, as shown in **Figures 10.1** and **10.2**.

Displaying Part of an Image

Dealing with 52 separate images can be a pain. In this example, all 52 images have been combined into one big image (**Figure 10.3**) and Java will select a single card to display. **Listing 10.2** and **Applet 10.2** show how to display just part of an image.

To display part of an image:

1. `ImageFilter cardFilter;`
   `ImageProducer cardProducer;`

   Here are two new classes we've never seen before. In order to select part of an image, Java needs to know two things: the dimensions of the desired area, and what image we want to act upon. These are the variables that will handle the selection area.

2. `playingCards = getImage`
   → `(getCodeBase(),"cards.gif");`

   Here we read in the big image.

3. `cardHeight =  61;`
   `cardWidth =  43;`

   To get just the image we want, we'll need the height and width of a single card.

4. `cardPos = (randomCard*cardWidth)+1;`

   The starting position of the desired image is calculated by multiplying the number of the card (starting from 0) we want by the width of the cards and then adding 1 to the result. For example, if we want the first card, **cardPos** is (0 x 43) + 1, or 1. For the fifth card, **cardPos** is (4 x 43) + 1, or 173. This number tells us how many pixels from the right our desired card starts.

Listing 10.2 This HTML calls the applet.

```
<html>
<head>
<title>Listing 10.2</title>
</head>
<body bgcolor="white">
<object classid="clsid:8AD9C840-044E-11D1-
→ B3E9-00805F499D93" width="47" height="65"
→ codetype="application/java">
 <param name="code" value="Applet2.class">
 <param name="type" value="application/x-java-
→ applet;version=1.3">
 <param name="scriptable" value="false">
 <embed type="application/x-java-applet;
→ version=1.3" code="Applet2.class" width="47"
→ height="65" scriptable="false" pluginspage=
→ "http://java.sun.com/products/plugin/1.3/
→ plugin-install.html">
 </embed>
</object>
</body>
</html>
```

Applet 10.2 This applet displays part of an image.

```
import java.awt.*;
import java.applet.*;
import java.awt.image.*;

public class Applet2 extends Applet {
  Image thisCard;

  public void init() {
    int randomCard,cardPos,cardWidth,
    → cardHeight;
    Image playingCards;
    ImageFilter cardFilter;
    ImageProducer cardProducer;

    setBackground(Color.black);

    playingCards = getImage(getCodeBase(),
    → "cards.gif");
    randomCard = (int)(java.lang.Math.random()
    → * 52);
    cardHeight =  61;
    cardWidth =  43;
    cardPos = (randomCard*cardWidth)+1;
    cardFilter = new CropImageFilter(cardPos,1,
    → cardWidth,cardHeight);
    cardProducer = new FilteredImageSource
    → (playingCards.getSource(),cardFilter);
    thisCard = createImage(cardProducer);
  }

  public void paint(Graphics g) {
    g.drawImage(thisCard,2,2,this);
  }
}
```

Figure 10.4 Just one card is shown here.

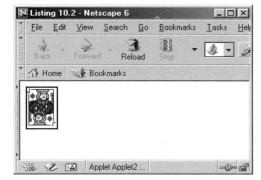

Figure 10.5 And another part of the larger image is shown.

5. `cardFilter = new CropImageFilter`
`→ (cardPos,1,cardWidth,cardHeight);`

The `cardFilter` variable is set up with the desired window into the big image. That is, `cardFilter` now contains the coordinates of the image we actually want so that we can grab just that area from within the full-size image.

6. `cardProducer = new`
`→ FilteredImageSource(playingCards.`
`→ getSource(),cardFilter);`

The `cardProducer` variable uses the `FilteredImageSource()` method with the source of the large image and the filter area from the last step.

7. `thisCard = createImage(cardProducer);`

The `cardProducer` from the previous step is passed to the `createImage()` method to create a new, small image of a single playing card, as shown in **Figures 10.4** and **10.5**.

Figure 10.3 The entire deck of cards is in this one image file.

DISPLAYING PART OF AN IMAGE

Drawing a Border Around an Image

In the previous two tasks, we made the image appear to have a border around it by simply making the applet area slightly larger than the image we were displaying. Obviously, this technique won't always work. In this example, as shown in **Listing 10.3** and **Applet 10.3**, we manually draw a border around our image, for a more versatile (and visually pleasing) effect.

To draw a border around an image:

◆ g.drawRoundRect(1,1,cardWidth+2,
→ cardHeight+2,5,5);

The drawRoundRect() method takes six parameters: the x and y of the starting point, the width of the frame, the height of the frame, and the width and height of the angle of the corners (i.e., distance from the edge). **Figures 10.6** and **10.7** display the single-pixel line around the image.

✔ Tips

■ If we wanted sharp corners instead of curved corners, this applet could use the drawRect() method instead of drawRoundRect(). The parameters of drawRect() are just the first four parameters of drawRoundRect().

■ The appearance of the frame can vary dramatically depending on the values passed for the height and width of the angle of the corners. The larger the numbers, the more rounded the frame. If the numbers are large enough, you'll end up with a circle instead of a rectangle.

Listing 10.3 Set up your HTML.

```
<html>
<head>
<title>Listing 10.3</title>
</head>
<body bgcolor="white">
<object classid="clsid:8AD9C840-044E-11D1-
→ B3E9-00805F499D93" width="300" height="100"
→ codetype="application/java">
 <param name="code" value="Applet3.class">
 <param name="type" value="application/x-java-
 → applet;version=1.3">
 <param name="scriptable" value="false">
 <embed type="application/x-java-applet;
 → version=1.3" code="Applet3.class" width="300"
 → height="100" scriptable="false" pluginspage=
 → "http://java.sun.com/products/plugin/1.3/
 → plugin-install.html">
 </embed>
</object>
</body>
</html>
```

Figure 10.6 This card shows a border of 1 pixel.

Figure 10.7 As does this card.

Applet 10.3 The code for the border applet.

```
                                          Applet
import java.awt.*;
import java.applet.*;
import java.awt.image.*;

public class Applet3 extends Applet {
 Image thisCard;
 int cardWidth=43,cardHeight=61;

 public void init() {
   int randomCard,cardPos;
   Image playingCards;
   ImageFilter cardFilter;
   ImageProducer cardProducer;

   setBackground(Color.white);

   playingCards = getImage(getCodeBase(),"cards.gif");
   randomCard = (int)(java.lang.Math.random() * 52);
   cardPos = (randomCard*cardWidth)+1;
   cardFilter = new CropImageFilter(cardPos,1,cardWidth,cardHeight);
   cardProducer = new FilteredImageSource(playingCards.getSource(),cardFilter);
   thisCard = createImage(cardProducer);
  }

 public void paint(Graphics g) {
   g.drawImage(thisCard,3,3,this);
   g.drawRoundRect(1,1,cardWidth+2,cardHeight+2,5,5);
  }
}
```

Displaying Multiple Images

If you can display a single image, it shouldn't be too difficult to display multiple images—all it takes is a few more calculations. In this example, **Listing 10.4** and **Applet 10.4** display five random images instead of one.

To display multiple images:

1. `Image thisCard[] = new Image[imgCt];`

Instead of creating `thisCard` as an `Image` object, we make `thisCard` an array of `Image` objects.

2. `boolean usedCards[] = new boolean[52];`

The `usedCards` array of Booleans (true/false values) stores whether a given card has already been displayed. All the values are initialized as `false`.

3.
```
for (i=0;i<imgCt;i++) {
 randomCard = (int)(java.lang.
 → Math.random() * 52);
 if (usedCards[randomCard]) {
  i--;
 }
```

For each card that we want to display, we go through this loop. A random card is picked, and then `usedCards` is checked to see if that one has already been used. If so, we subtract one from `i` so that this pass through the loop doesn't count.

4.
```
thisCard[i] = createImage
 → (cardProducer);
usedCards[randomCard] = true;
```

If this card hasn't been seen already, its image is put into the `thisCard` array and its usage in `usedCards` is set to `true`.

Listing 10.4 The HTML for Applet 10.4.

```
<html>
<head>
<title>Listing 10.4</title>
</head>
<body bgcolor="white">
<object classid="clsid:8AD9C840-044E-11D1-
 → B3E9-00805F499D93" width="600" height="100"
 → codetype="application/java">
 <param name="code" value="Applet4.class">
 <param name="type" value="application/x-java-
 → applet;version=1.3">
 <param name="scriptable" value="false">
 <embed type="application/x-java-applet;
 → version=1.3" code="Applet4.class" width="600"
 → height="100" scriptable="false" pluginspage=
 → "http://java.sun.com/products/plugin/1.3/
 → plugin-install.html">
 </embed>
</object>
</body>
</html>
```

Applet 10.4 This applet displays five random images.

```
import java.awt.*;
import java.applet.*;
import java.awt.image.*;

public class Applet4 extends Applet {
 int cardWidth=43,cardHeight=61,imgCt=5;
 Image thisCard[] = new Image[imgCt];

 public void init() {
   int randomCard,cardPos,i;
   Image playingCards;
   ImageFilter cardFilter;
   ImageProducer cardProducer;
   boolean usedCards[] = new boolean[52];

   setBackground(Color.white);
   playingCards = getImage(getCodeBase(),
   → "cards.gif");

   for (i=0;i<imgCt;i++) {
     randomCard = (int)(java.lang.Math.random()
     → * 52);
     if (usedCards[randomCard]) {
       i--;
     }
     else {
      cardPos = (randomCard*cardWidth)+1;
      cardFilter = new CropImageFilter
      → (cardPos,1,cardWidth,cardHeight);
      cardProducer = new FilteredImageSource
      → (playingCards.getSource(),cardFilter);
      thisCard[i] = createImage(cardProducer);
      usedCards[randomCard] = true;
     }
   }
 }

 public void paint(Graphics g) {
   int i,startPt;

   for (i=0;i<imgCt;i++) {
    startPt = (i*(cardWidth+10));
    g.drawImage(thisCard[i],startPt+3,3,this);
    g.drawRoundRect(startPt+1,1,cardWidth+2,
    → cardHeight+2,5,5);
   }
 }
}
```

5. ```startPt = (i*(cardWidth+10));
g.drawImage(thisCard[i],startPt+3,3,
→ this);
g.drawRoundRect(startPt+1,1,cardWidth
→ +2,cardHeight+2,5,5);```

Because there are five images, there's no fixed starting point at which to display each image. The `startPt` variable calculates where each should start, based on which pass through the loop we're on and the width of the cards.

The `drawImage()` and `drawRoundRect()` methods are similar to what we've seen before, except that the former now uses the `thisCard` array for the card to display, and both use `startPt` to know where to start drawing, as shown in **Figures 10.8** and **10.9**.

continued

✔ Tip

■ Note how easy it is to change the number of images that are displayed: Simply change `imgCt` from 5 to some other number, and everything else changes with it.

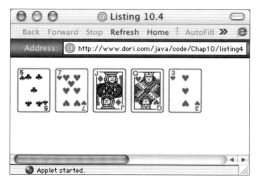

Figure 10.8 Pick a card, any card.

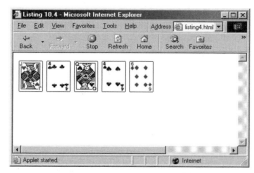

Figure 10.9 Another card on another platform.

Listing 10.5 The HTML you need to load the applet.

```
                    Listing
<html>
<head>
<title>Listing 10.5</title>
</head>
<body bgcolor="white">
<object classid="clsid:8AD9C840-044E-11D1-
➝ B3E9-00805F499D93" width="300" height="100"
➝ codetype="application/java">
 <param name="code" value="Applet5.class">
 <param name="type" value="application/x-java-
➝ applet;version=1.3">
 <param name="scriptable" value="false">
 <embed type="application/x-java-applet;
➝ version=1.3" code="Applet5.class" width="300"
➝ height="100" scriptable="false" pluginspage=
➝ "http://java.sun.com/products/plugin/1.3/
➝ plugin-install.html">
 </embed>
</object>
</body>
</html>
```

Threading and Animation

You may have noticed that all the examples you've seen so far in this chapter involve just putting something up on the screen. They don't move and they don't change. The key to making Java applets move and change is *threading*, as demonstrated by **Listing 10.5** and **Applet 10.5**.

When a computer does more than one thing at a time, it is referred to as *multi-threaded*. Each of the things it is doing is called a *thread*. Threads let programs play nice with other programs, and with other parts of the same program. Java (and your operating system) parcel out time to threads, making sure that each gets the time it needs without hogging your computer.

To make an applet threaded:

1. `public class Applet5 extends Applet`
   `➝ implements Runnable {`

   The big change here is that we're not just extending Applet any more, we're also *implementing* Runnable. This adds the run() method to the applet, which means that Java will now be able to do things while the applet is running. Previously, we've only been able to change the screen display when it was first displayed, or when the user caused an event to occur. Now, Java will be able to use run() to do just about anything.

2. `Thread runner;`

   This creates a new type of object, a thread called runner, which will handle the one thread that this applet needs.

   continued

Applet 10.5 . A threaded applet.

```
                                      Applet
import java.awt.*;
import java.applet.*;
import java.awt.image.*;

public class Applet5 extends Applet implements Runnable {
 int cardWidth=43,cardHeight=61,imgCt=10,thisPos;
 Image currImg,thisCard[] = new Image[imgCt];
 Thread runner;

 public void init() {
   int randomCard,cardPos,i;
   Image playingCards;
   ImageFilter cardFilter;
   ImageProducer cardProducer;
   boolean usedCards[] = new boolean [52];

   setBackground(Color.white);
   playingCards = getImage(getCodeBase(),"cards.gif");

   for (i=0;i<imgCt;i++) {
     randomCard = (int)(java.lang.Math.random() * 52);
     if (usedCards[randomCard]) {
       i--;
     }
     else {
       cardPos = (randomCard*cardWidth)+1;
       cardFilter = new CropImageFilter(cardPos,1,cardWidth,cardHeight);
       cardProducer = new FilteredImageSource(playingCards.getSource(),cardFilter);
       thisCard[i] = createImage(cardProducer);
       usedCards[randomCard] = true;
     }
   }
   thisPos = (int)(java.lang.Math.random() * 200);
   currImg = thisCard[0];
 }

 public void start() {
   runner = new Thread(this);
   runner.start();
 }

 public void run() {
   for (int i=1;i<imgCt;i++) {
     try {
      Thread.sleep(2000);
     }
     catch (InterruptedException e) {
     }

     thisPos = (int)(java.lang.Math.random() * 200);
     currImg = thisCard[i];
     repaint();
   }
 }

 public void paint(Graphics g) {
   g.drawImage(currImg,thisPos+3,3,this);
   g.drawRoundRect(thisPos+1,1,cardWidth+2,cardHeight+2,5,5);
 }
}
```

3.
```
public void start() {
   runner = new Thread(this);
   runner.start();
}
```

Because we're using threading, we now need to override the **start()** method for the first time. We create our new thread and tell it to start up.

4.
```
public void run() {
```

Here's where the action is. The code inside the **run()** method runs whenever other processes give this thread a chance to do something.

5.
```
for (int i=1;i<imgCt;i++) {
```

What we want to do is display our ten images, so we loop through them.

6.
```
try {
   Thread.sleep(2000);
}
```

Whenever you have a **run()** method, you have to have a **try/catch** statement. Other threads are giving up system time to your applet, so your applet should be a good neighbor and give control back to the system periodically.

Here we tell the thread to sleep for two seconds (2000 milliseconds). If something bad happens while the applet is sleeping, the **try** will throw the error to the **catch** statement.

7.
```
catch (InterruptedException e) {
}
```

If, during our two-second sleep, something interrupts the thread, an **InterruptedException** will be thrown, and so must be caught. Here we catch it, but because we don't care about interruptions, we don't have to do anything else with it.

continued

THREADING AND ANIMATION

165

8. `thisPos = (int)(java.lang.Math.`
   `→ random() * 200);`
   `currImg = thisCard[i];`
   `repaint();`

   The variable `thisPos` picks a random location at which to display `currImg`, our random card. We then call the `repaint()` method, which will clear the applet area and then call `paint()`. Because `repaint()` clears the applet area (by calling `update()`), only one card at a time is displayed, as shown in **Figures 10.10** and **10.11**.

✔ Tips

- You might wonder sometimes how to know what errors your applet needs to catch. Here's an easy way to figure out the most important ones: don't catch any errors. If some errors are required to be caught, your compiler will object and tell you what exceptions need to be caught before it will create your .class file.

- It's difficult for a screenshot of an animated applet to show the full result. For a better view, you can view the applets in action at <http://www.dori.com/java/>.

Figure 10.10 The cards appear ...

Figure 10.11 ... to move and change.

Listing 10.6 The HTML displays the applet.

```
<html>
<head>
<title>Listing 10.6</title>
</head>
<body bgcolor="white">
<object classid="clsid:8AD9C840-044E-11D1-
→ B3E9-00805F499D93" width="300" height="100"
→ codetype="application/java">
 <param name="code" value="Applet6.class">
 <param name="type" value="application/x-java-
→ applet;version=1.3">
 <param name="scriptable" value="false">
 <embed type="application/x-java-applet;
→ version=1.3" code="Applet6.class" width="300"
→ height="100" scriptable="false" pluginspage=
→ "http://java.sun.com/products/plugin/1.3/
→ plugin-install.html">
 </embed>
</object>
</body>
</html>
```

Double-Buffering Animation

You may have noticed that the images in the last example flickered when they were drawn on your screen. **Listing 10.6** and **Applet 10.6** show you how to use a technique called *double-buffering* to get rid of that flicker.

As mentioned in the previous task, the applet area is completely redrawn each time a new card is displayed. This is what causes the flickering effect. The double-buffering solution involves creating an off-screen (or "scratch") drawing area, updating that instead of the on-screen area, and then using the off-screen area to update the on-screen after everything has been drawn. This means that the on-screen area that the user sees is updated once, not twice, thus eliminating the flicker.

To double-buffer animation:

1. `Image currImg,thisCard[] = new`
   `→ Image[imgCt],winScratch;`
   `Graphics gScratch;`

   Here's where we create the off-screen scratch area in memory, with an `Image` object named `winScratch` and a `Graphics` object named `gScratch`.

2. `winScratch = createImage`
   `→ (this.getSize().width, this.`
   `→ getSize().height);`
   `gScratch = winScratch.getGraphics();`

   We initialize `winScratch`, our scratch area, to be an image with the exact dimensions of the applet area. `gScratch` is initialized using `winScratch`'s `getGraphics()` method.

   continued

Applet 10.6 This applet gets rid of the flicker.

```
                                         Applet
import java.awt.*;
import java.applet.*;
import java.awt.image.*;

public class Applet6 extends Applet implements Runnable {
 int cardWidth=43,cardHeight=61,imgCt=50,thisPos;
 Image currImg,thisCard[] = new Image[imgCt],winScratch;
 Graphics gScratch;
 Thread runner;

 public void init() {
   int randomCard,cardPos,i;
   Image playingCards;
   ImageFilter cardFilter;
   ImageProducer cardProducer;
   boolean usedCards[] = new boolean [52];

   winScratch = createImage(this.getSize().width,this.getSize().height);
   gScratch = winScratch.getGraphics();
   setBackground(Color.white);
   playingCards = getImage(getCodeBase(),"cards.gif");

   for (i=0;i<imgCt;i++) {
    randomCard = (int)(java.lang.Math.random() * 52);
    if (usedCards[randomCard]) {
     i--;
    }
    else {
     cardPos = (randomCard*cardWidth)+1;
     cardFilter = new CropImageFilter(cardPos,1,cardWidth,cardHeight);
     cardProducer = new FilteredImageSource(playingCards.getSource(),cardFilter);
     thisCard[i] = createImage(cardProducer);
     usedCards[randomCard] = true;
    }
   }
   thisPos = (int)(java.lang.Math.random() * 200);
   currImg = thisCard[0];
 }

 public void start() {
   runner = new Thread(this);
   runner.start();
 }

 public void run() {
   for (int i=1;i<imgCt;i++) {
    try {
     Thread.sleep(2000);
    }
    catch (InterruptedException e) {
    }

    thisPos = (int)(java.lang.Math.random() * 200);
    currImg = thisCard[i];
    repaint();
   }
 }

 public void paint(Graphics g) {
   gScratch.setColor(this.getBackground());
   gScratch.fillRect(0,0,this.getSize().width,this.getSize().height);
   gScratch.setColor(Color.black);

   gScratch.drawImage(currImg,thisPos+3,3,this);
   gScratch.drawRoundRect(thisPos+1,1,cardWidth+2,cardHeight+2,5,5);
   g.drawImage(winScratch,0,0,this);
 }

 public final void update(Graphics g) {
   paint(g);
 }
}
```

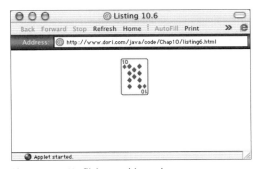

Figure 10.12 No flicker as this card...

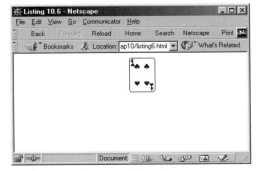

Figure 10.13 ...changes to this card.

3. gScratch.setColor(this.
→ getBackground());
gScratch.fillRect(0,0,this.getSize().
→ width,this.getSize().height);
gScratch.setColor(Color.black);

gScratch.drawImage(currImg, thisPos+3,
→ 3,this);
gScratch.drawRoundRect(thisPos+1,1,
→ cardWidth+2,cardHeight+2,5,5);
g.drawImage(winScratch,0,0,this);

Because we now have to handle all the screen updates manually, a few lines have been added to the `paint()` method. The big change is that instead of calling `g.drawImage()` (for instance), we're calling `gScratch.drawImage()`. This is where the double-buffering, i.e., the writing out to the off-screen buffer, is occurring. Only in the last line, when the off-screen area has been completely drawn, is `g.drawImage()` called, with a parameter of `winScratch`. This draws the off-screen image in the on-screen area, as demonstrated by **Figures 10.12** and **10.13**.

4. public final void update(Graphics g) {
    paint(g);
}

A required part of double-buffering is overriding the `update()` method. It's the `update()` method that clears the screen normally, so in order to stop that behavior, the method must be overridden. We still want drawing to take place, however, so we still call the `paint()` method.

Displaying Unlimited Images

Sometimes it's useful to only display a certain number of images. Other times, you'll want to continue the animation indefinitely. This example displays a random playing card every two seconds for as long as you're on the Web page.

To display non-stop animation:

1. `while (true) {`

    Instead of looping a certain number of times inside `run()`, this statement (which always evaluates to `true`, and so will run forever) forces the animation to display continuously.

2. `if (currImg != null) {`

    Because all the image initialization code has been moved to the `run()` method, there's a short amount of time when `paint()` has been called but `currImg` has not yet been set. Checking to see if `currImg` has been set before attempting to draw it on the screen avoids errors. **Figures 10.14** and **10.15** show how this applet appears on screen.

    For the most part, this example is very similar to the previous. Most of the changes just involve code that's been moved, not added, as seen in **Listing 10.7** and **Applet 10.7**.

Listing 10.7 Calls Applet 10.7.

```
<html>
<head>
<title>Listing 10.7</title>
</head>
<body bgcolor="white">
<object classid="clsid:8AD9C840-044E-11D1-
→ B3E9-00805F499D93" width="300" height="100"
→ codetype="application/java">
 <param name="code" value="Applet7.class">
 <param name="type" value="application/x-java-
 → applet;version=1.3">
 <param name="scriptable" value="false">
 <embed type="application/x-java-applet;
 → version=1.3" code="Applet7.class" width="300"
 → height="100" scriptable="false" pluginspage=
 → "http://java.sun.com/products/plugin/1.3/
 → plugin-install.html">
 </embed>
</object>
</body>
</html>
```

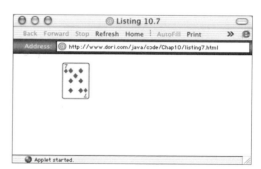

Figure 10.14 There's no end...

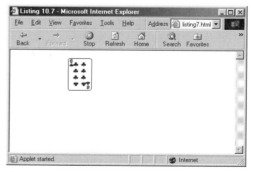

Figure 10.15 ... to this house of cards.

Applet 10.7 This applet is similar to Applet 10.6.

```
import java.awt.*;
import java.applet.*;
import java.awt.image.*;

public class Applet7 extends Applet implements Runnable {
 int cardWidth=43,cardHeight=61,thisPos;
 Image winScratch,playingCards,currImg;
 Graphics gScratch;
 Thread runner;

 public void init() {
   winScratch = createImage(this.getSize().width,this.getSize().height);
   gScratch = winScratch.getGraphics();
   setBackground(Color.white);
   playingCards = getImage(getCodeBase(),"cards.gif");
 }

 public void start() {
   runner = new Thread(this);
   runner.start();
 }

 public void run() {
   int randomCard,cardPos;
   ImageFilter cardFilter;
   ImageProducer cardProducer;

   while (true) {
    try {
      Thread.sleep(2000);
    }
      catch (InterruptedException e) {
    }

    thisPos = (int)(java.lang.Math.random() * 200);
    randomCard = (int)(java.lang.Math.random() * 52);
    cardPos = (randomCard*cardWidth)+1;
    cardFilter = new CropImageFilter(cardPos,1,cardWidth,cardHeight);
    cardProducer = new FilteredImageSource(playingCards.getSource(),cardFilter);
    currImg = createImage(cardProducer);
    repaint();
   }
 }

 public void paint(Graphics g) {
   if (currImg != null) {
    gScratch.setColor(this.getBackground());
    gScratch.fillRect(0,0,this.getSize().width,this.getSize().height);
    gScratch.setColor(Color.black);

    gScratch.drawImage(currImg,thisPos+3,3,this);
    gScratch.drawRoundRect(thisPos+1,1,cardWidth+2,cardHeight+2,5,5);
    g.drawImage(winScratch,0,0,this);
   }
 }

 public final void update(Graphics g) {
   paint(g);
 }
}
```

Controlling Animation

Letting your animation run on and on (and on and on...) is nice, but it's nicer to be able to start and stop the display. **Listing 10.8** and **Applet 10.8** include a button that allows the user to stop the display and then start it back up again. This is where the real power of a multi-threaded applet is revealed.

To start and stop animation:

1. `Button startStop;`
   `Boolean isRunning = true;`

   Two variables are declared here: `startStop`, a button which does exactly what it says, and `isRunning`, which keeps track of whether or not the applet is running. It's set to start off running.

2. `startStop = new Button("Stop");`
   `add(startStop);`

   The new button is added to the display with a label of "Stop."

3. `if (runner == null) {`

   Previously, we made the assumption that if `start()` was called, it was time to start up a new thread. Now, because the thread can be started and stopped, we have to check to see if it already exists before trying to create it.

4. `public void stop() {`
   `  runner = null;`
   `}`

   Here's a new method: `stop()`. Now that the thread can be stopped as well as started, we need to handle that option. In this case, all we're going to do is throw away our `runner` thread.

   continued on page 174

Listing 10.8 This HTML page loads Applet 10.8.

```
<html>
<head>
<title>Listing 10.8</title>
</head>
<body bgcolor="white">
<object classid="clsid:8AD9C840-044E-11D1-
→ B3E9-00805F499D93" width="300" height="100"
→ codetype="application/java">
<param name="code" value="Applet8.class">
<param name="type" value="application/x-java-
→ applet;version=1.3">
<param name="scriptable" value="false">
<embed type="application/x-java-applet;
→ version=1.3" code="Applet8.class" width="300"
→ height="100" scriptable="false" pluginspage=
→ "http://java.sun.com/products/plugin/1.3/
→ plugin-install.html">
</embed>
</object>
</body>
</html>
```

Applet 10.8 This applet lets your visitors stop and start the animations.

```
import java.awt.*;
import java.applet.*;
import java.awt.image.*;
import java.awt.event.*;

public class Applet8 extends Applet implements
→ Runnable, ActionListener {
  int cardWidth=43,cardHeight=61,thisPos;
  Image winScratch,playingCards,currImg;
  Graphics gScratch;
  Thread runner;
  Button startStop;
  boolean isRunning = true;

  public void init() {
    winScratch = createImage(this.getSize().
    → width,this.getSize().height);
    gScratch = winScratch.getGraphics();
    setBackground(Color.white);
    playingCards = getImage(getCodeBase(),
    → "cards.gif");
    startStop = new Button("Stop");
    startStop.addActionListener(this);
    add(startStop);
  }

  public void start() {
    if (runner == null) {
    runner = new Thread(this);
    runner.start();
```

Applet continues on next page

Applet 10.8 *continued*

```
  }
}

public void stop() {
  runner = null;
}

public void run() {
  int randomCard,cardPos;
  ImageFilter cardFilter;
  ImageProducer cardProducer;

  while (isRunning) {
    try {
      Thread.sleep(2000);
    }
    catch (InterruptedException e) {
    }

    thisPos = (int)(java.lang.Math.random() * 200);
    randomCard = (int)(java.lang.Math.random() * 52);
    cardPos = (randomCard*cardWidth)+1;
    cardFilter = new CropImageFilter(cardPos,1,cardWidth,cardHeight);
    cardProducer = new FilteredImageSource(playingCards.getSource(),cardFilter);
    currImg = createImage(cardProducer);
    repaint();
  }
}

public void paint(Graphics g) {
  if (currImg != null && isRunning) {
    gScratch.setColor(this.getBackground());
    gScratch.fillRect(0,0,this.getSize().width,this.getSize().height);
    gScratch.setColor(Color.black);

    gScratch.drawImage(currImg,thisPos+3,32,this);
    gScratch.drawRoundRect(thisPos+1,30,cardWidth+2,cardHeight+2,5,5);
    g.drawImage(winScratch,0,0,this);
  }
}

public final void update(Graphics g) {
  paint(g);
}

public void actionPerformed(ActionEvent e) {
  if (isRunning) {
    isRunning = false;
    startStop.setLabel("Start");
    stop();
  }
  else {
    isRunning = true;
    startStop.setLabel("Stop");
    start();
  }
}
}
```

5. `while (isRunning) {`

In the last example, we looped through `run()` forever. Now, we just want to do it while the `isRunning` flag is `true`.

6. `if (currImg != null && isRunning) {`

Along with not wanting to paint nonexistent images, we now also want to skip painting whenever the `isRunning` flag has been set to `false`. The results on the screen are displayed in **Figures 10.16** and **10.17**.

7. `if (isRunning) {`
   `isRunning = false;`
   `startStop.setLabel("Start");`
   `stop();`
`}`

When the Start/Stop button is pressed, we check to see if we're currently running or not. If we are, we want to stop the thread. In this case, the `isRunning` flag is turned off (`false`), the button label is reset to "Start," and `stop()` is called.

8. `else {`
   `isRunning = true;`
   `startStop.setLabel("Stop");`
   `start();`
`}`

If we were stopped, it's time to start back up again. We set the `isRunning` flag to on (`true`), reset the button label back to "Stop," and call the `start()` method to restart the thread.

✔ Tip

■ You can add another form field (a radio button, text box, etc.) to allow the user to modify how long the applet sleeps between redraws.

Figure 10.16 How the button looks in Internet Explorer on the Mac.

Figure 10.17 The same button in Netscape Navigator on Windows.

JAVA AND JAVASCRIPT

11

At first glance, Java and JavaScript might appear to be related, given the similarities in their names. The truth is that they have many more differences than similarities.

When Sun first introduced Java to the world in 1995 it was widely acknowledged as a major change in programming languages. Around the same time, Netscape introduced a scripting language called LiveScript, which was an add-on to HTML for Netscape. A few months later, those smart guys (and gals) at Netscape noticed that no one was paying attention to their new language due to the amount of buzz Java was getting, so they decided to borrow a little of that buzz for themselves by cutting a deal with Sun to allow them to change the name of their language to JavaScript. Mostly, they succeeded in badly confusing legions of would-be Web programmers.

However, JavaScript and Java can and do talk to each other, giving additional functionality to your pages. With this approach, you can use each language for its strengths, combining the two for a sum greater than the parts. One warning, though: different browsers can have radically different capabilities between versions and platforms. Each task in this chapter only works on certain browsers, and the best way to know where your code will work is to test on all your target configurations.

✔ Tip

■ If you're interested in learning more about JavaScript, a good place to start is *JavaScript for the World Wide Web, 4th Edition: Visual QuickStart Guide,* (Peachpit Press; 2001), written by Tom Negrino and me. For those looking for something more advanced, check out *The JavaScript Bible, 4th Edition* (Hungry Minds, 2001), by Danny Goodman.

Checking for Java

You can use JavaScript in your HTML page to check to see if Java is enabled. Doing this allows you to generate different pages on the fly, depending on whether or not the user has Java, as shown in **Listing 11.1**.

To check if Java is enabled:

1. `<script language="javascript"`
   → `type="text/javascript">`

   The `script` HTML tag tells the browser that whatever follows is scripting language, not text to be displayed in the browser window. The `language` attribute of the `script` tag tells the browser which scripting language we're using, which in this case is JavaScript. And just to be sure, the `type` attribute tells the browser that the following uses the `text/javascript` MIME type.

2. `<!-- Hide script from old browsers`

   The first line of a script should always start with a comment. This tells older browsers that don't understand JavaScript to skip the contents of the script. These browsers then treat the entire script as a comment.

3. `if (navigator.javaEnabled()) {`

   Here's the meat of the script. JavaScript has an object called `navigator`, which has a method called `javaEnabled()`. This method is either true or false, depending on whether this browser understands Java. If the check evaluates to `true`, the code within the following curly braces will be executed.

Listing 11.1 This code displays an applet if Java's enabled.

```
<html>
<head>
<title>Listing 11.1</title>
</head>
<body bgcolor="white">
 <script language="javascript" type=
 → "text/javascript">
  <!-- Hide script from old browsers

  if (navigator.javaEnabled()) {
  document.writeln('<object classid=
  → "clsid:8AD9C840-044E-11D1-B3E9-
  → 00805F499D93" width="500" height="100"
  → codetype="application/java">')
  document.writeln('<param name="code"
  → value="Applet5.class">')
  document.writeln('<param name="type" value=
  → "application/x-java-applet;version=1.3">')
  document.writeln('<param name="scriptable"
  → value="false">')
  document.writeln('<embed type=
  → "application/x-java-applet;version=1.3"
  → code="Applet5.class" width="500" height=
  → "100" scriptable="false" pluginspage=
  → "http://java.sun.com/products/plugin/1.3/
  → plugin-install.html">')
  document.writeln('<\/embed>')
  document.writeln('<\/object>')
}
  else {
  document.writeln('<img src="butterfly.gif"
  → width="32" height="26"><br>You would be
  → seeing something more impressive if you
  → had Java, so download a Java-enabled
  → browser now!')
}

  // End hiding script from old browsers -->
</script>

</body>
</html>
```

Figure 11.1 The applet in a Java-enabled browser.

Figure 11.2 The same page in Internet Explorer.

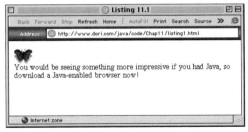

Figure 11.3 This message is displayed if the user has JavaScript turned on but not Java.

✔ Tips

- The else part of the script is optional. If there's nothing that you want to add if Java's disabled, leave off the else block.

- Most modern browsers allow the user to turn both JavaScript and Java on or off. The code above will work only if JavaScript is turned on but Java is turned off. If JavaScript is turned off, the code within the script tags is ignored.

4. `document.writeln('<object`
   `→ classid="clsid:8AD9C840-044E-11D1-`
   `→ B3E9-00805F499D93" width="500"`
   `→ height="100" codetype="`
   `→ application/java">')`

If JavaScript is enabled, the method `document.writeln()` will be executed. This method adds whatever's been passed to the page's HTML. In this case, we're adding an `object` tag—one referring to **Applet 7.5**, to be exact. **Figures 11.1** and **11.2** show the results in Java-enabled browsers. The lines up until the end of the `if true` section area write out the remainder of the object and embed tags.

5. `}`

This right curly brace ends the `if true` code segment.

6. `else {`

If the above check to see if Java is enabled fails (i.e., Java is not enabled), the code in the `else` code block is executed.

7. `document.writeln('<img src="`
   `→ butterfly.gif" width="32"`
   `→ height="26"><br>You would be seeing`
   `→ something more impressive if you`
   `→ had Java, so download a Java-enabled`
   `→ browser now!')`

This code displays an image and encourages the user to get a current version of a Java-enabled browser (**Figure 11.3**).

8. `}`

This right curly brace ends the `false` or `else` code segment.

9. `// End hiding script from old`
   `→ browsers -->`

For those older browsers that don't understand `script` tags, this ends the comment started above.

10. `</script>`

This ends the JavaScript part of the page.

JavaScript and Public Java Methods

If a user is running a Netscape browser with both JavaScript and Java enabled, JavaScript is able to access public Java methods. This is accomplished via a Netscape technology called *LiveConnect*. Unfortunately, this technique doesn't work with Internet Explorer. **Listing 11.2** shows how JavaScript can get access to the default Toolkit to find out the user's monitor's width, height, and resolution in dots per inch. This is useful information to have when you're using JavaScript to, for instance, open a window to its largest possible size. Given these measurements, JavaScript can open a new browser window to the correct dimensions to fill the user's screen.

To use public Java methods in JavaScript:

1. `sWidth = 0`
`sHeight = 0`
`sRes = 0`

This initializes our three variables, `sWidth`, `sHeight`, and `sRes`, to zero. Unlike Java, JavaScript uses loosely typed variables, which means that we don't need to explicitly declare them as integers, floats, or even as numbers at all.

2. `if (navigator.appName == "Netscape"`
`→ && navigator.javaEnabled()) {`

Because only Netscape supports this capability, the following code will cause errors in other browsers. Consequently, there's a check here to make sure that only Netscape executes the following block of code. Also, we check to see if Java's enabled; there's no point in trying to access Java methods if we know that Java won't run in this browser.

Listing 11.2 Without writing any Java code you can still find out the user's monitor width, height, and resolution.

```
<html>
<head>
<title>Listing 11.2</title>
</head>
<body bgcolor="white">
<script language="javascript" type=
→ "text/javascript">
  <!-- Hide script from old browsers

  sWidth = 0
  sHeight = 0
  sRes = 0

  if (navigator.appName == "Netscape" &&
  → navigator.javaEnabled()) {
    defToolkit = java.awt.Toolkit.
    → getDefaultToolkit()
    sWidth = defToolkit.getScreenSize().width
    sHeight = defToolkit.
    → getScreenSize().height
    sRes = defToolkit.getScreenResolution()
  }

  if (sWidth == 0 || sHeight == 0 || sRes == 0) {
    sWidth = 800
    sHeight = 600
    sRes = 96
  }

  document.writeln("<H1>Your screen dimensions
  → are " + sWidth + " x " + sHeight + ", with
  → a resolution of " + sRes + " dpi.<\/H1>")

  // End hiding script from old browsers -->
  </script>
</body>
</html>
```

3. `defToolkit = java.awt.Toolkit.`
`→ getDefaultToolkit()`

Here we initialize a new variable, `defToolkit`, based on the Java method that gets Java's known information about the user's system.

4. `sWidth = defToolkit.`
`→ getScreenSize().width`
`sHeight = defToolkit.`
`→ getScreenSize().height`

Given the default Toolkit, we can use the public Java method `getScreenSize()` to find out the height and width that the user's monitor currently displays.

5. `sRes = defToolkit.`
`→ getScreenResolution()`

Similarly, we can find out the screen resolution of the user's monitor by checking the public Java method `getScreenResolution()`.

6. `}`

The right curly brace closes the conditional code segment.

7. `if (sWidth == 0 || sHeight == 0 ||`
`→ sRes == 0) {`

If any of the three variables we care about are still set to zero, then we want to execute the code following this `if` statement. This can happen if the user's browser wasn't Netscape, if the user is running with JavaScript on but Java off, or if there was an error of some type while accessing Java.

continued

8. `sWidth = 800`
`sHeight = 600`
`sRes = 96`

In this case, we want to set all the variables to their most likely values. This is what will be displayed if, for some reason, the user's browser doesn't support this functionality. It won't be accurate all the time, but it will be most of the time.

9. `}`

And close the conditional.

10. `document.writeln("<H1>Your screen`
`→ dimensions are " + sWidth + " x "`
`→ + sHeight + ", with a resolution`
`→ of " + sRes + " dpi.<\/H1>")`

Here we use the JavaScript method `document.writeln` to print out our results, as shown in **Figure 11.4**.

✔ Tip

■ Even though no Java applet is explicitly called, anyone running Netscape version 4 or later will see a message that says that Java is loading. LiveConnect has to start up Java in order to check the Toolkit.

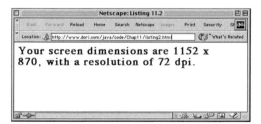

Figure 11.4 Using the code in Listing 11.2, the user's information is displayed in the window.

Listing 11.3 Use this code to ask the user to enter a string.

```
<html>
<head>
<title>Listing 11.3</title>
<script language="javascript" type=
→ "text/javascript">
  <!-- Hide script from old browsers

  function startUp() {
  document.myApplet.newText(prompt
  → ("What do you want to say?",""))
  }

  // End hiding script from old browsers -->
  </script>
</head>
<body onLoad="startUp()" bgcolor="white">
<applet code="Applet1.class" width="300"
→ height="50" name="myApplet">
</applet>
</body>
</html>
```

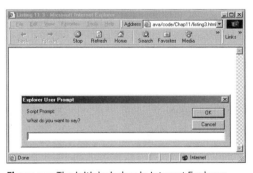

Figure 11.5 The initial window in Internet Explorer (Windows).

Figure 11.6 The same window in Netscape (Mac).

Passing Information from JavaScript to Java

We can also pass information between JavaScript and Java applets we've written. **Listing 11.3** and **Applet 11.1** demonstrate how text entered into a JavaScript prompt window can be displayed in the browser window by Java. **Listing 11.3** shows the JavaScript side of passing information to Java:

To pass information from JavaScript to Java (the JavaScript side):

1. `function startUp() {`

   This begins a new JavaScript function called `startUp()`.

2. `document.myApplet.newText(prompt`
   `→ ("What do you want to say?",""))`

   Two things are happening here. First, the JavaScript `prompt()` method creates a new window, as shown in **Figure 11.5**. The first parameter passed to `prompt()` is the window's prompt, and the second parameter is the default input—in this case, nothing. The method `prompt()` returns a string, which will be displayed in **Figure 11.6** when the user clicks on the OK button.

   The second thing is that we're calling the Java method `newText()`, which JavaScript knows by the name `document.myApplet.newText()`. The parameter passed to this is the string returned by the JavaScript method `prompt()`.

3. `}`

   This ends the `startUp()` function.

   continued

4. `<body onLoad="startUp()"`
→ `bgcolor="white">`

This is a normal HTML **body** tag, with the addition of an **onLoad** handler. This event handler is triggered when the page is completely loaded. If the page were set up to call **startUp()** directly, it might try to call the Java method **newText()** before the applet had completed loading. Putting the **onLoad** event handler in the **body** tag allows us to be sure that everything on the page has completed loading before the prompt is displayed.

5. `<applet code="Applet1.class"`
→ `width="300" height="50"`
→ `name="myApplet">`

This is again a normal HTML **applet** tag, with the addition of the **name** attribute. Giving the Java applet a name within HTML allows JavaScript to reference the applet, and thereby its public methods, as we did in step 2 above with `document.myApplet.newText()`.

Applet 11.1 This applet displays the string on the screen.

```
import java.applet.*;
import java.awt.*;

public class Applet1 extends Applet {
  Font f = new Font("TimesRoman",Font.BOLD,36);
  String whatToSay;

  public void init() {
    setBackground(Color.white);
  }

  public void paint(Graphics g) {
    g.setFont(f);
    g.drawString(this.whatToSay, 100 , 25);
  }

  public void newText(String s) {
    this.whatToSay = s;
    repaint();
  }
}
```

Figure 11.7 The text the user entered is now displayed by Java.

To pass information from JavaScript to Java (the Java side):

1. `String whatToSay;`

This declares a string, whatToSay, for future use.

2.
```
public void paint(Graphics g) {
  g.setFont(f);
  g.drawString(this.whatToSay, 100 , 25);
}
```
Whenever the Java applet needs to be painted, the string whatToSay will be drawn at a position 100 pixels over and 25 down.

3.
```
public void newText(String s) {
  this.whatToSay = s;
  repaint();
}
```
Whenever the method newText() is called by the JavaScript, it sets whatToSay to the passed parameter and forces a repaint() to update the applet window, as shown in **Figure 11.7**.

✔ Tip

■ This is the first time in this book we've seen an applet use the **applet** tag instead of the **object** tag. For some reason, at the time this was written, the browser makers have decided to support this functionality only through the **applet** tag and not the **object** tag.

Passing Information from Java to JavaScript

The previous pages showed an example in which JavaScript passed data to a Java applet. In this example, JavaScript passes data to Java, and then Java passes a response based on that data back to JavaScript, as shown in **Figures 11.8** and **11.9**. **Listing 11.4** shows the JavaScript side of receiving information from Java:

To pass information from Java to JavaScript (the JavaScript side):

1. `function passCheck(passForm) {`

   We start by creating a new function, `passCheck()`. This function will check password entry fields, returning `true` if the password is valid, and `false` otherwise. The parameter that's being passed in, `passForm`, is the Form object on the HTML page.

2. `goodPass = false`

   The content of the variable `goodPass` depends on whether or not the entered password is valid. We start by initializing it to `false`; i.e., the password is assumed to be bad.

3. `if (passForm.pass.value != "") {`

   We only want to call the Java applet if the password entry field contains something. If it's blank, by definition it's bad, so why bother checking? The password field in the form is referred to as `passForm.pass.value`. To evaluate this, we start by looking at the Form object `passForm`, taking its text entry object called `pass`, and then looking at the value of that object. This notation illustrates one of the similarities between Java and JavaScript: Objects are identified by starting with the most general and working towards the most specific, using dot notation.

Listing 11.4 On the HTML and JavaScript side, the user enters a password and clicks the Submit button...

```
<html>
<head>
 <title>Listing 11.4</title>
 <script language="javascript" type=
→ "text/javascript">
 <!-- Hide script from old browsers

  function passCheck(passForm) {
   goodPass = false
   if (passForm.pass.value != "") {
    goodPass = document.javaCheck.checkPass
→ (passForm.pass.value)
   }
   if (!goodPass) {
    alert("Invalid password")
    passForm.pass.focus()
    passForm.pass.select()
   }
   return goodPass
 }

   // End hiding script from old browsers -->
 </script>
</head>
<body bgcolor="white">
 You'll have to enter the secret password to
→ see that page...
 <br>
 <form method="post" action="javascript:
→ document.location=
→ 'http://www.dori.com/java/'" onSubmit=
→ "return passCheck(this)">
  Enter password: <input type="text" name=
→ "pass">
  <br><br>
  <input type="submit" value="Submit">
 </form>
 <applet code="Applet2.class" width="1"
→ height="1" name="javaCheck">
 </applet>
</body>
</html>
```

Applet 11.2 ... And the applet decides if an entry is valid.

```
import java.applet.*;

public class Applet2 extends Applet {

 public boolean checkPass(String s) {
  return (s.equals("peachpit"));
 }
}
```

Figure 11.8 The password page in Netscape (Mac).

Figure 11.9 The password page in Internet Explorer (Windows), with an invalid result.

4. `goodPass = document.javaCheck.`
`→ checkPass(passForm.pass.value)`

Here, `goodPass` is set to the value returned by the Java method `checkPass()` (which is discussed below). Again, the entered password is being referred to in the format `passForm.pass.value`, which is passed to `checkPass()`.

5. `}`

This right curly brace closes the conditional block.

6. `if (!goodPass) {`

If the user didn't enter a valid password, we'll want to execute the following statements.

7. `alert("Invalid password")`
`passForm.pass.focus()`
`passForm.pass.select()`

First, we put up a JavaScript alert window, letting the user know that their password just wasn't good enough. Next, we use the two JavaScript methods `focus()` and `select()`. The former puts the cursor into the chosen entry field, and the latter selects all the text in that field so that the user can automatically type over the existing entry.

8. `}`

That's all we want to do if they entered an invalid password.

9. `return goodPass`

Now `goodPass` is returned. It doesn't matter if the value is `true` or `false`, it just needs to be returned.

10. `}`

And that's the end of the `passCheck()` function.

continued

11. `<form method="post" action=`
→ `"javascript:document.location=`
→ `'http://www.dori.com/java/'"`
→ `onSubmit="return passCheck(this)">`

There are two pieces of JavaScript going on here. The `action` attribute of the `form` tag is calling a line of JavaScript that will load a new page into the browser by resetting `document.location` to the desired URL.

The second piece of JavaScript is the `onSubmit` event handler. When the form is submitted, the `passCheck()` function is called. If the function returns `false`, the form submission is aborted, and the form's action never occurs. If `passCheck()` returns `true`, the action is allowed to proceed. The value `this` is passed to `passCheck()`; as in Java, this implies the form currently being processed.

12. `<applet code="Applet2.class"`
→ `width="1" height="1"`
→ `name="javaCheck">`

This is a normal applet call, except that it's named `javaCheck` and its height and width are both set to 1. While the applet does need to be on the page, there's no need for it to have a visible height and width, as this applet isn't displayed on the screen.

To pass information from Java to JavaScript (the Java side):

◆
```
public boolean checkPass(String s) {
  return (s.equals("peachpit"));
}
```
This very simple Java method, as shown in **Applet 11.2**, accepts a string as a parameter, and returns whether or not the passed string is equal to "peachpit." If it is, the value `true` is returned; if not, the value `false` is returned.

✔ Tips

■ A straightforward enhancement to this applet would be to change it to accept two strings: the one that the user entered and an encrypted target string. The Java applet could then take the first string, run it through a one-way encryption algorithm, and compare it to the second, returning `true` if they're the same. This would allow this applet to be used on any Web page, with the right algorithm making it impossible to break the password.

■ In order to display the password in the figures, I've let it be seen in clear text. To make the password display as bullets, simply change the `type="text"` attribute of the `input` tag to `type="password"`.

USER
INTERFACE
DESIGN WITH SWING

As numerous examples in this book testify, traditional Java applets look different on every platform. To solve this problem, Sun created *Swing*, a user interface toolkit that allows developers a choice of how they want their applets to appear: either native to a platform, or with a similar appearance on all platforms. In this chapter, we'll cover simple Swing components and how they're used. If you want to learn more about Swing, I recommend *Graphic Java 2: Mastering the JFC, 3rd Edition (Volume 2: Swing)* by David M. Geary.

Your First Swing Applet

The differences between Java with and without Swing are subtle but important. **Listing 12.1** and **Applet 12.1** show a variant of the standard "Hello, World!" that we've grown to know and love.

To write your first Swing applet:

1. `import javax.swing.*;`

   Here's a new class to import: `javax.swing` and its associated classes. This will give us access to the Swing components.

2. `public class Applet1 extends JApplet {`

   Instead of extending `Applet`, as we've done previously, we're now extending `JApplet`. Swing components start with the letter J to distinguish them from the standard AWT components that we've seen in other chapters.

3. `JLabel helloLabel = new JLabel("Once` → `upon a time...");`

   In order to put out information to the screen, we need to create a label, or as Swing calls it, a `JLabel`. This string will later be displayed in our browser window, as shown in **Figure 12.1**.

4. `helloLabel.setToolTipText("The story` → `begins");`

   Because the point of Swing is to make writing user interface elements easy, it's simple to add a tool tip to any given label. This line sets up a tool tip so that any time the user's cursor is over our label (as in **Figure 12.2**), the tool tip is displayed.

Listing 12.1 This HTML file displays Applet 12.1.

```
<html>
<head>
 <title>Applet 12.1</title>
</head>
<body bgcolor="white">
<object classid="clsid:8AD9C840-044E-11D1-
→ B3E9-00805F499D93" width="400" height="50"
→ codetype="application/java">
 <param name="code" value="Applet1.class">
 <param name="type" value="application/x-java-
→ applet;version=1.3">
 <param name="scriptable" value="false">
 <embed type="application/x-java-applet;
→ version=1.3" code="Applet1.class"
→ width="400" height="50" scriptable="false"
→ pluginspage="http://java.sun.com/products/
→ plugin/1.3/plugin-install.html">
 </embed>
</object>
</body>
</html>
```

Applet 12.1 Once again, we start with displaying our hello message to the world.

```
import javax.swing.*;

public class Applet1 extends JApplet {
 public void init() {
  JLabel helloLabel = new JLabel("Once upon a
→ time...");
  helloLabel.setToolTipText("The story
→ begins");

  java.awt.Container contentPane=
→ getContentPane();
  contentPane.setBackground(java.awt.
→ Color.white);
  contentPane.add(helloLabel);
 }
}
```

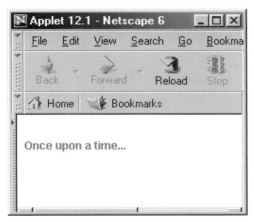

Figure 12.1 Here's our message displayed in the user's browser window.

Figure 12.2 And here's the help, just in case they want to know more about what's going on.

5. `java.awt.Container contentPane=`
   `➜ getContentPane();`
   `contentPane.setBackground(java.`
   `➜ awt.Color.white);`

   These two lines create a content pane for future use and set the background to white.

6. `contentPane.add(helloLabel);`

   And finally, our label is added to the pane, which displays the label's text in our browser window.

Setting Fonts with Swing

The previous example just dumped text on to the screen, but if that was all you could do with Swing, it wouldn't be much of an advantage. In **Listing 12.2** and **Applet 12.2**, we find that we can also change the font, the style, and the point size.

To set fonts with Swing:

1. `Font helloFont=new Font("San-Serif",`
   `→ Font.BOLD, 32);`

   Just as you can set the font attributes without Swing, you can set the font attributes with Swing. Here, we create a new font style, which is then set to 32-point bold sans serif.

2. `helloLabel.setFont(helloFont);`

   And here the new font style is applied to the label, just before it's displayed on the screen, as shown in **Figure 12.3**.

Listing 12.2 This calls Applet 12.2.

```
<html>
<head>
 <title>Applet 12.2</title>
</head>
<body bgcolor="white">
<object classid="clsid:8AD9C840-044E-11D1-
→ B3E9-00805F499D93" width="400" height="50"
→ codetype="application/java">
 <param name="code" value="Applet2.class">
 <param name="type" value="application/x-java-
→ applet;version=1.3">
 <param name="scriptable" value="false">
 <embed type="application/x-java-applet;
→ version=1.3" code="Applet2.class"
→ width="400" height="50" scriptable="false"
→ pluginspage="http://java.sun.com/products/
→ plugin/1.3/plugin-install.html">
 </embed>
</object>
</body>
</html>
```

Applet 12.2 This applet displays our message with the desired font attributes.

```
import java.awt.Container;
import java.awt.Font;
import javax.swing.*;

public class Applet2 extends JApplet {
 public void init() {
  JLabel helloLabel = new JLabel("Once upon a
→ time...");
  helloLabel.setToolTipText("The story begins");

  Font helloFont=new Font("San-Serif",
→ Font.BOLD, 32);
  helloLabel.setFont(helloFont);

  Container contentPane=getContentPane();
  contentPane.setBackground(java.awt.Color.
→ white);
  contentPane.add(helloLabel);
 }
}
```

Figure 12.3 Our message is now displayed big and bold in the browser window.

Sans Serif or San Serif?

The French word "sans" means "without." Therefore, the phrase "sans serif" means "without serif" or, fonts that don't have those little feet on the bottom. So, the text you're reading here is serif, but the heading for this sidebar is in a sans serif font.

For some reason, though, Java wants it spelled "san-serif," without the middle "s" that you'd normally expect. And while the default is sans serif text anyway, you might find yourself with some odd results if you try to switch back and forth between styles.

If you're used to using Cascading Style Sheets in your HTML, this becomes especially tricky to remember, as CSS requires that you use "sans-serif."

SETTING FONTS WITH SWING

Swing Checkboxes

The main goal of Swing is to create user interface elements, so it's time to start to show how this is done. **Listing 12.3** and **Applet 12.3** allow the user to set the style of the text.

To create checkboxes with Swing:

1. JCheckBox boldButton;
   JCheckBox italicButton;

   We want to add two new checkboxes to our page, the first to say whether the text should be bold and the second to say whether the text should be italic. As always, Swing components start with a "J."

2. boldButton = new JCheckBox("Bold");
   boldButton.setToolTipText("Makes text
   → appear bold.");

   The bold button is created here, with a label of "Bold" and a tool tip that lets the user know that its purpose is to make the text bold.

3. boldButton.setMnemonic('b');

   Along with making it easy to create tool tips, Swing also makes it easy to create shortcut keys. By calling setMnemonic('b'), the applet now knows that when the user presses Alt-B (Option-B on the Mac), it's equivalent to clicking the checkbox. As you can see in **Figures 12.4** and **12.5**, setting the keyboard shortcuts to a character in the label also automatically underlines that character in the label.

Listing 12.3 This HTML page calls Applet 12.3.

```
                        Listing
<html>
<head>
 <title>Applet 12.3</title>
</head>
<body bgcolor="white">
<object classid="clsid:8AD9C840-044E-11D1-
→ B3E9-00805F499D93" width="400" height="100"
→ codetype="application/java">
 <param name="code" value="Applet3.class">
 <param name="type" value="application/x-java-
→ applet;version=1.3">
 <param name="scriptable" value="false">
 <embed type="application/x-java-applet;
→ version=1.3" code="Applet3.class"
→ width="400" height="100" scriptable="false"
→ pluginspage="http://java.sun.com/products/
→ plugin/1.3/plugin-install.html">
 </embed>
</object>
</body>
</html>
```

Applet 12.3 This applet introduces us to checkboxes in Swing.

```
                    Applet
import java.awt.*;
import java.awt.event.*;
import javax.swing.*;

public class Applet3 extends JApplet
→ implements ItemListener{
 JCheckBox boldButton;
 JCheckBox italicButton;
 JLabel helloLabel;

 public void init() {
  helloLabel = new JLabel("This space for
→ rent");
  helloLabel.setToolTipText("Your message to
→ the world");

  Font helloFont=new Font("Serif", 0, 32);
  helloLabel.setFont(helloFont);

  boldButton = new JCheckBox("Bold");
  boldButton.setToolTipText("Makes text
→ appear bold.");
  boldButton.setMnemonic('b');
  boldButton.setContentAreaFilled(false);

  italicButton = new JCheckBox("Italic");
  italicButton.setToolTipText("Makes text
→ appear italic.");
  italicButton.setMnemonic('i');
  italicButton.setContentAreaFilled(false);

  boldButton.addItemListener(this);
  italicButton.addItemListener(this);

  Container contentPane=getContentPane();
  contentPane.setLayout(new FlowLayout());
  contentPane.setBackground(java.awt.Color.
→ white);
  contentPane.add(helloLabel, BorderLayout.
→ CENTER);
  contentPane.add(italicButton, BorderLayout.
→ EAST);
  contentPane.add(boldButton, BorderLayout.
→ WEST);
 }

 public void itemStateChanged(ItemEvent e) {
  int style=0;
  if (boldButton.isSelected()) style +=
→ Font.BOLD;
  if (italicButton.isSelected()) style +=
→ Font.ITALIC;
  Font helloFont=new Font("Serif", style, 32);
  helloLabel.setFont(helloFont);
 }
}
```

4. `boldButton.setContentAreaFilled`
`→ (false);`

Swing gives us a choice of whether or not we want the buttons to display transparent, or with rollover effects. We don't want rollover effects, so we set it to false.

5. `italicButton = new JCheckBox`
`→ ("Italic");`
`italicButton.setToolTipText("Makes`
`→ text appear italic.");`

The lines of code above are repeated here, this time for the italic checkbox. The new checkbox is created, and the tool tip is set.

6. `italicButton.setMnemonic('i');`
`italicButton.setContentAreaFilled`
`→ (false);`

The shortcut key for italic is set to "I", so that either Alt-I or Option-I will cause the box to be toggled, and the box is set to be transparent.

7. `boldButton.addItemListener(this);`
`italicButton.addItemListener(this);`

Two `ItemListeners` are added here, one for each of the buttons. With these lines, the applet will know to call `itemStateChanged` if the user clicks on a checkbox.

8. `contentPane.add(italicButton,`
`→ BorderLayout.EAST);`
`contentPane.add(boldButton,`
`→ BorderLayout.WEST);`

The two buttons are added to the browser window using `BorderLayout`, which was covered in Chapter 9.

continued

9. `if (boldButton.isSelected()) style`
`→ += Font.BOLD;`
`if (italicButton.isSelected()) style`
`→ += Font.ITALIC;`

Here's where the action actually takes place. If the user clicks on a box, we end up in `itemStateChanged`. Instead of having to do all the ugly checks that we did in **Applet 8.3**, we can simply check `isSelected()` for each button. If it's set, then we add the values for bold and/or italic to our style variable.

10. `Font helloFont=new Font("Serif",`
`→ style, 32);`

Now that we know which style is wanted, resetting the font automatically redisplays the text with the selected style.

Figure 12.4 The applet, as it first appears when the page is loaded.

Figure 12.5 And again, after the user has clicked the Bold button.

Listing 12.4 This HTML loads Applet 12.4.

```
                    Listing
<html>
<head>
 <title>Applet 12.4</title>
</head>
<body bgcolor="white">
<object classid="clsid:8AD9C840-044E-11D1-
→ B3E9-00805F499D93" width="450" height="150"
→ codetype="application/java">
 <param name="code" value="Applet4.class">
 <param name="type" value="application/x-java-
→ applet;version=1.3">
 <param name="scriptable" value="false">
 <embed type="application/x-java-applet;
→ version=1.3" code="Applet4.class"
→ width="450" height="150" scriptable="false"
→ pluginspage="http://java.sun.com/products/
→ plugin/1.3/plugin-install.html">
 </embed>
</object>
</body>
</html>
```

Figure 12.6 Choosing bold and sans serif produces this page on Internet Explorer for Mac.

Figure 12.7 While choosing italic and serif produces this Netscape for Windows page.

Radio Buttons with Swing

Another common user interface widget is the radio button, or more properly, a group of radio buttons. **Listing 12.4** and **Applet 12.4** show how to use Swing's radio buttons to pick between one of several options.

To create radio buttons with Swing:

1. JRadioButton sanSerifButton,
   → serifButton;

   Here we declare two radio buttons, which will be used to set whether the text should appear in a serif or sans serif font.

2. sanSerifButton = new JRadioButton
   → ("Sans Serif");
   sanSerifButton.setToolTipText
   → ("Display text with Sans Serif
   → typeface");
   sanSerifButton.setMnemonic('a');
   sanSerifButton.setContentAreaFilled
   → (false);

   The sans serif radio button is created here, with the label "Sans Serif," a tool tip that explains its usage, and a shortcut of "A."

   continued

3. `serifButton = new JRadioButton`
→ `("Serif");`
`serifButton.setToolTipText("Display`
→ `text with Serif typeface");`
`serifButton.setMnemonic('s');`
`serifButton.setContentAreaFilled`
→ `(false);`
`serifButton.setSelected(true);`

The above steps are repeated here, but this time for the serif button. The only differences are the shortcut key (now "S") and the last line, which sets this particular radio button to be selected.

4. `ButtonGroup btnGroup = new`
→ `ButtonGroup();`
`btnGroup.add(sanSerifButton);`
`btnGroup.add(serifButton);`

Radio buttons are different from checkboxes, in that only one of them can be set at any given time. Clicking on one turns it on and all the others off. In order to properly handle radio buttons, Java needs to know that they belong to a group. In this step, we create a group and add our two radio buttons to it.

5. `sanSerifButton.addItemListener(this);`
`serifButton.addItemListener(this);`

Adding `ItemListeners` to our radio buttons tells Java to call `itemStateChanged` whenever one is clicked.

Applet 12.4 Adding radio buttons to our page is easy with Swing.

```
Applet
import java.awt.*;
import java.awt.event.*;
import javax.swing.*;

public class Applet4 extends JApplet
→ implements ItemListener{
 JCheckBox boldButton;
 JCheckBox italicButton;
 JLabel helloLabel;
 JRadioButton sanSerifButton, serifButton;

 public void init() {
  helloLabel = new JLabel("BurmaShave");
  helloLabel.setToolTipText("Helpful tooltip
→ text message goes here");

  Font helloFont=new Font("Serif", 0, 32);
  helloLabel.setFont(helloFont);

  boldButton = new JCheckBox("Bold");
  boldButton.setToolTipText("Makes text appear
→ bold.");
  boldButton.setMnemonic('b');
  boldButton.setContentAreaFilled(false);

  italicButton = new JCheckBox("Italic");
  italicButton.setToolTipText("Makes text
→ appear italic.");
  italicButton.setMnemonic('i');
  italicButton.setContentAreaFilled(false);

  sanSerifButton = new JRadioButton("Sans
→ Serif");
  sanSerifButton.setToolTipText("Display text
→ with Sans Serif typeface");
  sanSerifButton.setMnemonic('a');
  sanSerifButton.setContentAreaFilled(false);

  serifButton = new JRadioButton("Serif");
  serifButton.setToolTipText("Display text
→ with Serif typeface");
  serifButton.setMnemonic('s');
  serifButton.setContentAreaFilled(false);
  serifButton.setSelected(true);

  ButtonGroup btnGroup = new ButtonGroup();
  btnGroup.add(sanSerifButton);
  btnGroup.add(serifButton);

  boldButton.addItemListener(this);
  italicButton.addItemListener(this);
  sanSerifButton.addItemListener(this);
  serifButton.addItemListener(this);
```

Applet continues on next page

RADIO BUTTONS WITH SWING

Applet 12.4 *continued*

```
┌──────────────────── Applet ─────────────────────┐

Container contentPane=getContentPane();
contentPane.setLayout(new BoxLayout
→ (contentPane, BoxLayout.Y_AXIS));

contentPane.setBackground(java.awt.
→ Color.white);
contentPane.add(helloLabel);

JPanel checkPanel=new JPanel();
checkPanel.setBackground(java.awt.
→ Color.white);
checkPanel.add(italicButton);
checkPanel.add(boldButton);

JPanel radioPanel=new JPanel();
radioPanel.setBackground(java.awt.
→ Color.white);
radioPanel.add(sanSerifButton);
radioPanel.add(serifButton);

contentPane.add(checkPanel);
contentPane.add(radioPanel);
}

public void itemStateChanged(ItemEvent e) {
  int style=0;
  String typeface="San-Serif";
  if (boldButton.isSelected()) style +=
→ Font.BOLD;
  if (italicButton.isSelected()) style +=
→ Font.ITALIC;
  if (serifButton.isSelected()) typeface=
→ "Serif";
  Font helloFont=new Font(typeface, style, 32);
  helloLabel.setFont(helloFont);
  }
}
```

6. `String typeface="San-Serif";`

   In `itemStateChanged`, we start with the default assumption that the user wants the text in a sans serif font, as shown in **Figure 12.6**.

7. `if (serifButton.isSelected())`
   `→ typeface="Serif";`

   If the serif radio button was clicked (as shown in **Figure 12.7**) the typeface is reset to "Serif."

8. `Font helloFont=new Font(typeface,`
   `→ style, 32);`
   `helloLabel.setFont(helloFont);`

   And here, the font is changed, and calling `setFont` will immediately change the way the text is displayed on the screen.

RADIO BUTTONS WITH SWING

Setting Look and Feel with Swing

The introduction to this chapter stated that one of the goals of Swing was to give you the choice of making your applets look the same on all platforms. That's done by setting the look and feel, as shown in **Listing 12.5** and **Applet 12.5**. It also demonstrates how to set up a menu bar, as well as how to ask a user to enter something in a text entry field.

To set the look and feel with Swing:

1. ```
   JMenuBar menuBar;
   JMenu fileMenu;
   JMenuItem nativeLookItem,
   → javaLookItem, newTextItem;
   ```

   Here's where the menu bar, menu, and menu items are declared. There's going to be one menu bar, with just a single menu on it, a file menu. The file menu will have three options: a choice of the native look and feel, the Java look and feel, or the ability to enter a new text string.

2. ```
   try {
       UIManager.setLookAndFeel
       → (UIManager.getSystemLookAndFeel
       → ClassName());
   }
   catch (Exception excep) { }
   ```

   We start off by setting the UI manager to be the native look and feel, which we've gotten by default in all of the previous examples. The native look and feel is shown in **Figures 12.8** and **12.9**.

3. ```
   menuBar = new JMenuBar();
   setJMenuBar(menuBar);
   fileMenu = new JMenu("File");
   fileMenu.setMnemonic('F');
   menuBar.add(fileMenu);
   ```

   Our new menu bar and file menu are created here and added to the page with a shortcut key of "F."

Listing 12.5 This HTML file calls Applet 12.5.

```
<html>
<head>
 <title>Applet 12.5</title>
</head>
<body bgcolor="white">
<object classid="clsid:8AD9C840-044E-11D1-
→ B3E9-00805F499D93" width="400" height="125"
→ codetype="application/java">
 <param name="code" value="Applet5.class">
 <param name="type" value="application/x-java-
→ applet;version=1.3">
 <param name="scriptable" value="false">
 <embed type="application/x-java-applet;
→ version=1.3" code="Applet5.class"
→ width="400" height="125" scriptable="false"
→ pluginspage="http://java.sun.com/products/
→ plugin/1.3/plugin-install.html">
 </embed>
</object>
</body>
</html>
```

Figure 12.8 The native look and feel on Macintosh OS X.

Figure 12.9 The native look and feel on Windows.
```

Applet 12.5 This code allows the user to choose their platform-specific look and feel, or the cross-platform Java look and feel.

```
                   Applet
import java.awt.*;
import java.awt.event.*;
import javax.swing.*;

public class Applet5 extends JApplet
→ implements ItemListener, ActionListener{
 JCheckBox boldButton, italicButton;
 JLabel textLabel;
 JRadioButton sanSerifButton, serifButton;
 JMenuBar menuBar;
 JMenu fileMenu;
 JMenuItem nativeLookItem, javaLookItem,
 → newTextItem;

 public void init() {
  try {
   UIManager.setLookAndFeel(UIManager.
   → getSystemLookAndFeelClassName());
  }
  catch (Exception excep) { }

  textLabel = new JLabel("Enter your message
  → here");
  textLabel.setToolTipText("It's what you
  → chose to say");

  Font helloFont=new Font("Serif", 0, 32);
  textLabel.setFont(helloFont);

  boldButton = new JCheckBox("Bold");
  boldButton.setToolTipText("Makes text appear
  → bold.");
  boldButton.setMnemonic('b');
  boldButton.setContentAreaFilled(false);

  italicButton = new JCheckBox("Italic");
  italicButton.setToolTipText("Makes text
  → appear italic.");
  italicButton.setMnemonic('i');
  italicButton.setContentAreaFilled(false);

  sanSerifButton = new JRadioButton("Sans
  → Serif");
  sanSerifButton.setToolTipText("Display text
  → with Sans Serif typeface");
  sanSerifButton.setMnemonic('a');
  sanSerifButton.setContentAreaFilled(false);

  serifButton = new JRadioButton("Serif");
  serifButton.setToolTipText("Display text
  → with Serif typeface");
  serifButton.setMnemonic('s');
  serifButton.setContentAreaFilled(false);
  serifButton.setSelected(true);
```

Applet continues on next page

4.
```
nativeLookItem = new JRadioButtonMenu
→ Item("Java Look");
nativeLookItem.addActionListener
→ (this);
javaLookItem = new JRadioButtonMenu
→ Item("Native Look", true);
javaLookItem.addActionListener(this);
```
Here are the first two options on the file menu: "Java Look" and "Native Look." Because you can only choose one or the other, they're set up as radio buttons. An `ActionListener` is added to each to catch any changes.

5.
```
newTextItem = new JMenuItem("New
→ Text...");
newTextItem.addActionListener(this);
```
The last item on the menu asks for new text to be entered.

6.
```
ButtonGroup lookGroup = new
→ ButtonGroup();
lookGroup.add(nativeLookItem);
lookGroup.add(javaLookItem);
```
In order for Java to handle the radio buttons properly, they need to be added to a group, and that's done here.

7.
```
fileMenu.add(nativeLookItem);
fileMenu.add(javaLookItem);
fileMenu.addSeparator();
fileMenu.add(newTextItem);
```
Four items are added to the file menu here: The first two are the radio buttons for native vs. Java look and feel. The third is a separator, which will display a line across the menu to separate the first two items from the last one. And finally, the last item is added, which asks the user for new text to display. **Figure 12.10** shows how the menu appears in OS X.

continued

Setting Look and Feel with Swing

201

Applet 12.5 *continued*

```
                    Applet
  ButtonGroup btnGroup = new ButtonGroup();
  btnGroup.add(sanSerifButton);
  btnGroup.add(serifButton);

  boldButton.addItemListener(this);
  italicButton.addItemListener(this);
  sanSerifButton.addItemListener(this);
  serifButton.addItemListener(this);

  Container contentPane=getContentPane();
  contentPane.setLayout(new BoxLayout
→ (contentPane, BoxLayout.Y_AXIS));
  contentPane.setBackground(java.awt.
→ Color.white);
  contentPane.add(textLabel);
  JPanel checkPanel=new JPanel();
  checkPanel.setBackground(java.awt.
→ Color.white);
  checkPanel.add(italicButton);
  checkPanel.add(boldButton);
  JPanel radioPanel=new JPanel();
  radioPanel.setBackground(java.awt.
→ Color.white);
  radioPanel.add(sanSerifButton);
  radioPanel.add(serifButton);
  contentPane.add(checkPanel);
  contentPane.add(radioPanel);

  menuBar = new JMenuBar();
  setJMenuBar(menuBar);
  fileMenu = new JMenu("File");
  fileMenu.setMnemonic('F');
  menuBar.add(fileMenu);
  nativeLookItem = new JRadioButtonMenuItem
→ ("Java Look");
  nativeLookItem.addActionListener(this);
  javaLookItem = new JRadioButtonMenuItem
→ ("Native Look", true);
  javaLookItem.addActionListener(this);
  newTextItem = new JMenuItem("New Text...");
  newTextItem.addActionListener(this);

  ButtonGroup lookGroup = new ButtonGroup();
  lookGroup.add(nativeLookItem);
  lookGroup.add(javaLookItem);

  fileMenu.add(nativeLookItem);
  fileMenu.add(javaLookItem);
  fileMenu.addSeparator();
  fileMenu.add(newTextItem);
}
```

Applet continues in next column

Applet 12.5 *continued*

```
                    Applet
public void itemStateChanged(ItemEvent e) {
  int style=0;
  String typeface="San-Serif";
  if (boldButton.isSelected()) style +=
→ Font.BOLD;
  if (italicButton.isSelected()) style +=
→ Font.ITALIC;
  if (serifButton.isSelected()) typeface=
→ "Serif";
  Font helloFont=new Font(typeface, style, 32);
  textLabel.setFont(helloFont);
}

public void actionPerformed (ActionEvent e) {
  if (e.getActionCommand()=="Native Look") {
    try {
      UIManager.setLookAndFeel(UIManager.
→ getSystemLookAndFeelClassName());
    }
    catch (Exception excep) { }
    SwingUtilities.updateComponentTreeUI
→ (getRootPane());
  }
  else if (e.getActionCommand()=="Java Look") {
    try {
      UIManager.setLookAndFeel(UIManager.
→ getCrossPlatformLookAndFeelClassName());
    }
    catch (Exception excep) { }
    SwingUtilities.updateComponentTreeUI
→ (getRootPane());
  }
  else if (e.getActionCommand()=="New
→ Text...") {
    String inputValue = JOptionPane.
→ showInputDialog("Please enter new
→ text to display");
    if (inputValue.equals("")) inputValue=
→ "Hello World";
    textLabel.setText(inputValue);
  }
 }
}
```

Figure 12.10 The menus are transparent in the native look and feel on OS X, but opaque when using Java's look and feel.

8. if (e.getActionCommand()=="Native
→ Look") {
  try {
  UIManager.setLookAndFeel
  → (UIManager.getSystemLookAndFeel
  → ClassName());
  }
  catch (Exception excep) { }

If the user chooses the native look, they end up here, where Java uses the UI manager to set the look and feel.

9. SwingUtilities.updateComponentTreeUI
→ (getRootPane());

Now that we've set the look and feel, updateComponentTreeUI tells Java to go through all the components of the applet and change them to the new UI.

10. else if (e.getActionCommand()=="Java
→ Look") {
  try {
  UIManager.setLookAndFeel
  → (UIManager.getCrossPlatformLook
  → AndFeelClassName());
  }
  catch (Exception excep) { }

As in step 8, if the user chooses the Java look, tell the UI manager to switch the look and feel.

11. SwingUtilities.updateComponent
→ TreeUI(getRootPane());

And once again, use updateComponent TreeUI to reset the UI for all the applet's components.

continued

SETTING LOOK AND FEEL WITH SWING

203

12. else if (e.getActionCommand()=="New
    → Text...") {
       String inputValue = JOptionPane.
    → showInputDialog("Please enter
    → new text to display");

If the user wants to enter new text to be displayed, they'll end up here, as shown in **Figure 12.11**. Calling showInputDialog puts up a window that prompts the user to enter something, which is then stored in inputValue.

13. if (inputValue.equals(""))
       → inputValue="Hello World";
       textLabel.setText(inputValue);

If nothing was entered, we reset inputValue to our old standby, "Hello World." Resetting the display is easy, as all we need to do is call **setText** and pass it the new string, as shown in **Figures 12.12** and **12.13**.

Figure 12.11 Swing makes it easy to ask the user to enter some text.

Figure 12.12 The Java look and feel on Mac OS X.

Figure 12.13 Here's the file menu, displayed on Windows with the Java look and feel.

Listing 12.6 This file calls Applet 12.6.

```
                    Listing
<html>
<head>
 <title>Applet 12.6</title>
</head>
<body bgcolor="white">
<object classid="clsid:8AD9C840-044E-11D1-
→ B3E9-00805F499D93" width="400" height="125"
→ codetype="application/java">
 <param name="code" value="Applet6.class">
 <param name="type" value="application/x-java-
→ applet;version=1.3">
 <param name="scriptable" value="false">
 <embed type="application/x-java-applet;
→ version=1.3" code="Applet6.class"
→ width="400" height="125" scriptable="false"
→ pluginspage="http://java.sun.com/products/
→ plugin/1.3/plugin-install.html">
 </embed>
</object>
</body>
</html>
```

Swing Animation

If you look back at **Applet 10.8**, there's a whole lot of code just to support double-buffering your animated images. Thankfully, Swing handles most of that work for us. **Listing 12.6** and **Applet 12.6** do similar work, but with much simpler code.

To animate images with Swing:

1. ImageIcon butterflyIcon;

   Using ImageIcon instead of Image allows us to benefit from Swing's double-buffering advantages.

2. Dimension size=getContentPane().
   → getSize();

   Store the size of the original content pane, because we'll need it later.

3. Container contentPane = new
   → AnimationPane();
   setContentPane(contentPane);
   contentPane.setBackground(Color.
   → white);
   contentPane.setSize(size);

   Create a pane with our new AnimationPane class (see below). Set the content pane to be the pane we just created, set the background color to white, and then reset the size to our saved value.

4. xPos = contentPane.getSize().width/2;
   yPos = contentPane.getSize().
   → height/2;

   We're going to want to put our butterfly image in the center, so we set xPos and yPos to be the coordinates where we want the image to start.

   continued

5. `butterflyIcon = new ImageIcon`
`→ (getImage(getCodeBase(),`
`→ "butterfly.gif"));`

If we try to load the image directly into our `ImageIcon`, we'll get a security violation error. So instead, we load `butterfly.`
`→ gif` into an `Image`, and then load that `Image` into the `ImageIcon`.

6. `startStop = new JButton("Stop");`
`contentPane.add(startStop);`
`startStop.addActionListener(this);`

Instead of letting the animation go on forever, we add a Stop button to the applet, as shown in **Figure 12.14**. If the user clicks on it, it will then turn itself into a Start button.

7. `xPos += changeBy();`
`yPos += changeBy();`
`repaint();`

In order to give the butterfly's movements a realistic feel, it's allowed to move a random value up, down, left, or right. Here, `changeBy()` (see below) is called, which will return a random number between −10 and 10. Calling `repaint()` causes the butterfly image to be repainted on the screen in its new location, giving the illusion of movement.

Applet 12.6 This Swing applet demonstrates starting and stopping a simple animation.

```
import java.awt.*;
import java.awt.event.*;
import javax.swing.*;

public class Applet6 extends JApplet
→ implements Runnable, ActionListener {
 int xPos, yPos;
 ImageIcon butterflyIcon;
 JButton startStop;
 Thread runner;
 boolean isRunning = true;

 public void init() {
  Dimension size=getContentPane().getSize();

  Container contentPane = new AnimationPane();
  setContentPane(contentPane);
  contentPane.setBackground(Color.white);
  contentPane.setSize(size);
  xPos = contentPane.getSize().width/2;
  yPos = contentPane.getSize().height/2;

  butterflyIcon = new ImageIcon
→ (getImage(getCodeBase(), "butterfly.gif"));

  startStop = new JButton("Stop");
  contentPane.add(startStop);
  startStop.addActionListener(this);
 }

 public void start() {
  if (runner == null) {
   runner = new Thread(this);
   runner.start();
  }
 }

 public void stop() {
  runner = null;
 }

 public void run() {
  while (isRunning) {
   try {
    Thread.sleep(10);
   }
   catch (InterruptedException e) {
   }

   xPos += changeBy();
   yPos += changeBy();
   repaint();
  }
 }
}
```

Applet continues on next page

SWING ANIMATION

Applet 12.6 *continued*

```
                        Applet
 int changeBy() {
   double myVal;

   if (java.lang.Math.random() < .5) {
     myVal = java.lang.Math.random() * -10;
   }
   else {
     myVal = java.lang.Math.random() * 10;
   }
   return (int) myVal;
 }

 public void actionPerformed(ActionEvent e) {
  if (isRunning) {
   isRunning = false;
   startStop.setText("Start");
   stop();
  }
  else {
   isRunning = true;
   startStop.setText("Stop");
   start();
  }
 }

 class AnimationPane extends JPanel {
  public void paintComponent(Graphics g) {
   super.paintComponent(g);
   butterflyIcon.paintIcon(this,g,xPos,yPos);
  }
 }
}
```

Figure 12.14 The butterfly moves randomly about the screen, while the user is given the choice of stopping the animation at any time.

8.
```
int changeBy() {
   double myVal;
   if (java.lang.Math.random() < .5) {
       myVal = java.lang.Math.
       → random() * -10;
   }
   else {
       myVal = java.lang.Math.
       → random() * 10;
   }
   return (int) myVal;
}
```

This simple routine starts off by taking a random number. If that number is less than .5 (which will happen half the time), the number it will return is negative. If it's greater than or equal to .5, it will return a positive number. Either way, another random number is selected and multiplied by ten, producing a result between 0 and 9, which is then returned.

9. `startStop.setText("Start");`

When the button is pressed, the thread is killed and the button's text is reset to "Start," as shown in **Figure 12.15**. In a similar fashion, if the button is then pressed again, the thread is restarted and the text is reset to "Stop."

10.
```
class AnimationPane extends JPanel {
   public void paintComponent
   → (Graphics g) {
    super.paintComponent(g);
    butterflyIcon.paintIcon(this,g,
    → xPos,yPos);
   }
}
```

The JPanel class needs to be extended so that we can override paintComponent. That allows us to display the butterflyIcon without having to override paint itself, as we did back in Chapter 10.

continued

SWING ANIMATION

✔ Tips

- Unlike most of the other applets in this book, there's an extra class here: AnimationPane. When you compile the applet, not only will you get a file called Applet6.class, but an additional file called Applet6$AnimationPane.class. When you upload your files to the server, make sure to upload them both, as all of the AnimationPane code is in the latter class file.

- As the previous tip states, you'll sometimes get multiple class files when compiling an applet. If you're ever going to be compiling or running an applet on a classic Mac OS system, be careful of that operating system's 31-character limitation on file name length. To make it worse, both the prefix (Applet6$) and suffix (.class) count towards the limit, so in this case, we're limited to a maximum of 17 characters in our class names.

- If you run this applet for a while, you may notice the butterfly fly outside the window. If you calculate the boundaries of the visible area, you can modify the applet to make sure that the butterfly always stays within the boundaries. Alternatively, you can have patience; the butterfly should eventually fly back in again.

Figure 12.15 When the user clicks to stop the animation, the button changes to "Start," and the butterfly stays still.

Listing 12.7 This file calls Applet 12.7.

```
                  Listing
<html>
<head>
 <title>Applet 12.7</title>
</head>
<body bgcolor="white">
<object classid="clsid:8AD9C840-044E-11D1-
→ B3E9-00805F499D93" width="600" height="500"
→ codetype="application/java">
 <param name="code" value="Applet7.class">
 <param name="type" value="application/x-java-
→ applet;version=1.3">
 <param name="scriptable" value="false">
 <embed type="application/x-java-applet;
→ version=1.3" code="Applet7.class"
→ width="600" height="500" scriptable="false"
→ pluginspage="http://java.sun.com/products/
→ plugin/1.3/plugin-install.html">
 </embed>
</object>
</body>
</html>
```

Swing in Action

To close out this chapter, I've included a relatively simple example of a Java applet using Swing in action, as shown in the Biorhythm Calculator in **Listing 12.7** and **Applet 12.7**. It implements many of the widgets that were introduced previously in this chapter in addition to a few that are new.

To see a Swing applet in action:

1. ```
   Cycle emotional, intellectual,
   → physical;
   Container contentPane;
   JTextField birthdayField,
   → targetDateField;
   ```
   Our variables are declared here, including three `Cycles`, a new data type that will be defined below. There are also two text fields to store the birth date and the target date.

2. ```
   Dimension size=getContentPane().
   → getSize();
   contentPane = new AnimationPane();
   ```
   Store the size of the original content pane so that we know how big it is, and then create a new pane with our `AnimationPane` class that overrides the `paintComponent` method.

3. ```
   setContentPane(contentPane);
   contentPane.setBackground(Color.
   → white);
   ```
   Set the content pane to the pane we just created, and set the background color to white.

4. ```
   DateFormat fmt = DateFormat.
   → getDateInstance(DateFormat.SHORT,
   → Locale.US);
   ```
   Set up `DateFormat` so that we can coerce the string to a `Date` object.

continued

5.
```
String birthdayString = new String
→ ("7/22/88");
```
Set the initial birthday as a string.

6.
```
try {
  birthday=fmt.parse(birthdayString);
}
catch(ParseException e){
  System.out.println(e);
}
```
Then try to parse the string as a **Date** value. If it was successful, the result is stored in **birthday**.

7.
```
birthdayField=new JTextField
→ (birthdayString);
birthdayField.setColumns(7);
birthdayField.setToolTipText
→ ("Enter the birthday to calculate
→ from.");
birthdayField.addActionListener(new
→ MyListener());
```
Create a birthday **JTextField** so the user can change the birthday value.

8.
```
targetDate = new Date();
targetDateField=new JTextField
→ (fmt.format(targetDate));
targetDateField.setColumns(7);
targetDateField.setToolTipText("Enter
→ the target date to display.");
targetDateField.addActionListener(new
→ MyListener());
```
Create a new **targetDate** to display, and then create a **targetDate JTextField** so the user can change the target date value. The default value of the **targetDate** is always the current date.

9.
```
contentPane.add(birthdayField);
contentPane.add(targetDateField);
```
Next, add the two date fields to the content pane.

Applet 12.7 This applet makes full use of Swing to display a biorhythm chart in the browser window.

```
import java.awt.*;
import java.awt.event.*;
import java.text.*;
import java.util.*;
import javax.swing.*;

public class Applet7 extends JApplet {
  Date birthday, targetDate;
  Cycle emotional, intellectual, physical;
  Container contentPane;
  JTextField birthdayField, targetDateField;

  public void init() {
    Dimension size=getContentPane().getSize();
    contentPane = new AnimationPane();

    setContentPane(contentPane);
    contentPane.setBackground(Color.white);

    DateFormat fmt = DateFormat.getDateInstance
    → (DateFormat.SHORT, Locale.US);

    String birthdayString = new String("7/22/88");
    try {
      birthday=fmt.parse(birthdayString);
    }
    catch(ParseException e){
      System.out.println(e);
    }
    birthdayField=new JTextField(birthdayString);
    birthdayField.setColumns(7);
    birthdayField.setToolTipText("Enter the
    → birthday to calculate from.");
    birthdayField.addActionListener(new
    → MyListener());

    targetDate = new Date();
    targetDateField=new JTextField(fmt.format
    → (targetDate));
    targetDateField.setColumns(7);
    targetDateField.setToolTipText("Enter the
    → target date to display.");
    targetDateField.addActionListener(new
    → MyListener());

    contentPane.add(birthdayField);
    contentPane.add(targetDateField);

    emotional=new Cycle("Emotional", 28,
    → Color.red);
    intellectual=new Cycle("Intellectual",33,
    → Color.blue);
    physical = new Cycle ("Physical", 23,
    → Color.green);
  }
```

Applet continues on next page

Applet 12.7 *continued*

```
                    Applet
class Cycle {
String name;
int duration;
Color color;
JCheckBox checkbox;

public Cycle(String nameVal, int durationVal,
→ Color colorVal) {
 name=nameVal;
 duration=durationVal;
 color=colorVal;

 checkbox = new JCheckBox(name);
 checkbox.setToolTipText("Toggles display of
 → " + name + " rhythm.");
 checkbox.setContentAreaFilled(false);
 checkbox.setSelected(true);
 checkbox.addItemListener(new MyListener());
 contentPane.add(this.checkbox);
}

public int dayInCycle (Date startDate, Date
→ targetDate) {
 int daysElapsed, cycleDay;
 long milliSecondsElapsed,
 → milliSecondsPerDay;
 milliSecondsPerDay=1000*60*60*24;
 milliSecondsElapsed=targetDate.getTime() -
 → startDate.getTime();
 daysElapsed=(int)(milliSecondsElapsed/
 → milliSecondsPerDay);
 cycleDay=daysElapsed % duration;
 if (cycleDay==0) cycleDay=duration;
 return cycleDay;
 }
}

class MyListener implements ItemListener,
→ ActionListener {
public void itemStateChanged(ItemEvent e) {
 contentPane.repaint();
}

public void actionPerformed(ActionEvent evt) {
 DateFormat fmt = DateFormat.getDateInstance
 → (DateFormat.SHORT, Locale.US);
 try {
  birthday=fmt.parse(birthdayField.
  → getText());
  targetDate=fmt.parse(targetDateField.
  → getText());
 }
 catch(ParseException ex){
  System.out.println(ex);
 }
```

Applet continues on next page

10. emotional=new Cycle("Emotional", 28,
→ Color.red);
intellectual=new Cycle("Intellectual",
→ 33, Color.blue);
physical = new Cycle ("Physical",
→ 23, Color.green);

Create three different biorhythm cycles: Emotional, Intellectual, and Physical, which respectively have 28, 33, and 23 day cycles, and will be displayed as red, blue, and green.

11. class Cycle {
String name;
int duration;
Color color;
JCheckBox checkbox;

Here's the Cycle class and its variable declarations.

12. public Cycle(String nameVal, int
→ durationVal, Color colorVal) {
name=nameVal;
duration=durationVal;
color=colorVal;

Calling Cycle requires three variables: the name of the cycle, the length of the cycle, and the color of the cycle.

13. checkbox = new JCheckBox(name);
checkbox.setToolTipText("Toggles
→ display of " + name + " rhythm.");
checkbox.setContentAreaFilled
→ (false);
checkbox.setSelected(true);
checkbox.addItemListener(new
→ MyListener());

Create a checkbox so users can toggle whether they see this particular cycle. Each cycle can be turned on and off without affecting the other two cycles.

14. contentPane.add(this.checkbox);

The checkbox is added to the content pane.

continued

Chapter 12

15. `public int dayInCycle (Date`
`→ startDate, Date targetDate) {`

The `dayInCycle()` method, when provided a `targetDate`, returns the current number of days into the cycle that target date is.

16. `int daysElapsed, cycleDay;`
`long milliSecondsElapsed,`
`→ milliSecondsPerDay;`

Java uses milliseconds to store the date value, so we can figure out how many days have passed by dividing by the number of milliseconds in one day.

17. `milliSecondsPerDay=1000*60*60*24;`
`milliSecondsElapsed=targetDate.`
`→ getTime() - startDate.getTime();`
`daysElapsed=(int)(milliSeconds`
`→ Elapsed/milliSecondsPerDay);`
`cycleDay=daysElapsed % duration;`
`if (cycleDay==0) cycleDay=duration;`
`return cycleDay;`

First, we define how many milliseconds there are in a day, then, find out how many milliseconds have elapsed between the dates. Next, turn the milliseconds into a number of days, and use the modulus (%) function (i.e., remainder) to figure out which day in the cycle it is. If there was no remainder, that means we're on the last day in the cycle. Finally, return the desired result.

18. `class MyListener implements`
`→ ItemListener, ActionListener {`

This class listens for events that change the checkboxes.

19. `public void itemStateChanged`
`→ (ItemEvent e) {`
`contentPane.repaint();`
`}`

We only need to `repaint` as the `paint` function checks whether the cycles should be displayed.

Applet 12.7 *continued*

```
contentPane.repaint();
 }
}

class AnimationPane extends JPanel {
 private void paintCycle(Graphics g, Cycle
→ currentCycle, int labelHeight) {
  int x,y,oldy,oldx;
  oldy=0;
  oldx=0;
  x=0;
  y=0;

  GregorianCalendar startCalendar,
→ targetCalendar;
  targetCalendar = new GregorianCalendar();
  targetCalendar.setTime(targetDate);
  startCalendar = new GregorianCalendar();
  startCalendar.setTime(birthday);

  int day;
  int dayInCycle;
  int daysToPaint=31;

  g.setColor(currentCycle.color);
  g.drawString(currentCycle.name,10,
→ labelHeight);

  Font myFont=new Font("San-Serif",
→ Font.PLAIN,9);
  g.setFont(myFont);
  int halfY=getContentPane().getSize().
→ height/2;

  for (day = 1; (day < daysToPaint); day++) {
   x=day*16;
   dayInCycle = currentCycle.dayInCycle
→ (startCalendar.getTime(),targetCalendar.
→ getTime());
   y =(int)((Math.sin(2 * Math.PI * dayInCycle/
→ currentCycle.duration) * 200 ) + halfY);
   y = getContentPane().getSize().height - y;
   if (x > 16) {
    g.drawLine(oldx,oldy,x,y);
    if (day%3==0) {
     g.setColor(Color.black);
     g.drawString(""+(targetCalendar.
→ get(Calendar.MONTH)+1)+"/"+target
→ Calendar.get(Calendar.DAY_OF_MONTH),
→ x,250);
     g.setColor(currentCycle.color);
   }
  }
```

Applet continues on next page

212

Applet 12.7 *continued*

```
oldy = y;
oldx = x;
targetCalendar.add(GregorianCalendar.
→ DATE, 1);
      }
   }

public void paintComponent(Graphics g) {
   super.paintComponent(g);
   g.setColor(Color.black);
   int halfY=getContentPane().getSize().
   → height/2;
   g.drawLine(0,halfY,getContentPane().
   → getSize().width,halfY);
   if (emotional.checkbox.isSelected()) {
    paintCycle(g, emotional, 10);
   }
   if (intellectual.checkbox.isSelected()) {
    paintCycle(g, intellectual, 20);
   }
   if (physical.checkbox.isSelected()) {
    paintCycle(g, physical, 30);
   }
  }
 }
}
```

20. `public void actionPerformed`
`→ (ActionEvent evt) {`

Here, we listen for events that change the date values.

21. `DateFormat fmt = DateFormat.`
`→ getDateInstance(DateFormat.SHORT,`
`→ Locale.US);`

Again, setup `DateFormat` so we can coerce the user's entry into a `Date` object.

22. `try {`
`    birthday= fmt.parse(birthdayField.`
`    → getText());`
`    targetDate= fmt.parse(targetDate`
`    → Field.getText());`
`  }`
`  catch(ParseException ex){`
`    System.out.println(ex);`
`  }`

Try and update the two `Date` objects to the latest values from the date fields on the panel.

23. `contentPane.repaint();`

And now, repaint the applet.

24. `class AnimationPane extends JPanel {`

As in **Applet 12.6**, we extend `JPanel` class so we can override `paintComponent` to display the cycles.

25. `private void paintCycle(Graphics g,`
`→ Cycle currentCycle, int`
`→ labelHeight) {`

`paintCycle` paints one biorhythm cycle, and so, will be called once for each of the three cycles.

26. `int x,y,oldy,oldx;`
`oldy=0;`
`oldx=0;`
`x=0;`
`y=0;`

Declare the point integers and set initial values.

continued

SWING IN ACTION

27.
```
GregorianCalendar startCalendar,
→ targetCalendar;
targetCalendar = new
→ GregorianCalendar();
targetCalendar.setTime(targetDate);
startCalendar = new
→ GregorianCalendar();
startCalendar.setTime(birthday);
```
Declare and set the Calendar objects.

28.
```
int day;
int dayInCycle;
int daysToPaint=31;
```
Declare some integers that will be used to calculate dates.

29.
```
g.setColor(currentCycle.color);
g.drawString(currentCycle.name,10,
→ labelHeight);
```
Set the color to be appropriate for the cycle, and draw the name of the cycle in the upper-left corner.

30.
```
Font myFont=new Font("San-Serif",
→ Font.PLAIN,9);
g.setFont(myFont);
```
Set the font to display the date in the middle of the display.

31.
```
int halfY=getContentPane().
→ getSize().height/2;
```
Determine the mid-way point in the component to display the centerline and the dates.

32.
```
for (day = 1; (day < daysToPaint);
→ day++) {
```
Loop through the number of days to paint, drawing the value for the cycle for each day.

33. `x=day*16;`
`dayInCycle = currentCycle.`
`→ dayInCycle(startCalendar.`
`→ getTime(),targetCalendar.`
`→ getTime());`

Set the value of x to be a factor of the day value; this makes the chart larger than it would be if x was set to the day. Then, figure out where we are in the cycle.

34. `y =(int)((Math.sin(2 * Math.PI *`
`→ dayInCycle/currentCycle.duration)`
`→ * 200 ) + halfY);`
`y = getContentPane().getSize().`
`→ height - y;`

Set y to the sine of (2 * PI * dayInCycle / duration of cycle), multiply by 200 to increase the size of the chart, and add halfY to position 0 in the middle of the chart. The initial value of y places the small values at the top of the screen and the large values at the bottom, but we want this reversed, so we subtract y from the height of the screen to place the smaller values at the bottom of the image.

35. `if (x > 16) {`
`   g.drawLine(oldx,oldy,x,y);`
`   if (day%3==0) {`

If we're not in the first instance of the loop then draw a line between the current value and the last value's location. If we're an increment of 3 then do the following to display the date's value in the center of the screen.

36. `g.setColor(Color.black);`
`g.drawString(""+(targetCalendar.`
`→ get(Calendar.MONTH)+1)+"/"+`
`→ targetCalendar.get(Calendar.`
`→ DAY_OF_MONTH),x,250);`
`g.setColor(currentCycle.color);`

First, set the color to black, then draw the date, and finally, reset the color back to the original line color.

continued

SWING IN ACTION

37. `oldy = y;`
`oldx = x;`

Remember this position for the next iteration through the loop

38. `targetCalendar.add`
→ `(GregorianCalendar.DATE, 1);`

Add one day to our target date within the loop to let us calculate the next value.

39. `public void paintComponent`
→ `(Graphics g) {`

`paintComponent` is called when we need to update the display.

40. `super.paintComponent(g);`
`g.setColor(Color.black);`
`int halfY=getContentPane().`
→ `getSize().height/2;`
`g.drawLine(0,halfY,getContentPane().`
→ `getSize().width,halfY);`

First, call our parent object's `paintComponent`, then set the color to black to display the zero line, find the halfway point on the screen, and finally draw the zero line.

41. `if (emotional.checkbox.isSelected()) {`
`   paintCycle(g, emotional, 10);`
` }`
`if (intellectual.checkbox.`
→ `isSelected()) {`
`   paintCycle(g, intellectual, 20);`
`}`
`if (physical.checkbox.isSelected()) {`
`   paintCycle(g, physical, 30);`
`}`

For each of the three cycles, check to see if that checkbox is selected. If it is, call `paintCycle` to draw the cycle, as shown in **Figure 12.16**.

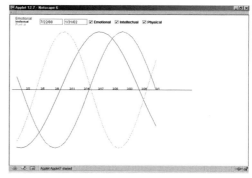

Figure 12.16 This person's biorhythm chart for January 31, 2002.

JavaServer
Pages and Servlets

The original hype for Java was all about the client side. Java within the browser or on the desktop would bring about the developer Holy Grail: Write Once, Run Anywhere (WORA). WORA turned out to be just about as mythical as that Grail; in practice, it's more like Write Once, Debug Everywhere.

Where Java has really taken hold is on the server side. It's still being used to add functionality to Web pages, but your code is executed on the server side instead of by the user's local Virtual Machine. That way, it doesn't matter what browser the person reading your site has, as it comes across as normal HTML.

There are two common ways to achieve this goal: JavaServer Pages (JSP) and Servlets. This chapter will cover how each works and why you'd want to use one instead of the other. These are complex topics, so, if you're interested in learning more, I recommend checking out *Core Servlets and JavaServer Pages* by Marty Hall (Prentice Hall, 2000).

Your First JavaServer Page

When you see your first JSP, you might think that it looks just like an HTML page. If so, you wouldn't be far off. **Listing 13.1** is an HTML page, with just a small amount of functionality added—that's the JSP in action. In practice, this makes it easy to learn how to write JSP when you already know HTML.

To write your first JavaServer Page:

1. <%

This little tag here is what tells JSP to execute the code inside the container. Everything else passes through as normal HTML, but whatever's inside this tag is looked at as Java.

2. out.println("Hello World!");

It's our first JSP, so it needs to say "Hello World." The code looks just like any other bit of Java, except that it's embedded inside an HTML page.

3. %>

This closes out this bit of Java on this page.

4. It is now <%= new java.util.Date() %>

If all you want to do with Java is use a simple expression, you start your tag slightly differently, using <%= instead of <%. That's all there is to it, and **Figure 13.1** shows the result.

Listing 13.1 Your very first JavaServer Page (called listing1.jsp) looks a lot like HTML, but with a little more smarts.

```
<html>
  <head>
    <title>Example 13.1</title>
  </head>
  <body bgcolor="white">
    <%
      out.println("Hello World!");
    %>
    <br>
    It is now <%= new java.util.Date() %>
  </body>
</html>
```

Figure 13.1 Here's your first JSP, printing out your message with the date and time.

✔ Tips

■ If you view the source of the page after it's loaded, there's really no way to know that this page was created on the fly (except for the file extension). Your little bits of Java code won't appear, just the HTML and/or text that they've generated.

■ It's important to remember that using the `<%=` tag will insert the results of the expression in the HTML stream without having to use `out.println`, but the `<%` tag will not.

Serving JavaServer Pages

Here's the good news/bad news of JSP: instead of depending on the user's browser to run your code, you're now depending on your Web server to do the trick.

So, you're probably wondering, how does your server know that it should be executing that Java code instead of just seeing it as text that should be pushed out to the browser? The answer is that you'll have to add one more piece to your serving strategy to make this happen.

What software you'll add all depends on what Web server you're using. If you, like most people, are using Apache, it's simple: download the open source program Tomcat from `http://jakarta.apache.org/tomcat/` and install it (**Figure 13.2**). Follow their directions to make it work with Apache, name your files to end with `.jsp`, and your code will automagically be processed before it's served.

If you're using some other Web server software, take a look at Sun's list at `http://java.sun.com/products/jsp/industry.html`. It lists all of the Web servers that officially support JSP, so you can find out what's compatible with your server.

Figure 13.2 When you first install Tomcat, you'll get this welcome message saying that everything's working.

JSP and Forms

One of the most common uses of JSP is to handle the results of HTML forms. This task sets up a JSP to read in the results submitted by your average HTML form.

To set up a form to call a JSP:

1. `<form action="listing2.jsp" method=`
   `→ "post">`

   Listing 13.2 is, once again, just a standard HTML form (**Figure 13.3**). About the only difference you'll find here compared with anything you've done before is that now your action is referring to a .jsp page.

2. `<input type="text" name="message">`

   Note that the text field being entered has the name message—that's how the JSP will refer to it. Consequently, you need to be careful about always giving your form elements unique names.

Listing 13.2 This file, named `listing2.html`, takes the information from your site's visitor.

```
<html>
 <head>
  <title>Example 13.2</title>
 </head>
 <body bgcolor="white">
  <form action="listing2.jsp" method="post">
   Enter a message:
   <p><input type="text" name="message"></p>
   <p><input type="submit" value="Submit"></p>
  </form>
 </body>
</html>
```

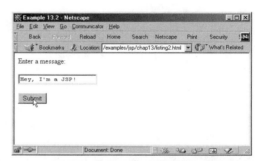

Figure 13.3 While this page isn't actually a JSP, after it's submitted, a JSP will display the message.

Listing 13.3 This file, named listing2.jsp, displays that same information (and a little more) after the user submits the form.

```
                    Listing
<html>
  <head>
    <title>Example 13.2</title>
  </head>
  <body bgcolor="white">
    <%= request.getParameter("message")
    → %><br>
    <%= request.getHeader("User-Agent")
    → %><br>
  </body>
</html>
```

Figure 13.4 And here's the resulting page, showing whatever the user entered.

To set up a JSP to use the results of a form:

1. `<%= request.getParameter("message") %>`

   In **Listing 13.3**, this simple Java statement in the midst of the HTML reads in the message field and displays it.

2. `<%= request.getHeader("User-Agent") %>`

   And just to get a little fancy, we'll also display the User-Agent information from the header, as shown in **Figure 13.4**.

✔ Tip

■ If you're not clear on how HTML forms work, check out *HTML 4 for the World Wide Web: Visual QuickStart Guide* by Elizabeth Castro.

JSP AND FORMS

221

Decisions with JSP

JSP doesn't have to just take whatever it's given; it can also make decisions based on the data it's passed. This example uses an HTML form (**Listing 13.4**) that is similar to **Listing 13.2** in the previous task, but **Listing 13.5** checks to see if the user entered anything. Based on that, different results can be passed back to the browser.

To make decisions with JSP:

1. `String helloMessage;`

   Now, instead of just grabbing and displaying whatever the user entered, we want to do a little bit of checking. Consequently, we start by creating a new string to store whatever was entered.

2. `helloMessage=request.getParameter`
   `→ ("message");`

   And here's where the new string is set, based on the user's entry in the form in **Figure 13.5**.

3. `if (helloMessage==null ||`
   `→ helloMessage.length()==0) {`

   If the user didn't enter anything, either of these two checks might be true (depending on a variety of factors). Just in case, we'll check them both. So, if `helloMessage` has no value, or if it has a value but it's an empty string, we want to execute the next line of code.

4. `helloMessage="Hello World!";`

   If no message was entered, it's reset here to our old standby.

Listing 13.4 This file, named `listing3.html`, once again takes in the user-entered data.

```
<html>
 <head>
  <title>Example 13.3</title>
 </head>
 <body bgcolor="white">
  <form action="listing3.jsp" method="post">
   Enter a message:
   <p><input type="text" name="message"></p>
   <p><input type="submit" value="Submit"></p>
  </form>
 </body>
</html>
```

Listing 13.5 This file, named `listing3.jsp`, checks to see whether the user actually entered something before displaying a message.

```
<html>
 <head>
  <title>Example 13.3</title>
 </head>
 <body bgcolor="white">
  <%
   String helloMessage;
   helloMessage=request.getParameter
   → ("message");

   if (helloMessage==null || helloMessage.
   → length()==0) {
    helloMessage="Hello World!";
   }

   out.println(helloMessage);
  %>
 </body>
</html>
```

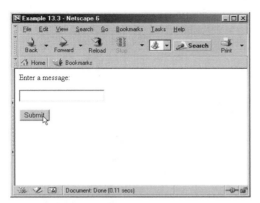

Figure 13.5 Nothing is stopping the user from submitting this form without entering something.

Figure 13.6 But in this example, the JSP sees that that's the case and displays something other than a blank page.

5. }

The `if` clause is closed here, so the following line of code is executed whether or not anything was entered.

6. `out.println(helloMessage);`

And the message is displayed here, as shown in **Figure 13.6**.

✔ Tip

■ One of the best reasons for making sure that you handle a situation where nothing was entered is for those folks who may have been to your site previously and bookmarked the JSP. In that case, JSP won't be able to find a parameter by that name, so you ought to make sure you have a graceful way to handle the situation.

DECISIONS WITH JSP

Writing Cookies with JSP

Another popular task for JSP is writing (and later reading) cookies in order to keep track of some information about the person visiting your site. **Listing 13.6** writes out two simple cookies to your visitor's browser, as shown in **Figure 13.7**.

To write cookies with JSP:

1. `String cookieMessage="I'm a temporary → value";`

   The first of the two cookies is a temporary cookie: because we don't set an expiration date, it will go away when your visitor quits their browser. A string value is set here that will shortly be stored in a new cookie.

2. `Cookie message = new Cookie → ("message", cookieMessage);`

   The new cookie is created here, with a name of `message`, and a value that's set to what's in `cookieMessage`.

3. `response.addCookie(message);`

   And here's where the cookie is actually written out when the browser loads the page.

4. `Cookie visitCount = new Cookie → ("visit count", "1");`

   Here's our second cookie. This one will keep track of how many visits have been made, so we'll call it `visit count` and start it off with a value of 1.

Listing 13.6 The `listing4.jsp` file writes two cookies out to the browser.

```
<html>
 <head>
  <title>Example 13.4</title>
 </head>
 <body bgcolor="white">
  <%
   String cookieMessage="I'm a temporary
   → value";
   Cookie message = new Cookie("message",
   → cookieMessage);
   response.addCookie(message);

   Cookie visitCount = new Cookie ("visit
   → count", "1");
   int secondsToLive=60*60*24;
   visitCount.setMaxAge(secondsToLive);
   response.addCookie(visitCount);
  %>
  Two cookie values set.
 </body>
</html>
```

Figure 13.7 Writing cookies is all behind-the-scenes work, so we add a message that two cookies have been written to let the user know what's going on.

5. `int secondsToLive=60*60*24;`

For this cookie, unlike the previous one, we'll set how long it will last on the user's system. A cookie's lifetime is calculated in seconds, so to make it last one day we set `secondsToLive` by multiplying the number of seconds in a minute, the number of minutes in an hour, and the number of hours in day, to produce a result of the number of seconds in a day. This way, the browser will keep track of this value for the next 24 hours, but no longer.

6. `visitCount.setMaxAge(secondsToLive);`

Here's where the maximum age is set for the `visitCount` cookie.

7. `response.addCookie(visitCount);`

And here's where the `visitCount` is written out.

Reading Cookies with JSP

There's not much point to writing cookies unless you plan to read them back in again at a later date. **Listing 13.7** reads in the cookies that were written out in the previous task, and then displays them in the browser as shown in **Figure 13.8**.

To read cookies with JSP:

1. Cookie[] cookies = request.
→ getCookies();

    This line creates an array of cookie objects, and assigns them to the values of the cookies that can be read for this domain.

2. int i;
Cookie currentCookie;

    Two variables are initialized here: one integer i and one cookie, currentCookie.

3. for(i=0; i < cookies.length; i++) {

    For each of the cookies that we were able to read, we want to loop once through the cookie array.

4. currentCookie=cookies[i];

    Here, currentCookie is set to whatever the current cookie is that we want to look at. The first time through the loop, it'll be the 0th cookie, the second time it'll be the 1st cookie, and so on. If, for example, there were 5 cookies, they'd be stored as 0 through 4 in the array.

5. if (currentCookie.getName().equals
→ ("visit count")) {

    Now that we have a cookie, we want to look at its name. If it's visit count, then execute the next few lines of code.

Listing 13.7 The listing5.jsp file reads the cookies set in the previous task.

```
                        Listing
<html>
  <head>
    <title>Example 13.5</title>
  </head>
  <body bgcolor="white">
    <table border=1>
      <tr>
        <th>Name</th>
        <th>Value</th>
      </tr>
      <%
        Cookie[] cookies = request.
        → getCookies();
        int i;
        Cookie currentCookie;

        for(i=0; i < cookies.length; i++) {
          currentCookie=cookies[i];
          if (currentCookie.getName().equals
          → ("visit count")) {
            int count=Integer.parseInt
            → (currentCookie.getValue());
            count++;
            currentCookie.setValue(Integer.
            → toString(count));
            int secondsToLive=60*60*24;
            currentCookie.setMaxAge
            → (secondsToLive);
            response.addCookie
            → (currentCookie);
          }
          out.println("<tr><td>" +
          → currentCookie.
          → getName() + "</td>");
          out.println("<td>" +
          → currentCookie.getValue() +
          → "</td></tr>");
        }
      %>
    </table>
  </body>
</html>
```

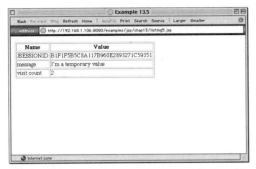

Figure 13.8 All the cookies set by Java are displayed in an HTML table.

6. `int count=Integer.parseInt`
   `→ (currentCookie.getValue());`

   If we're here, we've found the visit counter, so we'll want to bump it up by one (because we've visited another page). Here, count is set to the value of the cookie, which we first need to cast as an integer because cookie values are stored as strings.

7. `count++;`

   Next, count is bumped up by one.

8. `currentCookie.setValue(Integer.`
   `→ toString(count));`

   And then it's written back out again with the new value.

9. `int secondsToLive=60*60*24;`

   Because we've rewritten the cookie, we also want to rewrite its expiration date, so we once again figure out when it should expire.

10. `currentCookie.setMaxAge`
    `→ (secondsToLive);`

    And again, the cookie's maximum age is set to 24 hours in the future.

11. `response.addCookie(currentCookie);`

    And then the cookie is written back out to the browser.

12. `out.println("<tr><td>" +`
    `→ currentCookie.getName() + "</td>");`

    Besides writing a new visit count cookie, we also want to display all the cookies that are accessible from this domain. That's a good use for a table, so we'll start writing a row here with the name of the cookie.

    continued

READING COOKIES WITH JSP

13. `out.println("<td>" + currentCookie.`
`→ getValue() + "</td></tr>");`

Here's the rest of the row, with the value of the cookie. Note that every cookie that can be read by this domain is being displayed, not just the `visit count` cookie.

✔ Tips

■ Cookies have a bad rap, but they're actually almost entirely secure (minus a few people with ancient browsers they haven't updated). You can't, for instance, use this JSP to read cookies written by other domains.

■ No, you're not imagining things, there is one more cookie being displayed here than you wrote out in the previous task. That `JSESSIONID` you see in **Figure 13.8** is a cookie that was written out by Java itself in order to keep track of session info.

■ If you reload this page, you should notice that the visit count is incremented every time (so long as you're reloading it within 24 hours of the previous visit, that is).

Listing 13.8 The listing6.html file calls listing6.jsp when it's submitted.

```
┌──────────────── Listing ────────────────┐
<html>
  <head>
    <title>Example 13.6</title>
  </head>
  <body bgcolor="white">
    <form action="listing6.jsp" method="post">
      Enter a message:
      <p><input type="text" name="message"></p>
      <p><input type="submit" value="Submit">
      → </p>
    </form>
  </body>
</html>
```

Listing 13.9 The listing6.jsp file uses XML syntax to display the message in the browser window.

```
┌──────────────── Listing ────────────────┐
<jsp:root xmlns:jsp="http://java.sun.com/
→ JSP/Page" version="1.2">
<html>
  <head>
  <title>Example 13.6</title>
  </head>
  <body bgcolor="white">
    <jsp:scriptlet>
      String helloMessage;
      helloMessage=request.getParameter
      → ("message");

      if (helloMessage==null || helloMessage.
      → length()==0) {
        helloMessage="Hello World!";
      }
    </jsp:scriptlet>

    <jsp:expression>
      helloMessage
    </jsp:expression>
  </body>
</html>
</jsp:root>
```

XML and JSP

JSP can also use XML (eXtensible Markup Language) syntax instead of the standard syntax that we've seen previously. **Listings 13.8** and **13.9** produce the same result as **Listings 13.4** and **13.5**, but this time, our file is in XML.

To create XML with JSP:

1. `<jsp:scriptlet>`

   The actual name for what we've been writing here is *scriptlets*, so XML uses this syntax instead of <%. **Table 13.1** covers the equivalent syntax for each type of JSP.

2. ```
   String helloMessage;
   helloMessage=request.
   → getParameter("message");
   if (helloMessage==null ||
   → helloMessage.length()==0) {
     helloMessage="Hello World!";
   }
   ```

   These lines are identical to those in **Listing 13.5**, and do the same thing.

3. `</jsp:scriptlet>`

   It should be unsurprising at this point that this line of code is equivalent to %>.

4. `<jsp:expression>`

   Where **Listing 13.5** used the line `out.println(helloMessage);` it's also possible to instead just display an *expression*. Using the original syntax, this would have been written as <%= (as in **Listing 13.1**); here it's done by saying explicitly using XML that this is an expression coming up.

   continued
   ```

5. helloMessage

   And here's the expression that we want displayed on our visitor's page, as shown in **Figures 13.9** and **13.10**.

6. </jsp:expression>

   And the expression ends with this line.

Table 13.1

JSP Scripting Elements	
STANDARD SYNTAX	XML SYNTAX
<%	<jsp:scriptlet>
<%=	<jsp:expression>
<%!	<jsp:declaration>
<%@	<jsp:directive>

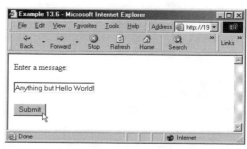

Figure 13.9 Once again, a message is entered.

Figure 13.10 And once again, it's displayed.

Listing 13.10 The file `listing7.html` has our usual HTML form, but this time, calls a servlet instead of a JSP.

```
<html>
  <head>
    <title>Example 13.7</title>
  </head>
  <body bgcolor="white">
    <form action="/examples/servlet/HelloWorld"
    → method="post">
      Enter a message:
      <p><input type="text" name="message"></p>
      <p><input type="submit" value=
      → "Submit"></p>
    </form>
  </body>
</html>
```

Listing 13.11 The file `HelloWorld.java` (compiled into `HelloWorld.class`) handles the input from either a GET or POST request and displays the page.

```
import java.io.*;
import javax.servlet.*;
import javax.servlet.http.*;

public class HelloWorld extends HttpServlet {

  public void doGet (HttpServletRequest request,
  → HttpServletResponse response) throws
  → ServletException, IOException {
    String formText,htmlText;

    response.setContentType("text/html");
    PrintWriter output=response.getWriter();

    formText=request.getParameter("message");

    if (formText==null || formText.length()==0) {
      formText="Hello World!";
    }

    htmlText="<html> \n <head><title>HelloWorld
    → </title></head>";
    htmlText+= "<body bgcolor='white'>" +
    → formText + "</body>";
    htmlText+= "</html>";

    output.println(htmlText);
  }

  public void doPost (HttpServletRequest
  → request, HttpServletResponse response)
  → throws ServletException, IOException {
    doGet(request, response);
  }
}
```

Your First Servlet

Servlets are a little different from JSP, in that you're back to writing actual Java code that needs to be compiled. The advantage is that you can do things that are considerably more complex than JSP can handle. In **Listings 13.10** and **13.11**, though, we'll take it slow and easy to introduce you to the new concepts.

To call your first servlet:

◆ `<form action="/examples/servlet/HelloWorld" method="post">`

Figure 13.11 shows another HTML form, just like our other HTML forms, with one difference: servlets can't handle relative links. Even if our HTML file was in the same directory as the `/examples/servlet` directory, it would still have to use the full syntax, as servlets don't map to URLs in the same fashion as JSP or regular HTML pages. While you don't have to use the full path (i.e., you don't have to specify the domain name), you do need to start from the root level of the server.

To write your first servlet:

1. `import java.io.*;`
   `import javax.servlet.*;`
   `import javax.servlet.http.*;`

   As always, we start off by importing a few classes. These are ones we haven't used before, but it's clear what they handle: i/o (input and output), servlets, and http handling for servlets.

2. `public class HelloWorld extends → HttpServlet {`

   This is the standard HelloWorld servlet, so it needs to extend `HttpServlet`.

   continued

3. `public void doGet`
→ `(HttpServletRequest request,`
→ `HttpServletResponse response)`
→ `throws ServletException,`
→ `IOException {`

If the servlet is called either by going directly to this page or by a form using a GET request, then the doGet() method gets called.

4. `String formText,htmlText;`

Two strings are defined here: formText for input, and htmlText for output.

5. `response.setContentType`
→ `("text/html");`

Tell the browser that it should expect everything coming through as HTML. If we needed to, this could be just about any MIME type, such as an image.

6. `PrintWriter output=response.`
→ `getWriter();`

We need to send our response somewhere, so here we create a PrintWriter object named output to send the response to.

7. `formText=request.getParameter`
→ `("message");`

Here, formText is set to whatever the user entered as the message in the HTML form.

8. `if (formText==null || formText.`
→ `length()==0) {`
`  formText="Hello World!";`
`}`

Again, if the user didn't enter anything, or if the user came to this page directly, set up a dummy message as the default.

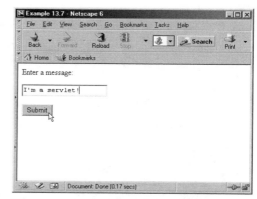

Figure 13.11 It's just another HTML form, from the outside.

Figure 13.12 Internally, though, this page was built by a servlet.

9. `htmlText="<html> \n <head><title>`
`→ HelloWorld</title></head>";`
`htmlText+= "<body bgcolor='white'>"`
`→ + formText + "</body>";`
`htmlText+= "</html>";`

Servlets need to build and return an entire HTML page. Here's where the page is put together.

10. `output.println(htmlText);`

And this line sends the result back to the browser, as shown in **Figure 13.12**.

11. `public void doPost`
`→ (HttpServletRequest request,`
`→ HttpServletResponse response)`
`→ throws ServletException,`
`→ IOException {`

If this page was called by a POST request, the doPost() method is called instead of doGet(). We want identical results, though, and the simplest way to ensure that is to have doPost() only run a single line of Java.

12. `doGet(request, response);`

And here's that single line: a call to the doGet() method.

✔ Tips

■ There's no special reason that the doGet() method does all the work and the doPost() method just calls doGet().Switching the order and functionality would have worked just fine, too.

■ Now that you've seen both JSP and servlets, here's the secret as to how the former work: when Tomcat sees a JSP, it translates it into Java and creates a servlet. So, while you start from different places, you end up with the same result. Which one you decide to use depends on whether you want to add a little bit of Java to your HTML (JSP), or a little bit of HTML to your Java (servlets).

Surveys with Servlets

A common use of servlets on a Web site is to take surveys of your site's readers. This handy survey allows you to ask your readers to choose between several options. After they've done so, they can see what others have picked, or they can choose to go straight to the results without having voted at all.

One of the slickest details of this survey servlet is that you don't have to rewrite the servlet every time you put up a new survey. Simply change the HTML form (as in **Listing 13.12**) to reflect the new options, delete the file where you've stored the previous responses, and voila—you're starting over again.

To set up a survey form:

1. ```
   <form action="/examples/servlet/
   ➔ PollCounter" method="post">
   ```

   Voting for one of the actors in this poll calls our **Listing 13.13** servlet and passes in the user's choice, as shown in **Figures 13.13**, **13.14**, and **13.15**.

2. ```
   <a href="/examples/servlet/
   ➔ PollCounter?results=actor">See
   ➔ Results</a>
   ```

   If you want to see the results without voting, clicking on this link will cause the servlet to display the chart without incrementing anyone's total. Note that there's a `results` parameter being passed here, which isn't the case when the visitor is voting.

Listing 13.12 The file, `listing8.html`, displays the survey options to the visitor.

```
┌─────────────────── Listing ───────────────────┐
<html>
  <head>
    <title>Example 13.8</title>
  </head>
  <body bgcolor="white">
    <form action="/examples/servlet/
    ➔ PollCounter" method="post">
      <p>Who's your favorite Star Trek
      ➔ Actor?</p>
      <p>
        <input type="radio" name="actor"
        ➔ value="John de Lancie"> John de
        ➔ Lancie<br>
        <input type="radio" name="actor"
        ➔ value="William Shatner"> William
        ➔ Shatner<br>
        <input type="radio" name="actor"
        ➔ value="Patrick Stewart"> Patrick
        ➔ Stewart<br>
        <input type="radio" name="actor"
        ➔ value="Wil Wheaton"> Wil Wheaton
      </p>
      <input type="submit" value="Vote">
      <p><a href="/examples/servlet/
      'PollCounter?results=actor">See Results
      ➔ </a></p>
    </form>
  </body>
</html>
```

Listing 13.13 The file, `PollCounter.java` (compiled into `PollCounter.class`), tabulates the results and displays the page.

```
                    Listing
import java.io.*;
import javax.servlet.*;
import javax.servlet.http.*;
import java.util.*;

public class PollCounter extends HttpServlet {
 Map names = Collections.synchronizedSortedMap
 → (new TreeMap());
 static int votesTotal = 0;
 File filename = new File("pollresults.bin");

 public void init() throws ServletException {
   if (filename.exists()) {
     try {
       ObjectInputStream in= new
       → ObjectInputStream(new FileInputStream
       → (filename));

       synchronized(names) {
         if (names.size()==0) {
           System.out.println("PollCounter:
           → Reading in old poll results.");
           names = (Map) in.readObject();
         }
         in.close();

         Iterator namesIter= names.keySet().
         → iterator();
         while (namesIter.hasNext()) {
           String itemName = (String)
           → namesIter.next();
           Integer itemVotes=(Integer)
           → names.get(itemName);
           votesTotal+=itemVotes.intValue();
         }
       }
     }
     catch(ClassNotFoundException e) {
       System.out.println(e);
     }
     catch(IOException e) {
       System.out.println(e);
     }
   }
 }
```

Listing continues on next page

To use a servlet to tabulate a survey:

1. ```
   import java.io.*;
   import javax.servlet.*;
   import javax.servlet.http.*;
   import java.util.*;
   ```
   We start off by importing the standard classes this servlet will need.

2. ```
   public class PollCounter extends
   → HttpServlet {
   ```
   Our servlet is called `PollCounter`, and it extends `HttpServlet`.

3. ```
   Map names = Collections.
   →synchronizedSortedMap(new
   → TreeMap());
   ```
   Create a synchronized sorted map to store the current votes for the list of names. It needs to be synchronized because it's likely that more than one servlet thread may be running at any given time. It's a sorted map so that we'll always get the list back in alphabetical order.

4. ```
   static int votesTotal = 0;
   ```
   Set the total number of votes to zero. This will be used later to calculate percentages for each name.

5. ```
   File filename = new File("pollresults.
   → bin");
   ```
   Here we create a `File` object that we'll use to store the results when the server shuts down. This keeps the poll from resetting if we need to stop the server for some reason.

6. ```
   public void init() throws
   → ServletException {
   ```
   The `init()` method is called when the servlet is first run. It's not called for each page request, instead, only when the servlet is launched in order to restore the vote count from any previous runs.

   continued

7. `if (filename.exists()) {`
    `try {`

If the filename exists, try to run the following code.

8. `ObjectInputStream in= new`
    `→ ObjectInputStream(new`
    `→ FileInputStream(filename));`

Create an input stream to read the values in.

9. `synchronized(names) {`

Synchronize our access to `names` so we're thread safe (i.e., so that the workings of one person voting (a thread) doesn't overwrite or run into another person's voting at the same time). While there's no chance of another servlet running the `init()` method, we must synchronize our access to `names` because we declared the map as a synchronized object.

10. `if (names.size()==0) {`
    `System.out.println("PollCounter:`
    `→ Reading in old poll results.");`
    `names = (Map) in.readObject();`
    `}`

Check to be sure that the count of `names` is really zero. If so, put up a notification message in the console that we're reading in the old poll results, and set the `names` map to the value of the only object in the file.

11. `in.close();`

We're done with it, so close the input stream.

12. `Iterator namesIter= names.`
    `→ keySet().iterator();`

We want to update the `votesTotal` count so we have an accurate count of all the votes, and that starts by creating an iterator to run through the list of names and values.

Listing 13.13 *continued*

```
┌─────────────────── Listing ───────────────────┐

  public void destroy() {
    try {
      System.out.println("PollCounter: Saving
      → current poll results");
      ObjectOutputStream out = new
      → ObjectOutputStream(new FileOutputStream
      → (filename));
      out.writeObject(names);
      out.close();
    }
    catch(IOException e) {
      System.out.println(e);
    }
  }

  public void doPost(HttpServletRequest
  → request, HttpServletResponse response)
  → throws ServletException, IOException {
    doGet(request, response);
  }

  public void doGet(HttpServletRequest request,
  → HttpServletResponse response) throws
  → ServletException, IOException {
    if (request.getParameter("results")
    → == null) {
      updateCount(request);
    }
    response.setContentType("text/html");
    PrintWriter out = response.getWriter();
    out.println("<html><head><title>Poll
    → Results</title></head><body bgcolor=
    → 'white'>");
    out.println(displayVoteResults(request));
    out.println("</body></html>");
  }

  private void updateCount(HttpServletRequest
  → request) {
    Enumeration paramNames = request.
    → getParameterNames();

    while (paramNames.hasMoreElements()) {
      String paramName = (String) paramNames.
      → nextElement();
      String[] paramValues = request.
      → getParameterValues(paramName);
      for (int i = 0; i<paramValues.length;
      → i++) {
        incrVote(paramValues[i]);
      }
    }
  }
}
```

Listing continues on next page

Listing 13.13 *continued*

```
                         Listing
private void incrVote(String voteName) {
  Integer storedValue;

  synchronized(names) {
    if (names.containsKey(voteName)) {
      storedValue = (Integer) names.
      → get(voteName);
      storedValue = new Integer(storedValue.
      → intValue()+1);
      names.put(voteName, storedValue);
    }
    else {
      names.put(voteName, new Integer(1));
    }
    votesTotal++;
  }
}

private String displayVoteResults
→ (HttpServletRequest request) {
  String results = "<table cellspacing=10>
  → \n\t<tr><th align='left'>Name</th>";
  results += "<th align='left'>Votes</th>
  → <th align='left'>Percent</th></tr>\n";
  Iterator namesIter= names.keySet()
  → iterator();

  while (namesIter.hasNext()) {
    String itemName = (String) namesIter.
    → next();
    Integer votes=(Integer) names.
    → get(itemName);

    int percent = 100 * votes.intValue() /
    → votesTotal;
    results += "\t<tr><td>" + itemName +
    → "</td><td>" + votes + "</td>";
    results += "<td><img src='/examples/
    → images/lilRed.gif' width='";
    results += percent + "' height='10'> " +
    → percent + "</td></tr>\n";
  }
  results += "</table>\n";
  return results;
  }
}
```

13. `while (namesIter.hasNext()) {`
`    String itemName = (String)`
`    → namesIter.next();`
`    Integer itemVotes=(Integer)`
`    → names.get(itemName);`
`    votesTotal +=itemVotes.`
`    → intValue();`
`}`

For every name, create a string with the name as its value, to use to get the vote count. Next, create an integer to contain the vote count for the current item, and update the total number of votes to include the count of the latest item.

14. `catch(ClassNotFoundException e) {`
`    System.out.println(e);`
`    }`

Catch the class not found exception and print it out, just in case.

15. `catch(IOException e) {`
`    System.out.println(e);`
`    }`

Again, in case of a possible I/O exception, catch it and print it out.

16. `}`
`}`

And that's all there is to the `init()` method.

17. `public void destroy() {`

The `destroy()` method is called when the servlet is being unloaded from memory, usually when the server is shutting down.

continued

18. try {
   System.out.println("PollCounter:
   → Saving current poll results");
   ObjectOutputStream out = new
   → ObjectOutputStream(new
   → FileOutputStream(filename));
   out.writeObject(names);
   out.close();
}

When that happens, we want to save the current vote count. First, notify that we're attempting to save the results. Then, create an output stream to save the results to, write the names map that holds our current values, and close the output stream.

19. catch(IOException e) {
   System.out.println(e);
}

There's the possibility of an I/O error, so if it happens, catch it and print it out. That's all there is to destroy().

20. public void doPost
   → (HttpServletRequest request,
   → HttpServletResponse response)
   → throws ServletException,
   → IOException {
  doGet(request, response);
}

If the calling HTML page sent a POST request, the doPost() method is called. Just like the previous example, we want both POST and GET to do the same thing, so doPost() just calls doGet().

21. public void doGet(HttpServletRequest
   → request, HttpServletResponse
   → response) throws ServletException,
   → IOException {

The doGet() method is called each time the servlet is called from the browser.

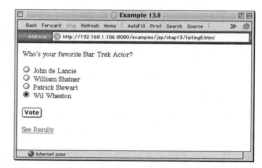

Figure 13.13 The survey, as shown in Classic Internet Explorer for Mac.

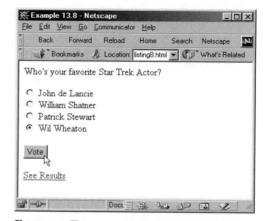

Figure 13.14 The same survey, as shown in Netscape 4 for Windows.

SURVEYS WITH SERVLETS

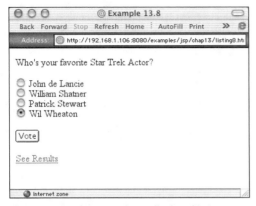

Figure 13.15 And once again, as displayed in Internet Explorer for Mac OS X.

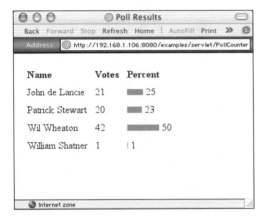

Figure 13.16 And here's the result of our voting.

22. `if (request.getParameter("results")`
`→ == null) {`
`updateCount(request);`
`}`

If there's no **results** parameter (see step 2 under "Setting up a survey form"), the user wants to actually vote. In that case, call **updateCount()** to handle the actual voting.

23. `response.setContentType`
`→ ("text/html");`

Whether they've voted or not, the user wants to see the results. The page being passed back is HTML, so tell that to the browser.

24. `PrintWriter out = response.`
`→ getWriter();`

Here, we get a **PrintWriter** object so we can send text to the browser.

25. `out.println("<html><head><title>Poll`
`→ Results</title></head><body`
`→ bgcolor='white'>");`
`out.println(displayVoteResults`
`→ (request));`
`out.println("</body></html>");`

The first line in this section begins the HTML text on the page. The second calls the **displayVoteResults()** method, which formats the results into more HTML text, and the last line finishes off the results page. This is the end of the line, control is returned back to the user, and the page is displayed, as shown in **Figure 13.16**.

26. `private void updateCount`
`→ (HttpServletRequest request) {`

The **updateCount()** method is called when the servlet has new votes to count.

continued

27. `Enumeration paramNames =`
`→ request.getParameterNames();`

We start by creating an **enumeration** (that's an object built in to Java that contains a collection of objects) that we'll use later to iterate through the form fields passed to the servlet.

28. `while (paramNames.hasMoreElements()) {`

So long as there are more elements to process, keep going through the fields.

29. `String paramName = (String)`
`→ paramNames.nextElement();`
`String[] paramValues = request.`
`→ getParameterValues(paramName);`

Create a string that's the parameter's name and an array of `String` objects that contain the parameter's values. An array is used here to allow more than one vote per field, in case your form allowed you to vote for multiple choices.

30. `for (int i = 0; i<paramValues.`
`→ length; i++) {`
`    incrVote(paramValues[i]);`
`}`

Next, iterate through the parameter's values and increment the votes for that person by calling the `incrVote()` method.

31. `private void incrVote(String`
`→ voteName) {`

The `incrVote()` method increments the vote for a single name.

32. `Integer storedValue;`

We start by declaring an integer, `storedValue`, to hold the most recently stored vote count for this name.

33. `synchronized(names) {`

Synchronize on the `names` map so we don't collide with other servlet threads.

SURVEYS WITH SERVLETS

34.
```
if (names.containsKey(voteName)) {
    storedValue = (Integer) names.
    → get(voteName);
    storedValue = new Integer
    → (storedValue.intValue()+1);
    names.put(voteName, storedValue);
}
```

If the names map contains voteName already, then we have a value that's been stored. When that's the case, set storedValue to the last vote count and then coerce storedValue to an integer and increment it. Finally, use names.put() to replace the old values in the names map with the new values.

35.
```
else {
    names.put(voteName, new
    → Integer(1));
}
```

If we're here, it's a new name, so use names.put() to add it to the list with a single vote.

36.
```
votesTotal++;
```

Increment the total number of votes cast. At this point, we've completed tabulating the voting.

37.
```
private String displayVoteResults
→ (HttpServletRequest request) {
```

The displayVoteResults() method takes the current vote count and turns it into an HTML table and bar graph.

38.
```
String results = "<table cellspacing=
→ 10>\n\t<tr><th align='left'>Name
→ </th>";
results += "<th align='left'>Votes
→ </th><th align='left'>Percent</th>
→ </tr>\n";
```

In these lines, we begin the table and write out the table headings.

continued

39. `Iterator namesIter= names.`
`→ keySet().iterator();`

Create an iterator so we can cycle through the list of names.

40. `while (namesIter.hasNext()) {`

And then go through this while loop once for each name.

41. `String itemName = (String) namesIter.`
`→ next();`
`Integer votes=(Integer) names.`
`→ get(itemName);`

`int percent = 100 * votes.`
`→ intValue() / votesTotal;`

First, set itemName to the name of the item, and then set votes to the value of the number of votes for this item. Lastly, calculate the percentage of votes out of the total for this item.

42. `results += "\t<tr><td>" + itemName +`
`→ "</td><td>" + votes + "</td>";`
`results += "<td><img src='/`
`→ examples/images/lilRed.gif'`
`→ width='";`
`results += percent + "' height=`
`→ '10'> " + percent + "</td>`
`→ </tr>\n";`

Here's where our row of HTML is written out for each item with a vote. The first cell in the table contains the name. The second contains the number of votes they've received. The third cell contains a single pixel gif with a variable width. That is, it's stretched out based on what percentage of the total votes this person has received. Finally, the actual percentage is displayed.

43. `results += "</table>\n";`
`return results;`

When the loop is complete, the table is closed, and the resulting HTML is returned.

SURVEYS WITH SERVLETS

Using Java with Visual Tools

Now that we're in the 21st century, most Web pages are written using visual editors such as Macromedia Dreamweaver and Adobe GoLive. However, neither product has made adding Java applets to your pages as easy as, say, adding a table. This chapter will cover how to add applets (using the Paper/Rock/Scissors game from Applet 6.8) to your pages using these visual tools.

If, after reading this chapter, you decide that you want to learn more about WYSIWYG tools, I recommend the following books: *Dreamweaver 4 for Windows and Macintosh: Visual QuickStart Guide* by J. Tarin Towers, *Real World Adobe GoLive 5* by Jeff Carlson and Glenn Fleishman, and *Adobe GoLive 5 for Windows and Macintosh: Visual QuickStart Guide* by Shelly Brisbin, all of which are available from Peachpit Press.

Adding Applet Tags with Dreamweaver

One problem with WYSIWYG tools is that they assume that when you want to add Java applets, you want to use the `applet` tag. As discussed in Chapter 3, this may or may not be the right approach for your project. In this example, we'll assume that you really do want to use Java via an applet tag on your page, and that you're using Macromedia's Dreamweaver.

To add an applet tag with Dreamweaver:

1. In Dreamweaver, open and save your first empty page. **Figure 14.1** shows a brand-spanking-new Dreamweaver page.

2. Since none of the Common tools on the Objects panel will create an applet tag, you'll need to switch to the Special tools, as shown in **Figures 14.2** and **14.3**.

Listing 14.1 The resulting applet from Macromedia Dreamweaver.

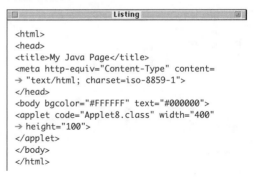

```html
<html>
<head>
<title>My Java Page</title>
<meta http-equiv="Content-Type" content=
→ "text/html; charset=iso-8859-1">
</head>
<body bgcolor="#FFFFFF" text="#000000">
<applet code="Applet8.class" width="400"
→ height="100">
</applet>
</body>
</html>
```

Figure 14.1 Here's what you see as you board the Dreamweaver train.

Figure 14.2 Switching from Common to Special will get you the applet icon.

Figure 14.3 Click the coffee cup icon to get the tool you need.

Figure 14.4 From this window, choose the .class file you want to add to your page.

Figure 14.5 Your page is beginning to take shape here.

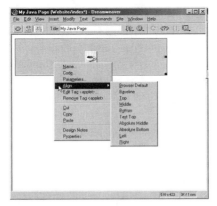

Figure 14.6 You can change the applet's parameters by choosing them from the popup menu.

3. Click the icon that looks like a coffee cup (it's actually called the Applet button) in the top left of the panel to get the tool for creating applet tags. You'll get a window similar to the one shown in **Figure 14.4**.

4. Select the class file of your choice, and click Select. Your page should now look like the one in **Figure 14.5**. At the bottom of the figure is the Property Inspector, which you'll use to change the attributes of your applet.

5. In the Property Inspector, change the height and width; the defaults aren't large enough. Other attributes you can change in the Property Inspector are the name, base, alignment, and alternate text. If you right-click (Windows) or Control-click (Macintosh) on the applet itself (**Figure 14.6**), you'll see that you can also add parameters to the applet (**Figure 14.7**). In this simple case, just increasing the size of the applet is sufficient, and the resulting Web page is shown in **Figure 14.8** and **Listing 14.1**.

continued

✔ Tips

- Note that even though Dreamweaver knows that this is a Java applet, it doesn't display the contents of the applet in the Design View. Unfortunately, at least in the currently shipping versions of the application, you'll always have to switch back to the browser to see how your page will appear.

- If you double-click on the coffee cup icon in the Property Inspector, more options will appear for you to modify: hspace and vspace (the amount of horizontal and vertical spacing you want around your applet). You can get to the applet's parameters from there, too.

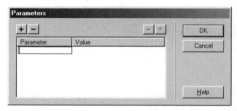

Figure 14.7 Parameter values can be added via this window.

Figure 14.8 And here's our applet, as expected!

Cross-platform Tools

The WYSIWYG tools being shown in this chapter are both cross-platform; they'll work happily on either Windows or Classic Mac. As of this writing, neither has been updated for Mac OS X, but both vendors have said that their next versions will be OS X compatible.

Given how similar each product is cross-platform, it seemed redundant to show an entire task on Windows, and then again on the Mac. In every case, the most that would have to be changed (besides the screen shots) is a replacement of right-click for Control-click and vice versa.

Consequently, I've shown one product on one platform, and the other on, well, the other. If you prefer Dreamweaver on the Mac, or GoLive on Windows, you should be able to easily translate the screenshots in this book into what you're seeing on your screen.

Figure 14.9 This time, we add an ActiveX icon.

Figure 14.10 Checking the Embed checkbox adds an embed tag to your page.

Figure 14.11 Add the classid into the ClassID field.

Figure 14.12 In Dreamweaver, you can manually edit a single tag's code without having to view the entire page.

Adding Object Tags with Dreamweaver

As we've done throughout most of this book, the generally accepted way to add Java applets to your pages is with the object tag, not the (long-deprecated) applet tag. Adding an object tag to call a Java applet is a little convoluted with Dreamweaver, but it can be done.

To add an object tag with Dreamweaver:

1. In the blank, saved Dreamweaver page (**Figure 14.1**), select the Active X icon under the Special tools (**Figure 14.3**). This icon does double-duty as a place-holder for a generic object tag. Simply clicking on it will add an object tag to our page, as shown in **Figure 14.9**.

2. Click the Embed checkbox next to the Src text entry field (**Figure 14.10**). That creates an embed tag that's embedded within the object tag.

3. Add the classid attribute to your object tag by typing in the ClassID text entry field; for our applets, it's set to clsid:8AD9C840-044E-11D1-B3E9- → 00805F499D93. Thankfully, Dreamweaver will remember this ugly thing, so you shouldn't ever have to type it in again (**Figure 14.11**).

4. Add the codetype attribute to your object tag. codetype should be set to application/java. Unfortunately, Dreamweaver doesn't offer a slick text entry field for this one, so you'll have to type it in manually, as shown in **Figure 14.12**.

continued

ADDING OBJECT TAGS WITH DREAMWEAVER

5. Add the three usual parameters to object, by either clicking on the Parameters button in the Property Inspector, or by right-clicking/Control-clicking and choosing Parameters from the drop-down menu. **Figure 14.13** shows the three parameters after they've been added. Dreamweaver knows what it's doing here, and correctly adds the parameters to both the object and the embed tags.

6. Add the remaining attribute: the embed tag. There is no property inspector for the embed tag, so you'll have to add this attribute manually. Go into Code View by clicking on the <> button in the top left, just under the word File. You can then type pluginspage="http://java.sun.
→ com/products/plugin/1.3/plugin-
→ install.html" directly into the embed tag, as shown in **Listing 14.2**.

✔ Tips

■ You might be wondering at this point why you simply can't put the class file into the Src text field. The reason is that Dreamweaver takes the file you enter there and uses it solely as the value for the src attribute of the embed tag. The applet doesn't need this, so there's no point in doing it.

■ If you find yourself frequently using Dreamweaver to add applets to your pages, look into its extensibility features. With a little bit of custom-written HTML and JavaScript, you can make your own objects with exactly the tags, attributes, and defaults you want. You'll never have to look at the Code View again!

Listing 14.2 And here's the resulting Dreamweaver file.

```
                  Listing
<html>
<head>
<title>My Java Page</title>
<meta http-equiv="Content-Type" content=
→ "text/html; charset=iso-8859-1">
</head>
<body bgcolor="#FFFFFF" text="#000000">
<object width="400" height="100" codetype=
→ "application/java" classid="clsid:8AD9C840-
→ 044E-11D1-B3E9-00805F499D93">
  <param name="code" value="Applet8.class">
  <param name="type" value="application/
  → x-java-applet;version=1.3">
  <param name="scriptable" value="false">
  <embed width="400" height="100" code=
  → "Applet8.class" type="application/x-java-
  → applet;version=1.3" scriptable="false"
  → pluginspage="http://java.sun.com/
  → products/plugin/1.3/plugin-install.html">
  </embed>
</object>
</body>
</html>
```

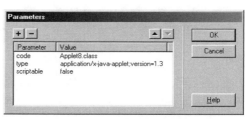

Figure 14.13 Here's where the parameters are added to both the embed and object tags at once.

Listing 14.3 The GoLive HTML page with your Java applet.

```
                    Listing
<html>

 <head>
  <meta http-equiv="content-type" content=
  → "text/html;charset=ISO-8859-1">
  <meta name="generator" content="Adobe
  → GoLive 5">
  <title>My Java Page</title>
 </head>

 <body bgcolor="#ffffff">
 <p><applet code="Applet8.class" width="400"
 → height="100"></applet></p>
 </body>

</html>
```

Adding Applet Tags with GoLive

Another popular cross-platform WYSIWYG tool is Adobe GoLive. In this task, we'll use GoLive to add an applet tag to our page.

To add an applet tag with GoLive:

1. In a brand-new GoLive window (**Figure 14.14**), from the Objects Palette select the icon that can charitably be considered to look like a coffee bean. Drag the icon onto your page to create a template for your applet (**Figure 14.15**).

continued

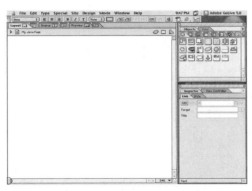

Figure 14.14 Starting out our GoLive adventure with a new blank document.

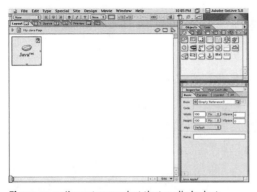

Figure 14.15 I'm not sure what that really is, but Adobe says that that icon is a coffee bean.

2. In GoLive's Inspector Window, change the attributes of your applet. In this case, set the width to 400 and the applet's source to `Applet8.class`. The resulting page will look like the one shown in **Figure 14.16** and **Listing 14.3**.

3. Unlike Dreamweaver, we can use GoLive to see how our applet works in the browser. Click on the Preview tab, and the page will be displayed as you'll see it in action. **Figures 14.17** and **14.18** show that you can even play the game!

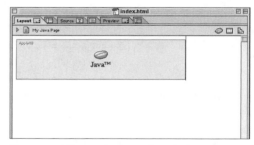

Figure 14.16 The result of our efforts is this page.

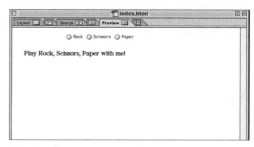

Figure 14.17 You can preview your work within GoLive.

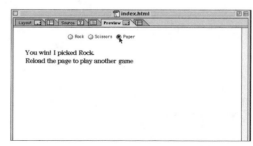

Figure 14.18 Not only can you see your applet, but you can run it, too!

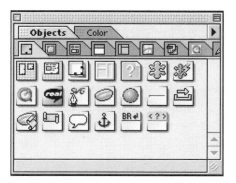

Figure 14.19 This time, we want the plug-in object, so look for the puzzle piece icon.

Figure 14.20 Make sure you add both the object and embed tags.

Figure 14.21 Add all the parameter values in the Attribs tab, and double-check your spelling!

Adding Object Tags with GoLive

While it's handy that you can use GoLive to display your applets, it's when you're adding the object/embed tag combination that GoLive really falls down on the job. Unfortunately, there's no simple way to support this functionality in the current version, on either platform. This task will show some ways to work around this problem.

To add an object tag with GoLive:

1. Open a new GoLive document, as shown in **Figure 14.14** in the previous task. Drag the object that looks like a puzzle piece from the Objects Palette to the new document. That's the plug-in object, and it will do double duty as we start out trying to add our object tag, as shown in **Figure 14.19**. You'll need to be careful with this and the following step, because GoLive will only allow you one shot at getting them right—otherwise, you'll need to start again from the beginning.

2. Use the HTML pull-down menu in the Inspector Palette (**Figure 14.20**) to choose both the object and embed tags. At the same time, set the width and the class attributes.

3. Choose the Attribs tab in the Inspector Palette. From here, we can set the applet's parameters. Click the New button three times, and change the default values to the parameter name and value pairs that we want (**Figure 14.21**). Be careful to get them right, because after the following step, you won't be able to change them again.

continued

4. Click on the Source tab of the document window. Once you do this, your plug-in object changes to an object object, and you'll lose access to some of the inspectors that you just had. You'll have to add three things in the Source view: the `codetype` attribute of the `object` tag, the `pluginspage` attribute of the `embed` tag, and the closing `embed` tag.

5. If you try to go back to the Layout tab, you will see a warning message of "Cannot create object" as shown in **Figure 14.22**. Don't worry; that just means that you can't view the applet in action within GoLive the way you could in the previous task. **Listing 14.4** shows the end result of your work.

✔ Tips

■ You need to do the fancy footwork with the plug-in object in steps 2 and 3 because that's the only way I've found to add an `object`/`embed` tag combination within GoLive. Unfortunately, once GoLive has converted that object, there's no way to go back.

■ Yes, it's really called an object object.

■ According to Adobe, the next version of GoLive should include, along with OS X support, the ability to add Java applets to your pages with the `object`/`embed` tag combination in a completely WYSIWYG fashion.

Listing 14.4 And here's the resulting GoLive HTML page with the object/embed tag combination.

```
<html>

  <head>
  <meta http-equiv="content-type" content=
→ "text/html;charset=ISO-8859-1">
  <meta name="generator" content="Adobe
→ GoLive 5">
  <title>My Java Page</title>
  </head>

  <body bgcolor="#ffffff">
  <p><object width="400" height="100" classid=
→ "clsid:8AD9C840-044E-11D1-B3E9-
→ 00805F499D93" codetype="application/java">
  <param name="scriptable" value="false">
  <param name="code" value="Applet8.class">
  <param name="type" value="application/
→ x-java-applet;version=1.3" >
  <embed width="400" height="100" type=
→ "application/x-java-applet;version=1.3"
→ code="Applet8.class" scriptable="false"
→ pluginspage="http://java.sun.com/
→ products/plugin/1.3/plugin-install.html">
  </embed>
  </object></p>
  </body>

</html>
```

Figure 14.22 Don't worry about this warning message, although you may get tired of it.

Tic-Tac-Toe

While snippets of code are useful when you're learning how to do small things, it's not until you tie what you've learned together that Java applets really get impressive (not to mention useful). This and the following chapters each take a fully realized Java applet and analyze what's going on step by step.

Playing a Game of Tic-Tac-Toe

Listing 15.1 and **Applet 15.1**, from Sun Microsystems, play a (not particularly good) game of Tic-Tac-Toe with a user. As you can see from **Figures 15.1**, **15.2**, **15.3**, and **15.4**, it is possible for the player to beat the computer, unlike most other human versus computer versions of Tic-Tac-Toe that usually end in a tied game.

To play a game of Tic-Tac-Toe:

1. `final static int moves[] = {4, 0, 2,`
   `→ 6, 8, 1, 3, 5, 7};`

   First we create an array named moves, which contains the given numbers. As it is declared final, the array cannot change—that is, it is a constant. This array determines which Tic-Tac-Toe square the computer will choose to take if neither player has a winning move. All of the possible moves are stored, in order of preference.

2. `static boolean won[] = new boolean[1`
   `→ << 9];`

   `static final int DONE = (1 << 9) - 1;`

   Here two variables (one array and one int) are defined, both of which use the left shift operator for initialization. In both cases, this means that number 1 is shifted left 9 times (for the nine squares on the board), giving a result in binary of 1000000000 (1 followed by 9 zeros), which evaluates to 512 in decimal. Therefore, the array won consists of 512 Booleans (true/false values), and the int DONE is initialized to 512-1 or 511.

   DONE could have been set explicitly to 511, but this approach keeps consistency with all the other places that need to identify separate squares.

Listing 15.1 This HTML page at http://java.sun.com/applets/jdk/1.2/demo/applets/TicTacToe/example1.html runs a Tic-Tac-Toe applet.

```
<html>
 <head>
  <title>TicTacToe v1.1</title>
  </head>
<body>
  <h1>TicTacToe v1.1</h1>
  <hr>
  <applet code="TicTacToe.class" width="120"
  → height="120">
  → alt="Your browser understands the
  → &lt;APPLET&gt; tag but isn't running
  → the applet, for some reason."
  → Your browser is completely ignoring
  → the &lt;APPLET&gt; tag!
  </applet>
  <hr>
  <a href="TicTacToe.java">The source.</a>
 </body>
</html>
```

Figure 15.1 Running Tic-Tac-Toe brings up the applet.

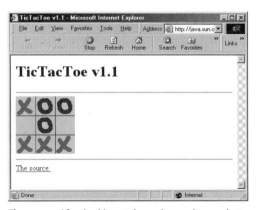

Figure 15.2 After looking at the code, you know what the applet's strategies are.

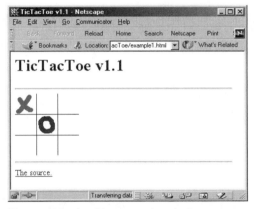

Figure 15.3 So then it's easy to play winning games...

Figure 15.4 ...and if you choose, the same winning game over and over again.

3.
```
static void isWon(int pos) {
    for (int i = 0 ; i < DONE ; i++) {
        if ((i & pos) == pos) {
            won[i] = true;
        }
    }
}
```

This step and the next use the 512 bits in won to keep track of all the possible winning combinations.

4.
```
static {
    isWon((1 << 0) | (1 << 1) | (1 << 2));
    isWon((1 << 3) | (1 << 4) | (1 << 5));
    isWon((1 << 6) | (1 << 7) | (1 << 8));
    isWon((1 << 0) | (1 << 3) | (1 << 6));
    isWon((1 << 1) | (1 << 4) | (1 << 7));
    isWon((1 << 2) | (1 << 5) | (1 << 8));
    isWon((1 << 0) | (1 << 4) | (1 << 8));
    isWon((1 << 2) | (1 << 4) | (1 << 6));
}
```

There are eight possible ways to win, as shown above. Each box is numbered from 0 to 8, so if one player has boxes 0, 1, and 2, for example, they've won. The call to isWon sets up the won array.

For example, if one player has squares 0, 1 and 2, they have the entire top row for a win. We take the value of 1 followed by the number of zeros equal to the square number. So, the first isWon() call could instead read isWon(1 | 10 | 100);.The "|" (or or) combines the three numbers together, with a one in any position that any of the three contain a one, with a result that the line could alternatively have been rewritten as isWon(7); (7 being the decimal equivalent of 111 in binary). The isWon() method is passed each of these values encoding a win, goes through the 512 possible positions for each side, and marks which ones are winning positions.

continues on page 262

Applet 15.1 Yes, Sun's comments really do say that this Tic-Tac-Toe applet should not be used to control aircraft or nuclear facilities.

```
/*
 * @(#)TicTacToe.java        1.4 98/06/29
 *
 * Copyright (c) 1997, 1998 Sun Microsystems, Inc. All Rights Reserved.
 *
 * Sun grants you ("Licensee") a non-exclusive, royalty free, license to use,
 * modify and redistribute this software in source and binary code form,
 * provided that i) this copyright notice and license appear on all copies of
 * the software; and ii) Licensee does not utilize the software in a manner
 * which is disparaging to Sun.
 *
 * This software is provided "AS IS," without a warranty of any kind. ALL
 * EXPRESS OR IMPLIED CONDITIONS, REPRESENTATIONS AND WARRANTIES, INCLUDING ANY
 * IMPLIED WARRANTY OF MERCHANTABILITY, FITNESS FOR A PARTICULAR PURPOSE OR
 * NON-INFRINGEMENT, ARE HEREBY EXCLUDED. SUN AND ITS LICENSORS SHALL NOT BE
 * LIABLE FOR ANY DAMAGES SUFFERED BY LICENSEE AS A RESULT OF USING, MODIFYING
 * OR DISTRIBUTING THE SOFTWARE OR ITS DERIVATIVES. IN NO EVENT WILL SUN OR ITS
 * LICENSORS BE LIABLE FOR ANY LOST REVENUE, PROFIT OR DATA, OR FOR DIRECT,
 * INDIRECT, SPECIAL, CONSEQUENTIAL, INCIDENTAL OR PUNITIVE DAMAGES, HOWEVER
 * CAUSED AND REGARDLESS OF THE THEORY OF LIABILITY, ARISING OUT OF THE USE OF
 * OR INABILITY TO USE SOFTWARE, EVEN IF SUN HAS BEEN ADVISED OF THE
 * POSSIBILITY OF SUCH DAMAGES.
 *
 * This software is not designed or intended for use in on-line control of
 * aircraft, air traffic, aircraft navigation or aircraft communications; or in
 * the design, construction, operation or maintenance of any nuclear
 * facility. Licensee represents and warrants that it will not use or
 * redistribute the Software for such purposes.
 */

import java.awt.*;
import java.awt.event.*;
import java.awt.image.*;
import java.net.*;
import java.applet.*;

/**
 * A TicTacToe applet. A very simple, and mostly brain-dead
 * implementation of your favorite game! <p>
 *
 * In this game a position is represented by a white and black
 * bitmask. A bit is set if a position is ocupied. There are
 * 9 squares so there are 1<<9 possible positions for each
 * side. An array of 1<<9 booleans is created, it marks
 * all the winning positions.
 *
 * @version     1.2, 13 Oct 1995
 * @author Arthur van Hoff
 * @modified 04/23/96 Jim Hagen : winning sounds
 * @modified 02/10/98 Mike McCloskey : added destroy()
 */
public
class TicTacToe extends Applet implements MouseListener {
    /**
```

Applet continues on next page

Applet 15.1 *continued*

```
                          Applet
   * White's current position. The computer is white.
   */
  int white;

  /**
   * Black's current position. The user is black.
   */
  int black;

  /**
   * The squares in order of importance...
   */
  final static int moves[] = {4, 0, 2, 6, 8, 1, 3, 5, 7};

  /**
   * The winning positions.
   */
  static boolean won[] = new boolean[1 << 9];
  static final int DONE = (1 << 9) - 1;
  static final int OK = 0;
  static final int WIN = 1;
  static final int LOSE = 2;
  static final int STALEMATE = 3;

  /**
   * Mark all positions with these bits set as winning.
   */
  static void isWon(int pos) {
   for (int i = 0 ; i < DONE ; i++) {
     if ((i & pos) == pos) {
        won[i] = true;
     }
    }
  }

  /**
   * Initialize all winning positions.
   */
  static {
   isWon((1 << 0) | (1 << 1) | (1 << 2));
   isWon((1 << 3) | (1 << 4) | (1 << 5));
   isWon((1 << 6) | (1 << 7) | (1 << 8));
   isWon((1 << 0) | (1 << 3) | (1 << 6));
   isWon((1 << 1) | (1 << 4) | (1 << 7));
   isWon((1 << 2) | (1 << 5) | (1 << 8));
   isWon((1 << 0) | (1 << 4) | (1 << 8));
   isWon((1 << 2) | (1 << 4) | (1 << 6));
  }

  /**
   * Compute the best move for white.
   * @return the square to take
   */
  int bestMove(int white, int black) {
    int bestmove = -1;
```

Applet continues on next page

Applet 15.1 *continued*

```
                                          Applet
     loop:
     for (int i = 0 ; i < 9 ; i++) {
         int mw = moves[i];
         if (((white & (1 << mw)) == 0) && ((black & (1 << mw)) == 0)) {
             int pw = white | (1 << mw);
             if (won[pw]) {
                // white wins, take it!
                return mw;
             }
             for (int mb = 0 ; mb < 9 ; mb++) {
                 if (((pw & (1 << mb)) == 0) && ((black & (1 << mb)) == 0)) {
                     int pb = black | (1 << mb);
                     if (won[pb]) {
                        // black wins, take another
                        continue loop;
                     }
                 }
             }
             // Neither white nor black can win in one move, this will do.
             if (bestmove == -1) {
               bestmove = mw;
             }
         }
     }
     if (bestmove != -1) {
       return bestmove;
     }

     // No move is totally satisfactory, try the first one that is open
     for (int i = 0 ; i < 9 ; i++) {
       int mw = moves[i];
       if (((white & (1 << mw)) == 0) && ((black & (1 << mw)) == 0)) {
           return mw;
       }
     }

     // No more moves
     return -1;
}

/**
 * User move.
 * @return true if legal
 */
boolean yourMove(int m) {
  if ((m < 0) || (m > 8)) {
    return false;
  }
  if (((black | white) & (1 << m)) != 0) {
    return false;
  }
  black |= 1 << m;
  return true;
}
```

Applet continues on next page

Applet 15.1 *continued*

```
                                  Applet
   /**
    * Computer move.
    * @return true if legal
    */
   boolean myMove() {
     if ((black | white) == DONE) {
       return false;
     }
     int best = bestMove(white, black);
     white |= 1 << best;
     return true;
   }

   /**
    * Figure what the status of the game is.
    */
   int status() {
     if (won[white]) {
       return WIN;
     }
     if (won[black]) {
       return LOSE;
     }
     if ((black | white) == DONE) {
       return STALEMATE;
     }
     return OK;
   }

   /**
    * Who goes first in the next game?
    */
   boolean first = true;

   /**
    * The image for white.
    */
   Image notImage;

   /**
    * The image for black.
    */
   Image crossImage;

   /**
    * Initialize the applet. Resize and load images.
    */
   public void init() {
     notImage = getImage(getCodeBase(), "images/not.gif");
     crossImage = getImage(getCodeBase(), "images/cross.gif");

     addMouseListener(this);
   }
```

Applet continues on next page

Applet 15.1 *continued*

```
                                  Applet
    public void destroy() {
        removeMouseListener(this);
    }

    /**
     * Paint it.
     */
    public void paint(Graphics g) {
      Dimension d = getSize();
      g.setColor(Color.black);
      int xoff = d.width / 3;
      int yoff = d.height / 3;
      g.drawLine(xoff, 0, xoff, d.height);
      g.drawLine(2*xoff, 0, 2*xoff, d.height);
      g.drawLine(0, yoff, d.width, yoff);
      g.drawLine(0, 2*yoff, d.width, 2*yoff);

      int i = 0;
      for (int r = 0 ; r < 3 ; r++) {
        for (int c = 0 ; c < 3 ; c++, i++) {
          if ((white & (1 << i)) != 0) {
            g.drawImage(notImage, c*xoff + 1, r*yoff + 1, this);
          }
          else if ((black & (1 << i)) != 0) {
            g.drawImage(crossImage, c*xoff + 1, r*yoff + 1, this);
          }
        }
      }
    }

    /**
     * The user has clicked in the applet. Figure out where
     * and see if a legal move is possible. If it is a legal
     * move, respond with a legal move (if possible).
     */
    public void mouseReleased(MouseEvent e) {
      int x = e.getX();
      int y = e.getY();

      switch (status()) {
      case WIN:
      case LOSE:
      case STALEMATE:
          play(getCodeBase(), "audio/return.au");
          white = black = 0;
          if (first) {
            white |= 1 << (int)(Math.random() * 9);
          }
          first = !first;
          repaint();
          return;
      }

      // Figure out the row/column
      Dimension d = getSize();
```

Applet continues on next page

Applet 15.1 *continued*

```
                                        Applet

      int c = (x * 3) / d.width;
      int r = (y * 3) / d.height;
      if (yourMove(c + r * 3)) {
        repaint();

        switch (status()) {
          case WIN:
            play(getCodeBase(), "audio/yahoo1.au");
            break;
          case LOSE:
            play(getCodeBase(), "audio/yahoo2.au");
            break;
          case STALEMATE:
            break;
          default:
            if (myMove()) {
              repaint();
          switch (status()) {
          case WIN:
            play(getCodeBase(), "audio/yahoo1.au");
            break;
          case LOSE:
            play(getCodeBase(), "audio/yahoo2.au");
            break;
          case STALEMATE:
            break;
          default:
            play(getCodeBase(), "audio/ding.au");
            }
          } else {
              play(getCodeBase(), "audio/beep.au");
          }
        }
      } else {
          play(getCodeBase(), "audio/beep.au");
      }
    }

    public void mousePressed(MouseEvent e) {
    }

    public void mouseClicked(MouseEvent e) {
    }

    public void mouseEntered(MouseEvent e) {
    }

    public void mouseExited(MouseEvent e) {
    }

    public String getAppletInfo() {
      return "TicTacToe by Arthur van Hoff";
    }
}
```

PLAYING A GAME OF TIC-TAC-TOE

5.
```
int bestMove(int white, int black) {
    int bestmove = -1;
    loop:
        for (int i = 0 ; i < 9 ; i++) {
```

Here the applet decides on its next move. There are nine boxes, so each has to be checked. The int i refers to the box we're checking, while bestmove is initialized to −1 to show that we haven't yet decided on the best possible move.

The white and black signify the computer and the player, respectively. They can't be referred to as X or O, as who goes first changes each game.

6.
```
int mw = moves[i];
if (((white & (1 << mw)) == 0) &&
→ ((black & (1 << mw)) == 0)) {
```

The first line uses the moves array to get the best possible next move. The preferred position is the middle, then the top left, the top right, the bottom left, the bottom right, the top middle, the middle left, the middle right, and finally the bottom middle. The next line checks to see if this square is already taken. If so, there's no need to check it.

7.
```
int pw = white | (1 << mw);
if (won[pw]) {
    // white wins, take it!
    return mw;
}
```

The variable pw (possible white) is set for this move. Using the won array, the applet determines if this move would win the game for white; if so, the applet chooses it and ends the game.

8.
```
for (int mb = 0 ; mb < 9 ; mb++) {
    if (((pw & (1 << mb)) == 0) &&
→    ((black & (1 << mb)) == 0)) {
        int pb = black | (1 << mb);
```
If there's no easy white move to win, we want to check to see if there's an easy black move to win that this suggested white move doesn't block. This code loops through the possible black moves.

9.
```
if (won[pb]) {
    // black wins, take another
    continue loop;
}
```
If there's a possible black move to win, then we don't want to take the white move that we've been saving. The statement `continue loop;` returns the flow of control back up to the `loop` label and goes through the next iteration of the `for` loop checking for a better possible move.

10.
```
// Neither white nor black can win in
→ one move, this will do.
if (bestmove == -1) {
    bestmove = mw;
}
```
The code should only make it here if there are no possible moves that either white or black can make that would win the game. If this is true, we save the current candidate as `bestmove`.

11.
```
if (bestmove != -1) {
    return bestmove;
}
```
If `bestmove` has been set, then that's the one to take.

continued

PLAYING A GAME OF TIC-TAC-TOE

12.
```
// If no move is totally satisfactory,
→ try the first one that is open
for (int i = 0 ; i < 9 ; i++) {
    int mw = moves[i];
    if (((white & (1 << mw)) == 0) &&
    → ((black & (1 << mw)) == 0)) {
        return mw;
    }
}
```

If the applet hasn't found a good move yet, it'll just take the preferred empty square.

13.
```
// No more moves
return -1;
```

If no moves are available, the game has ended in a stalemate, so return -1.

14.
```
boolean yourMove(int m) {
    if ((m < 0) || (m > 8)) {
        return false;
    }
    if (((black | white) & (1 << m))
    → != 0) {
        return false;
    }
    black |= 1 << m;
    return true;
}
```

This checks to see if the move that the user entered is valid. If a square lower than 0 or greater than 8 was picked, it's an invalid move. Or, if that square was already taken, it's also an invalid move. Otherwise, we set that square to indicate that it was taken by black and return that the move was valid.

15.
```
boolean myMove() {
    if ((black | white) == DONE) {
        return false;
    }
    int best = bestMove(white, black);
    white |= 1 << best;
    return true;
}
```

Here's where the applet handles its move. If black or white is DONE, that means that there's a stalemate, so false is returned to show that there are no possible valid moves. Otherwise, we get the next move by calling bestMove, set white to show that that move has been taken, and return true.

16.
```
int status() {
    if (won[white]) {
        return WIN;
    }
    if (won[black]) {
        return LOSE;
    }
    if ((black | white) == DONE) {
        return STALEMATE;
    }
    return OK;
}
```

A call to status() returns the game's status. If white has won, WIN is returned; if black has won, LOSE is returned. If black or white is DONE, STALEMATE is returned; otherwise, the game is in progress and the status is OK.

continued

PLAYING A GAME OF TIC-TAC-TOE

17.
```
Dimension d = getSize();
g.setColor(Color.black);
int xoff = d.width / 3;
int yoff = d.height / 3;
g.drawLine(xoff, 0, xoff, d.height);
g.drawLine(2*xoff, 0,
→ 2*xoff,d.height);
g.drawLine(0, yoff, d.width, yoff);
g.drawLine(0, 2*yoff, d.width,
→ 2*yoff);
```

The paint() method handles drawing the applet in the browser window. In this code, the applet gets the size of the applet area and divides it by three. Four lines are then drawn, dividing the area into thirds both horizontally and vertically.

18.
```
int i = 0;
for (int r = 0 ; r < 3 ; r++) {
    for (int c = 0 ; c < 3 ; c++,
    → i++) {
        if ((white & (1 << i)) != 0) {
            g.drawImage(notImage,
            → c*xoff + 1, r*yoff + 1,
            → this);
        }
        else if ((black & (1 <<
        → i)) != 0) {
            g.drawImage(crossImage,
            → c*xoff + 1, r*yoff + 1,
            → this);
        }
    }
}
```

In the remainder of the paint() method, the Xs and Os are drawn. The r loop counts rows and the c loop counts columns. In each square that white has claimed, an O is drawn, and in each square that black has claimed, an X is drawn.

19.
```
switch (status()) {
    case WIN:
    case LOSE:
    case STALEMATE:
      play(getCodeBase(),
      → "audio/return.au");
      white = black = 0;
      if (first) {
          white |= 1 << (int)(Math.
          → random() * 9);
      }
      first = !first;
      repaint();
      return;
}
```

The mouseReleased() method handles the main event check in this applet. If the game has already come to a conclusion and the user clicks the mouse in the playing area, a new game is started. Any result of status() (described in Step 16) other than OK causes a sound to play and white and black to be set to unplayed. If it's now white's (the applet's) turn to go first, white is set to a random square. Then, the variable first is reset to keep track of who will go first next time, and repaint() is called to clear the playing board.

20.
```
// Figure out the row/column
Dimension d = getSize();
int c = (x * 3) / d.width;
int r = (y * 3) / d.height;
if (yourMove(c + r * 3)) {
    repaint();
```

If it's the user's turn to go first, the applet needs to handle their move. The placement of mouseReleased () needs to be calculated and then checked for validity. If it's valid, the applet is repainted with the user's new X.

continued

21.
```
switch (status()) {
    case WIN:
        play(getCodeBase(),
        → "audio/yahoo1.au");
        break;
    case LOSE:
        play(getCodeBase(),
        → "audio/yahoo2.au");
        break;
    case STALEMATE:
        break;
```

Now that the user has made a move, status() is once again checked. If the result is a win or loss, a sound congratulating the winner is played (the winning sound is much more enthusiastic than the losing sound).

22.
```
default:
    if (myMove()) {
        repaint();
```

In the default case, the game is still in progress, so the computer takes its turn by calling myMove() and repainting the window.

23.
```
switch (status()) {
    case WIN:
        play(getCodeBase(),
        → "audio/yahoo1.au");
        break;
    case LOSE:
        play(getCodeBase(),
        → "audio/yahoo2.au");
        break;
    case STALEMATE:
        break;
    default:
        play(getCodeBase(),
        → "audio/ding.au");
```

Now that the computer has taken its turn, it's time to check status() again. The only difference between this and the code above in step 21 is that here when the code falls into the default block, a sound plays to tell the user that it's now their turn.

✔ **Tip**

■ Both "|" and "||" are valid Java operators, as are "&" and "&&". The doubled versions are logical operators: you can set hasPet to be true if a person has a cat *or* a dog, or you can set isGeek to be true if a person has both a pocket protector *and* a propeller beanie. The single versions operate only on numbers, which are then internally converted to their binary values (that is, all 1's and 0's) and compared character by character, resulting in a binary combination of the numbers.

A SIMPLE
CALCULATOR

16

This simple applet puts a small calculator on a user's Web page. Given this basic design, you'll only need to add a few buttons to turn it into a mortgage calculator, decimal/hexadecimal/octal converter, tax calculator, or whatever your site requires.

A Simple Calculator

This applet gives you the functionality of a simple four-function calculator (plus a little extra) and the framework to add your own keys. Start with **Applet 16.1**, calculator.java, and just expand the size of the grid, add your new buttons, and add handlers in the calc() method. That's all there is to it!

To build a simple Java calculator:

1.
```
setBackground(Color.white);
display = new TextField("0",6);
display.setEditable(false);
add(display);
```

   In this initialization code, we start by changing the applet's background to white to blend in with the page. Then we add the calculator's display field, giving it an initialized display of zero and setting it to not be editable.

2.
```
Panel p = new Panel();
p.setLayout(new GridLayout(5, 4));
```

   Next, we create a new panel for the buttons, which will go into a 5 by 4 GridLayout (see Chapter 9 for more about GridLayout).

3.
```
for (int i = 1; i <= 9; i++) {
    Button num=new Button("" + i);
    num.addActionListener(this);
    p.add(num);
    if (i==3) {
      Button plus=new Button("+");
      plus.addActionListener(this);
      p.add(plus);
    }
    if (i==6) {
      Button minus=new Button("-");
      minus.addActionListener(this);
      p.add(minus);
    }
}
```

   The numbers 1 through 9 are then added in three rows. The final button at the end of each row is one of the main functions, so they end up in a neat column, as shown in **Figures 16.1** and **16.2**.

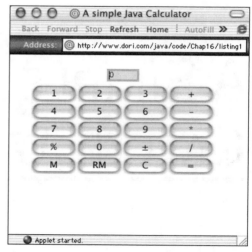

Figure 16.1 The calculator as seen in Internet Explorer for Mac OS X.

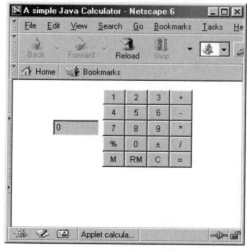

Figure 16.2 The calculator as seen in Netscape for Windows 98.

Applet 16.1 A simple Java calculator.

Applet

```
import java.awt.*;
import java.awt.event.*;
import java.applet.*;

public class calculator extends Applet
implements ActionListener {
 TextField display;
 int saveNum = 0;
 int memNum = 0;
 char op = '=';
 char lastOp = '=';
 boolean newNum = true;

 public void init() {
  setBackground(Color.white);

  display = new TextField("0",6);
  display.setEditable(false);
  add(display);

  Panel p = new Panel();
  p.setLayout(new GridLayout(5, 4));
  for (int i = 1; i <= 9; i++) {
   Button num=new Button("" + i);
   num.addActionListener(this);
   p.add(num);
   if (i==3) {
     Button plus=new Button("+");
     plus.addActionListener(this);
     p.add(plus);
   }
   if (i==6) {
    Button minus=new Button("-");
    minus.addActionListener(this);
    p.add(minus);
   }
  }
  Button times=new Button("*");
  times.addActionListener(this);
  p.add(times);
  Button percent=new Button("%");
  percent.addActionListener(this);
  p.add(percent);
  Button zero=new Button("0");
  zero.addActionListener(this);
  p.add(zero);
  Button inverse=new Button("±");
  inverse.addActionListener(this);
  p.add(inverse);
  Button division=new Button("/");
  division.addActionListener(this);
  p.add(division);
  Button memory=new Button("M");
  memory.addActionListener(this);
  p.add(memory);
  Button remindMemory=new Button("RM");
```

Applet 16.1 *continued*

Applet

```
  remindMemory.addActionListener(this);
  p.add(remindMemory);
  Button clear=new Button("C");
  clear.addActionListener(this);
  p.add(clear);
  Button equals=new Button("=");
  equals.addActionListener(this);
  p.add(equals);
  add(p);
 }

 public void actionPerformed(ActionEvent evt) {
  if (evt.getActionCommand() instanceof
  → String) {
   String s = (String) evt.getActionCommand();
   if (s.charAt(0) >= '0' && s.charAt(0) <=
   → '9') {
    if (newNum)
      display.setText(s);
    else
      display.setText(display.getText() + s);
    newNum = false;
   }
   else {
    if (s.charAt(0) == '-' && newNum) {
      display.setText("-");
      newNum = false;
    }
    else {
      op = s.charAt(0);
      calc(Integer.parseInt(display.
      → getText()));
      newNum = true;
    }
    lastOp = op;
   }
  }
  return;
 }

 public void calc(int n) {
  switch (op) {
   case '+':
   case '-':
   case '*':
   case '/':
   case '%':
    saveNum = n;
    return;
   }

   if (op == '=')
   op = lastOp;
   switch (op) {
    case '+':
    saveNum += n;
```

Applet continues on next page

4.
```
Button times=new Button("*");
times.addActionListener(this);
p.add(times);
Button percent=new Button("%");
percent.addActionListener(this);
p.add(percent);
Button zero=new Button("0");
zero.addActionListener(this);
p.add(zero);
Button inverse=new Button("±");
inverse.addActionListener(this);
p.add(inverse);
Button division=new Button("/");
division.addActionListener(this);
p.add(division);
Button memory=new Button("M");
memory.addActionListener(this);
p.add(memory);
Button remindMemory=new Button("RM");
remindMemory.addActionListener(this);
p.add(remindMemory);
Button clear=new Button("C");
clear.addActionListener(this);
p.add(clear);
Button equals=new Button("=");
equals.addActionListener(this);
p.add(equals);
add(p);
```

Then the rest of the buttons are added one by one, in the order we choose. The ± key changes the sign, the M key stores the current value in memory, the RM key recalls the saved memory, and the C key clears the display by resetting it to 0. The panel is then added, and that's all for the init() method.

5.
```
if (evt.getActionCommand() instanceof
→ String) {
```

Inside the actionPerformed() method, the only type of events we need to handle are those involving strings (i.e., the buttons we created). Otherwise, Java can handle them just fine with its default behavior.

Applet 16.1 *continued*

```
                    Applet
    break;
  case '-':
    saveNum -= n;
    break;
  case '*':
    saveNum *= n;
    break;
  case '/':
    saveNum /= n;
    break;
  case '%':
    saveNum %= n;
    break;
  case 'M':
    memNum = n;
    saveNum = n;
    break;
  case 'R':
    saveNum = memNum;
    break;
  case 'C':
    saveNum = 0;
    break;
  case '±':
    saveNum = -n;
    break;
  }
  display.setText("" + saveNum);
  }
}
```

6.
```
String s = (String) evt.
→ getActionCommand();
if (s.charAt(0) >= '0' && s.charAt(0)
→ <= '9') {
```

If the string caught by the event handler is a character between 0 and 9, then the user must have clicked on a number key.

7.
```
if (newNum)
    display.setText(s);
else display.setText(display.
→ getText() + s);
newNum = false;
```

The Boolean variable newNum tells the applet whether or not the number being entered should overwrite the existing value. For instance, if the display currently contains 0 and the user is trying to enter the number 15, we want newNum to start off as true. In this case, clicking on the 1 key will overwrite the 0. However, when the user clicks on the 5 key, we want the 5 appended to the 1 to display the desired result. Consequently, as soon as one good number has been entered, newNum is set to false.

8.
```
if (s.charAt(0) == '-' && newNum) {
    display.setText("-");
    newNum = false;
}
```

If the key pressed was non-numeric, we start to handle it here. In this section, if the user clicked on the - (dash) key before typing in a number, we assume that they want to enter a negative number. In this case, we put the - in the display and turn off newNum to end the overwriting.

continued

9.
```
op = s.charAt(0);
calc(Integer.parseInt(display.getText
→ ()));
newNum = true;
```

If we make it to this section, the user clicked on an operator that needs to be handled. The operator is stored in op, and the calc() method (explained below) is called with a parameter set to the integer value of the display field. When this is complete, the newNum flag is set back to true, so that the next number entered will again write over the contents of the display field.

10.
```
        lastOp = op;
    }
}
    return;
```

When we've completed handling the operator, the last operator chosen is saved in lastOp. Then, when everything's completed, we return.

11.
```
public void calc(int n) {
    switch (op) {
      case '+':
      case '-':
      case '*':
      case '/':
      case '%':
        saveNum = n;
    return;
    }
```

Here's the meat of the applet: the calc() method, where the actual work is done. There are two types of operators: unary, which operates on one number, and binary, which requires two numbers. With binary operators, no calculation is actually done until both numbers have been entered. So here we handle the five binary operators by saving the number currently in the display field. The operator being processed will be saved by the calling method.

12. `if (op == '=')`
      `op = lastOp;`

If the user clicked on the = (equals) key, we should now have enough information to handle the last operator entered.

13.
```
switch (op) {
    case '+':
        saveNum += n;
        break;
    case '-':
        saveNum -= n;
        break;
    case '*':
        saveNum *= n;
        break;
    case '/':
        saveNum /= n;
        break;
    case '%':
        saveNum %= n;
        break;
```

These five cases are virtually identical. In each case, the applet takes the number saved in step 11 above, the current value of the display field, and the operator entered between them to update the display field.

14.
```
case 'M':
    memNum = n;
    saveNum = n;
    break;
```

When the user chooses to store the display field in memory, nothing appears to happen on the screen but the applet stores the current value in memNum.

15.
```
case 'R':
    saveNum = memNum;
    break;
```

When the user then chooses to retrieve this number, we simply set **saveNum** to memNum to redisplay the stored value.

continued

16. `case 'C':`
    `saveNum = 0;`
    `break;`

To clear the display field, we zero out `saveNum`.

17. `case '±':`
    `saveNum = -n;`
    `break;`

To change the sign of the number in the display field, we set `saveNum` to the negative value of the current display field. This will set positive numbers to their negative values, and negative numbers to their positive values.

18. `display.setText("" + saveNum);`

The last step is to display the number as modified by the operator the user chose.

REAL WORLD JAVA— JAVA— HIERARCHICAL MENU

A common use of Java on Web sites is to display a hierarchical menu, that is, a menu that displays a list of submenus when the cursor is moved over it. This applet, based on an applet originally written by Patrick Chan for Sun Microsystems, handles a single submenu level.

Java Hierarchical Menu

A hierarchical menu allows you to use both a menu and a submenu within a limited area on your Web page, as shown in **Figures 17.1**, **17.2**, and **17.3**. **Applet 17.1** gets the menu information from the calling HTML file in **Listing 17.1**, which allows a single applet to be used by multiple pages with different menus.

To create a hierarchical menu:

1. `image = getImage(getCodeBase(),`
   `→ getParameter("image"));`

   First we read the name of the image from the calling HTML file, then load the image (**Figure 17.4**) itself. For the name and associated value of this and the following parameters, see **Table 17.1**.

2. `marginH = Integer.parseInt`
   `→ (getParameter("marginh"));`
   `marginV = Integer.parseInt`
   `→ (getParameter("marginv"));`

   Then we read in the `marginh` and `marginv` values from the HTML file.

3. `ints = parseInt(getParameter`
   `→ ("bg-color"), " ");`
   `bgColor = new Color(ints[0], ints[1],`
   `→ ints[2]);`

   The applet uses five color fields, each defined by a set of three numbers (red, green, and blue values), which can be any number from 0 to 255. This format allows for over 16 million different colors. The array `ints` gets the three values, and then the `Color()` method turns those numbers into a Java color. This same code is then repeated for each of the four other color fields.

Figure 17.1 The hierarchical menu as it appears when the page is loaded—at first, it looks just like a normal menu...

Figure 17.2 ...until the user moves the cursor over a field, possibly expecting to see just a simple rollover...

Figure 17.3 ...but instead, more options automagically appear.

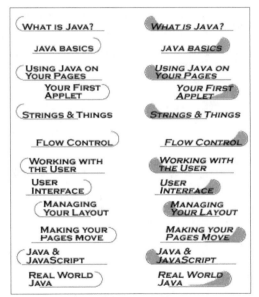

Figure 17.4 This is what the menu graphic looks like, under the hood.

4.
```
bbuf = createImage(getSize().width,
→ getSize().height);
bbufG = bbuf.getGraphics();
```
This creates a buffer area for double-buffering the menu graphic.

5.
```
int fh = Integer.parseInt
→ (getParameter("font-height"));
int i = fh;
```
Here we read in the font height and save it for future use.

6.
```
while (i > 10) {
  f = new Font(getParameter("font"),
  → Font.PLAIN, i);
  fm = getFontMetrics(f);
  if (fm.getHeight() <= fh) {
    break;
  }
  i--;
}
```
We need to calculate the actual font size based on the font height. This code loops around, checking to see if a font of this size has the height requested. If so, we exit the loop using **break**. Otherwise, we subtract 1 from the font size and try again.

7.
```
for (i=0; ; i++) {
  if (getParameter("menu"+i) ==
  → null) {
    hitArea = new Rectangle[i];
    srcRect = new Rectangle[i];
    dstPt = new Point[i];
    url = new String[i];
    down = new boolean[i];
    itemUrl = new String[i][];
    item = new String[i][];
    break;
  }
}
```
This loop counts the number of **menuX** parameters being passed by the calling HTML file, and then creates new arrays of the required size.

continued

Table 17.1

APPLET PARAMETERS		
PARAMETER	**DESCRIPTION**	**EXAMPLE**
bg-color	Specifies a color to paint behind the background image. This color is only visible if the background image has transparent pixels or if the applet is larger than the background image.	
bg-hi-menu-color	The color to paint the background of highlighted menu items. The color is specified by an RGB triplet of three decimal numbers in the range 0–255.	`<param name="bg-hi-menu-color"` `→ value="10 10 10">`
bg-menu-color	The color to paint the background of the menu items. The color is specified by an RGB triplet of three decimal numbers in the range 0–255.	`<param name="bg-menu-color"` `→ value="0 255 0">`
fg-hi-menu-color	The color to paint the text of highlighted menu item labels. The color is specified by an RGB triplet of three decimal numbers in the range 0–255.	`<param name="fg-hi-menu-color"` `→ value="255 255 255">`
fg-menu-color	The color to paint the text of the menu item labels. The color is specified by an RGB triplet of three decimal numbers in the range 0–255.	`<param name="fg-menu-color"` `→ value="0 0 0">`
font	The font type to use for the menu items. There are only three possible values: Helvetica, TimesRoman, and Courier.	`<param name="font" value="Helvetica">`
font-height	The pixel height of the font to use for the menu items.	`<param name="font-height" value="14">`
image	Names the file containing the background image and the rollover images.	`<param name="image"` `→ value="background.gif">`
marginh	The number of pixels to the left and right of the menu item labels.	`<param name="marginh" value="2">`
marginv	The number of pixels above and below each menu item label.	`<param name="marginv" value="2">`

menuX	X starts at 0 and increases upwards by 1. The value of this parameter is made up of five non-optional values, separated by the separator character described below. There may also be a pair of optional values that specify the menu items for the menu. If no values are specified, no menu will appear when the cursor moves into the hotbox. These pairs are repeated for each menu label. See Table 17.2 for the values of the fields.	`<param name="menu0"`
		`→ value="0 0 148 18|148 0 148 18|0 0|d|/`
		`→ nav/whatis/index.html|Intro FAQ|/`
		`→ nav/whatis/introfaq.html|Java Story|/`
		`→ nav/whatis/index.html">`

newline	Specifies the character used to force a newline in a menu item.	`<param name="newline" value="^">`
separator	Specifies the character used to separate items in menuX parameters.	`<param name="separator" value="|">`
target	If present, specifies the target frame that will show the new URL.	`<param name="target"` `→ value="otherframe">`

Table 17.2

Menu Parameters	
PARAMETER	DESCRIPTION
downUp	A parameter specifying whether the menu should be drawn downward or upward from dstPt.
dstPt	A set of two numbers specifying the location on the image where srcImage should appear. The two numbers are x and y.
hotbox	A set of four numbers specifying a rectangle on the image. When the cursor rolls into the hotbox, a menu is displayed. The four numbers are x, y, width, and height.
label	The menu label; it can appear on more than one line by using the newline parameter described in Table 17.1.
mainURL	The URL that the applet will send the browser to when the user clicks in the hotbox.
srcImage	A set of four numbers specifying a rectangle on the image. When the cursor rolls into the hotbox, the sub-image defined by srcImage is drawn over the main image. The location is defined by dstPt. The four numbers are –x, y, width, and height.
url	The URL that the applet will send the browser to when the user clicks on the menu item.

8. `for (i=0; i<hitArea.length; i++) {`

For each `menuX` parameter in the calling HTML file, the applet will execute the code in steps 9 and 10.

9. ```
String[] fields = parse(getParameter
→ ("menu"+i), getParameter
→ ("separator"));
```

```
ints = parseInt(fields[0], " ");
hitArea[i] = new Rectangle(ints[0],
→ ints[1], ints[2], ints[3]);
```

```
ints = parseInt(fields[1], " ");
srcRect[i] = new Rectangle(ints[0],
→ ints[1], ints[2], ints[3]);
```

```
ints = parseInt(fields[2], " ");
dstPt[i] = new Point(ints[0],
→ ints[1]);
down[i] = fields[3].equals("d");
url[i] = fields[4];
```

```
item[i] = new String
→ [(fields.length-5)/2];
itemUrl[i] = new String[(fields.
→ length-5)/2];
```

We read in each of the `menuX` parameters, as described in **Table 17.2**.

10. ```
for (int j=0; j<item [i].length;
→ j++) {
    item[i][j] = fields[j*2+5];
    itemUrl[i][j] = fields[j*2+6];
}
```

For each item in each `menuX` parameter, we set the `item` and `itemURL` arrays.

11. ```
addMouseMotionListener(this);
addMouseListener(this);
```

Along with the rest of our initialization steps, we need to tell Java to listen for the user's mouse movements. That's done here.

*continued*

JAVA HIERARCHICAL MENU
```

Listing 17.1

```
                                    Listing
<html>
<head>
  <title>Xeo Menu</title>
</head>
<body bgcolor="white">
<applet codebase="." code="XeoMenu" width="160" height="364">
<param name="bg-color" value="255 255 255">
<param name="image" value="menu.gif">
<param name="separator" value="|">
<param name="newline" value="^">
<param name="font" value="Helvetica">
<param name="font-height" value="14">
<param name="marginh" value="2">
<param name="marginv" value="2">
<param name="fg-menu-color" value="0 0 0">
<param name="bg-menu-color" value="255 255 255">
<param name="fg-hi-menu-color" value="0 0 0">
<param name="bg-hi-menu-color" value="150 150 150">


<param name="menu0" value="0 0 150 24|150 0 150 24|0 0|d|chap01.html|Cans & Can'ts|chap011.html|
→ Secure Sandbox|chap012.html">
<param name="menu1" value="0 24 150 24|150 24 150 24|0 24|d|chap02.html|OO|chap021.html|Applet|
→ chap022.html|Glossary|chap023.html">
<param name="menu2" value="0 53 150 34|150 53 150 34|0 53|d|chap03.html|Calling Java|chap031.html|
→ Displaying HTML|chap023.html|Placing Applets|chap033.html|Passing Params|chap034.html">
<param name="menu3" value="0 86 150 24|150 86 150 24|0 86|d|chap04.html|Hello World!|chap041.html|
→ Changing^Font Face|chap042.html|Setting back-^ground color|chap043.html|HTML to Java|
→ chap044.html|Adding comments|chap045.html|Font styles|chap046.html|Font colors|chap047.html">
<param name="menu4" value="0 111 150 24|150 111 150 24|0 111|d|chap05.html|Declaring^variables|
→ chap051.html|Strings|chap052.html|Variable scope|chap053.html|String methods|chap054.html|
→ Numbers|chap055.html|String^conversions|chap056.html|Numeric^conversions|chap057.html|
→ Conversion^by casting|chap058.html|Arrays|chap059.html">
<param name="menu5" value="0 139 150 30|150 139 150 30|0 139|d|chap06.html|If/then|chap061.html|
→ If/then/else|chap062.html|For loops|chap063.html|While loops|chap064.html|Do/while loops|
→ chap065.html|Break &^Continue|chap066.html|Switch/Case|chap067.html">
<param name="menu6" value="0 175 150 30|150 175 150 30|0 175|u|chap07.html|Drawing lines|
→ chap071.html|2 Dimensions|chap072.html|Freehand drawing|chap073.html|Capturing keys|
→ chap074.html|Arrow keys|chap075.html|Varying speed|chap076.html">
<param name="menu7" value="0 209 150 24|150 209 150 24|0 209|d|chap08.html|Password^protection|
→ chap081.html|Text fields|chap082.html|Checkboxes|chap083.html|Radio buttons|chap084.html|
→ Pulldown menus|chap085.html|On-the-fly menus|chap086.html|Text areas|chap087.html|Lists|
→ chap088.html">
<param name="menu8" value="0 236 150 24|150 236 150 24|0 236|d|chap09.html|No Layout|chap091.html|
→ FlowLayout|chap092.html|More FlowLayout|chap093.html|Border Layout|chap094.html|Grid Layout|
→ chap095.html|Insets|chap096.html|Panels|chap097.html|CardLayout|chap098.html|GridBagLayout|
→ chap099.html">
<param name="menu9" value="0 264 150 30|150 264 150 30|0 264|d|chap10.html|Java animation|
→ chap101.html|Threading|chap102.html|Double-buffering|chap103.html">
<param name="menu10" value="0 296 150 30|150 296 150 30|0 296|d|chap11.html|Checking on Java|
→ chap111.html|Public Java methods|chap112.html|JavaScript to Java|chap113.html|Using Java
→ methods|chap114.html">
<param name="menu11" value="0 325 150 30|150 325 150 30|0 325|d|chap12.html|Tic-Tac-Toe|
→ chap12.html|Calculator|chap13.html|Hierarchical^Menu|chap14.html">

</applet>
</body>
</html>
```

Applet 17.1

```
import java.applet.*;
import java.awt.*;
import java.awt.event.*;
import java.util.*;
import java.net.*;

public class XeoMenu extends Applet implements
→ MouseListener, MouseMotionListener {
    // The background image.  This had better
    → not be null.
    Image image;

    // These two fields are used to do double-
    → buffering.
    // The dimensions of bbuf is exactly the
    → dimensions of the applet.
    Image bbuf;
    Graphics bbufG;

    // This field is set to true only when the
    → background image has
    // completely loaded.
    boolean imageDone;

    /* Menu data */
    Rectangle[] hitArea;
    Rectangle[] srcRect;
    Point[] dstPt;
    boolean[] down;
    String[] url;

    /* Submenu data */
    String[][] itemUrl;
    String[][] item;

    // If >= 0, this fields holds the index of
    → the current menu.
    // If -1, no menu is current.
    int curMenu;

    // If >= 0, this fields holds the index of
    → the current menu item.
    // If -1, no menu item is current.
```

Applet continues on next page

12. `String[] parse(String s, String`
`→ sep) {`

This creates a new method, `parse()`, which is passed two strings: The first is the string to parse, and the second is a separator used to define how the first should be parsed. It returns an array of strings. In other words, if the two strings passed are "a|b|c" and "|", the pipe character ("|") is used to split up the first string, with the result being an array consisting of three strings: "a", "b", and "c."

13. `StringTokenizer st = new`
`→ StringTokenizer(s, sep);`
`String result[] = new`
`→ String[st.countTokens()];`

The variable `st` is set to the number of strings that will be returned by calling the `StringTokenizer()` method. Then, given `st`, the `result` array is created with the correct length.

14. `for (int i=0; i<result.length;`
`→ i++) {`
`    result[i] = st.nextToken();`
`}`
`return result;`

This loop sets the `result` array, and then we return `result` to end the method.

15. `int[] parseInt(String s, String`
`→ sep) {`

This method is similar to `parse()`, except that the first string is a list of integers, so the result is an array of ints.

16. `StringTokenizer st = new`
`→ StringTokenizer(s, sep);`
`int[] result = new`
`→ int[st.countTokens()];`

Again, the `StringTokenizer()` method is used to break apart the input string, and a `result` array is declared.

continued

17.
```
for (int i=0; i<result.length;
→ i++) {
    result[i] = Integer.parseInt
    → (st.nextToken());
}
```
Here, the `result` array is set based on the parsed input string.

18.
```
public void paint(Graphics g) {
    imageDone = false;
    update(g);
}
```
The overridden `paint()` method does just two simple things: It resets `imageDone` to `false` and then calls the `update()` method.

19.
```
public void update(Graphics g) {
    Graphics g2;

    if (!imageDone) {
        imageDone = g.drawImage
        → (image, 0, 0, this);
        return;
    }
```
We want to make sure that the menu image is completely loaded before displaying it on-screen. Here, we check to see if the menu image has been loaded; if not, `drawImage()` is called.

20.
```
bbufG.setColor(bgColor);
bbufG.fillRect(0, 0, getSize().width,
→ getSize().height);
bbufG.drawImage(image, 0, 0, this);
```
The buffer is filled with the chosen background color, and then the menu image is drawn in the buffer.

21.
```
if (curMenu >= 0) {
```
The variable `curMenu` contains the current menu item that the cursor is pointing to. If `curMenu` is nonzero, then we want to draw the hierarchical submenu.

Applet 17.1 *continued*

```
int curMenuItem;

// This is an array of rectangles - one
→ rectangle for each menu item.
// Each rectangle specifies the
// location (relative to the left-corner
→ of the applet) of a menu item.
//
// menuItemRect is null when curMenu is -1.
// It becomes non-null when curMenu >= 0.
//
// Note: it would have been better
→ programming to define classes for
// the menu and menu items.  However, I
→ decided for this little applet
// to keep the number of class files to a
→ minimum to minimize the download
// time.
Rectangle[] menuItemRect;

// This is the color to paint "behind"
→ the image.
Color bgColor;

// [0] is the text color of a menu item;
→ [1] is the text color of a highlighted
// menu item.
Color fgMenuColor[] = new Color[2];

// This is the background of a menu item;
→ [1] is the background color of a
// highlighted menu item.
Color bgMenuColor[] = new Color[2];

// marginH is the number of pixels on the
→ left and right edges of the menu.
// marginV is the number of pixels on the
→ top and bottom edges of the menu.
int marginH, marginV;

// This is the font used to display the
→ menu item labels.
Font f;

// This is the font metrics of 'f'.
FontMetrics fm;

public void init() {
    int[] ints;

    // Grab applet parameters.
    image = getImage(getCodeBase(),
    → getParameter("image"));
    marginH = Integer.parseInt(getParameter
    → ("marginh"));
    marginV = Integer.parseInt(getParameter
    → ("marginv"));
```

Applet continues on next page

Applet 17.1 *continued*

```
                    Applet
    // Get color parameters.
    ints = parseInt(getParameter("bg-
    → color"), " ");
    bgColor = new Color(ints[0], ints[1],
    → ints[2]);
    ints = parseInt(getParameter("fg-menu-
    → color"), " ");
    fgMenuColor[0] = new Color(ints[0],
    → ints[1], ints[2]);
    ints = parseInt(getParameter("fg-hi-
    → menu-color"), " ");
    fgMenuColor[1] = new Color(ints[0],
    → ints[1], ints[2]);
    ints = parseInt(getParameter("bg-menu-
    → color"), " ");
    bgMenuColor[0] = new Color(ints[0],
    → ints[1], ints[2]);
    ints = parseInt(getParameter("bg-hi-
    → menu-color"), " ");
    bgMenuColor[1] = new Color(ints[0],
    → ints[1], ints[2]);

    // Create back buffer for double-
    → buffering.
    bbuf = createImage(getSize().width,
    → getSize().height);
    bbufG = bbuf.getGraphics();

    // Determine the font from the font-
    → height.
    int fh = Integer.parseInt(getParameter
    → ("font-height"));
    int i = fh;
    while (i > 10) {
      f = new Font(getParameter("font"),
      → Font.PLAIN, i);
      fm = getFontMetrics(f);
      if (fm.getHeight() <= fh) {
        break;
      }
      i--;
    }

    // Get the menu parameters.
    for (i=0; ; i++) {
      if (getParameter("menu"+i) == null) {
        hitArea = new Rectangle[i];
        srcRect = new Rectangle[i];
        dstPt = new Point[i];
        url = new String[i];
        down = new boolean[i];
        itemUrl = new String[i][];
        item = new String[i][];

        break;
      }
    }
```

Applet continues on next page

22. `g2 = bbuf.getGraphics();`
`g2.clipRect(dstPt[curMenu].x,`
`→ dstPt[curMenu].y,`
`→ srcRect[curMenu].width,`
`→ srcRect[curMenu].height);`
`g2.drawImage(image, dstPt`
`→ [curMenu].x-srcRect[curMenu].x,`
`→ dstPt[curMenu].y-srcRect`
`→ [curMenu].y, this);`
`g2.dispose();`

`g2 = bbuf.getGraphics();`

Now we paint the overlay image.

23. `for (int i=0; i<menuItemRect.`
`→ length; i++) {`
`    drawMenuItem(g2, i);`
`}`

For each line in the submenu, we call the *drawMenuItem()* method.

24. `    g2.dispose();`
`    }`
`g.drawImage(bbuf, 0, 0, this);`

Then we finish off setting up the submenu and display it on the screen.

25. `void drawMenuItem(Graphics g,`
`→ int i) {`

This creates the *drawMenuItem()* method, which handles creating and drawing the submenus.

26. `String[] line = parse(item[curMenu]`
`→ [i], getParameter("newline"));`

We get the **newline** character from the calling HTML file.

continued

27. `int hi = 0;`
```
if (i == curMenuItem) {
    hi = 1;
    getAppletContext().showStatus
    ➝ (itemUrl[curMenu][i]);
}
```
If the submenu item that we're currently processing is the same menu item that the cursor is currently on, we call **showStatus()** to display the URL in the browser's status area, and set the highlight variable **hi** to 1.

28. `g.setColor(bgMenuColor[hi]);`
```
g.fillRect(menuItemRect[i].x,
➝ menuItemRect[i].y,
➝ menuItemRect[i].width,
➝ menuItemRect[i].height);
```
These lines set the background color based on **hi** and fill the rectangle with that color.

29. `g.setColor(fgMenuColor[hi]);`
```
g.drawRect(menuItemRect[i].x,
➝ menuItemRect[i].y,
➝ menuItemRect[i].width,
➝ menuItemRect[i].height);
```
These lines set the color for the text and box, and draw a box around the menu item.

30. `g.setFont(f);`
`y = menuItemRect[i].y + marginV;`
These lines set the font and initialize the y-placement of the text.

31. `for (i=0; i<line.length; i++) {`
This is a loop, because there may be more than one line for a single submenu item.

Applet 17.1 *continued*

```
                    Applet
for (i=0; i<hitArea.length; i++) {
    String[] fields = parse(getParameter
    ➝ ("menu"+i), getParameter
    ➝ ("separator"));

    // Get the hit area.
    ints = parseInt(fields[0], " ");
    hitArea[i] = new Rectangle(ints[0],
    ➝ ints[1], ints[2], ints[3]);

    // Get the source image.
    ints = parseInt(fields[1], " ");
    srcRect[i] = new Rectangle(ints[0],
    ➝ ints[1], ints[2], ints[3]);

    // Get the destination point.
    ints = parseInt(fields[2], " ");
    dstPt[i] = new Point(ints[0],
    ➝ ints[1]);
    down[i] = fields[3].equals("d");
    url[i] = fields[4];

    item[i] = new String[(fields.length-
    ➝ 5)/2];
    itemUrl[i] = new String
    ➝ [(fields.length-5)/2];
    for (int j=0; j<item[i].length; j++) {
        item[i][j] = fields[j*2+5];
        itemUrl[i][j] = fields[j*2+6];
    }
}
addMouseMotionListener(this);
addMouseListener(this);

}


// s is a string containing 'sep'
➝ separators.  This method
// breaks up the string at the separators
➝ and returns the resulting
// strings in an array.  The result may
➝ have zero length but is never null.
String[] parse(String s, String sep) {
    StringTokenizer st = new StringTokenizer
    ➝ (s, sep);
    String result[] = new String
    ➝ [st.countTokens()];

    for (int i=0; i<result.length; i++) {
        result[i] = st.nextToken();
    }
    return result;
}
```

Applet continues on next page

JAVA HIERARCHICAL MENU

Applet 17.1 *continued*

```
‖▓▓▓▓▓▓▓▓▓ Applet ▓▓▓▓▓▓▓▓▓▓ ▣‖
// This method is similar to parse()
→ except that the strings are
  // assumed to be decimal integers.  This
  → method coverts these integer
  // strings into integers and returns them
  → in an array.
  // The result may have zero length but is
  → never null.
  int[] parseInt(String s, String sep) {
    StringTokenizer st = new StringTokenizer
    → (s, sep);
    int[] result = new int[st.countTokens()];

    for (int i=0; i<result.length; i++) {
      result[i] = Integer.parseInt
      → (st.nextToken());
    }
    return result;
  }

  public void paint(Graphics g) {
    imageDone = false;
    update(g);
  }

  public void update(Graphics g) {
    Graphics g2;

    if (!imageDone) {
      imageDone = g.drawImage(image, 0, 0,
      → this);
      return;
    }

    bbufG.setColor(bgColor);
    bbufG.fillRect(0, 0, getSize().width,
    → getSize().height);
    bbufG.drawImage(image, 0, 0, this);

    if (curMenu >= 0) {
      g2 = bbuf.getGraphics();
      // Paint the overlay image
      g2.clipRect(dstPt[curMenu].x, dstPt
      → [curMenu].y, srcRect[curMenu].width,
      → srcRect[curMenu].height);
      g2.drawImage(image, dstPt[curMenu].
      → x-srcRect[curMenu].x, dstPt
      → [curMenu].y-srcRect[curMenu].y,
      → this);
      g2.dispose();

      g2 = bbuf.getGraphics();
      for (int i=0; i<menuItemRect.length;
      → i++) {
        drawMenuItem(g2, i);
      }
```

Applet continues on next page

32.
```
g.drawString(line[i],
→ menuItemRect[i].x+menuItemRect[i].
→ width-fm.stringWidth(line[i])-
→ marginH, y + fm.getAscent());
y += fm.getHeight();
```

Here we draw the submenu text at the correct location, and increment the y-location for the next line.

33.
```
public void mouseExited(MouseEvent
→ evt) {
  curMenuItem = curMenu = -1;
  repaint();
  return;
}
```

The **mouseExited** event is triggered when the cursor leaves the menu area. In this case, the cursor isn't over a menu option anymore, so **curMenuItem** and **curMenu** are both set to -1, and the applet is repainted.

34.
```
public void mousePressed
→ (MouseEvent evt) {
  try {
```

The **mousePressed** event is triggered when the user clicks a mouse button while the cursor is over the menu.

35.
```
String u = null;
if (curMenuItem >= 0 && itemUrl
→ [curMenu].length > 0) {
  u = itemUrl[curMenu]
  → [curMenuItem];
}
```

If the user has triggered the **mouseDown** event over an area where there's an active submenu URL, we set **u** to that URL.

36.
```
else
  if (curMenu >= 0) {
    u = url[curMenu];
  }
```

Otherwise, we set **u** to the generic URL for that menu item.

continued

37. `if (u != null) {`
    `URL url = new URL`
      `→ (getDocumentBase(), u);`

If we have an URL, we call the `getDocumentBase()` method using u to get the complete URL.

38. `if (getParameter("target") !=`
  `→ null) {`
    `getAppletContext().`
      `→ showDocument(url,`
      `→ getParameter("target"));`
`}`

If the calling HTML file specified a target for the URL, we set it up.

39. `else {`
    `getAppletContext().`
      `→ showDocument(url);`
`}`

Otherwise, we call `showDocument()` without a target.

40. `catch (Exception e) {`
    `e.printStackTrace();`
`}`

If an exception was triggered, we have an unrecoverable problem, so we just call `printStackTrace()`.

41. `public void mouseMoved(MouseEvent`
  `→ evt) {`

The mouseMoved event is triggered every time the mouse is moved while the cursor is over the menu. This is where a great deal of the applet's most complex work is done.

Applet 17.1 *continued*

```
    g2.dispose();
  }
  g.drawImage(bbuf, 0, 0, this);
}

void drawMenuItem(Graphics g, int i) {
  int x, y, w, height;
  // break the menu item label into lines.
  String[] line = parse(item[curMenu][i],
  → getParameter("newline"));

  int hi = 0;
  if (i == curMenuItem) {
    hi = 1;
    getAppletContext().showStatus
    → (itemUrl[curMenu][i]);
  }
  g.setColor(bgMenuColor[hi]);
  g.fillRect(menuItemRect[i].x,
  → menuItemRect[i].y,
  → menuItemRect[i].width,
  → menuItemRect[i].height);

  // set color for text and box
  g.setColor(fgMenuColor[hi]);

  // draw box around menu item.
  g.drawRect(menuItemRect[i].x,
  → menuItemRect[i].y,
  → menuItemRect[i].width,
  → menuItemRect[i].height);

  // draw label
  g.setFont(f);
  y = menuItemRect[i].y + marginV;
  for (i=0; i<line.length; i++) {
    g.drawString(line[i], menuItemRect[i]
    → .x+menuItemRect[i].width-fm.
    → stringWidth(line[i])-marginH,
    → y + fm.getAscent());
    y += fm.getHeight();
  }
}

public void mouseExited(MouseEvent evt) {
  curMenuItem = curMenu = -1;
  repaint();
  return;
}

public void mouseEntered(MouseEvent evt) {
  return;
}

public void mouseClicked(MouseEvent evt) {
  return;
}
```

Applet continues on next page

Applet 17.1 *continued*

```
                    Applet

public void mouseReleased(MouseEvent evt) {
  return;
}

public void mousePressed(MouseEvent evt) {
  try {
    String u = null;

    if (curMenuItem >= 0 && itemUrl
→ [curMenu].length > 0) {
      u = itemUrl[curMenu][curMenuItem];
    }
    else
      if (curMenu >= 0) {
        u = url[curMenu];
      }
    if (u != null) {
      URL url = new URL (getDocumentBase
→ (), u);

      if (getParameter("target") != null) {
        getAppletContext().
→ showDocument(url,
→ getParameter("target"));
      }
      else {
        getAppletContext().
→ showDocument(url);
      }
    }
  }
  catch (Exception e) {
    e.printStackTrace();
  }
  return;
}

public void mouseDragged(MouseEvent evt) {
  return;
}

public void mouseMoved(MouseEvent evt) {
  int x = evt.getX();
  int y = evt.getY();
  if (curMenu >= 0) {
    int sm = inMenu(menuItemRect, x, y);

    if (curMenuItem != sm) {
      curMenuItem = sm;
      repaint();
    }
    if (sm >= 0) {
      return;
    }
    curMenu = -1;
  }
```

Applet continues on next page

42.
```
int x = evt.getX();
int y = evt.getY();
if (curMenu >= 0) {
    int sm = inMenu(menuItemRect,
→ x, y);
```
We first need the x and y coordinates of the mouse movement that triggered this event. Then, if we've been working on a submenu already, we calculate the new cursor location by calling the `inMenu()` method.

43.
```
if (curMenuItem != sm) {
    curMenuItem = sm;
    repaint();
}
```
If the location of the cursor has changed the submenu to be highlighted, we reset `curMenuItem` and repaint the applet.

44.
```
if (sm >= 0) {
    return;
}
curMenu = -1;
```
If sm is a number other than -1, it means that the mouse has moved elsewhere in the already-drawn submenu. If this is the case, all that needs to happen is for the highlighting to be redrawn, so we then return. Otherwise, we reinitialize curmenu to -1.

45.
```
int m = inMenu(hitArea, x, y);
if (m != curMenu) {
    curMenu = m;

    if (m >= 0) {
```
We use the `inMenu()` method to calculate the new menu, and if one is found we perform steps 46–55.

continued

46. `int maxWidth = 50;`
`int maxHeight = 0;`

`menuItemRect = new Rectangle`
`→ [item[curMenu].length];`

These lines initialize maxWidth and maxHeight, and declare the new menuItemRect array.

47. `for (int i=0; i<menuItemRect.`
`→ length; i++) {`

This tells the applet to do the following for each submenu option.

48. `String[] line = parse(item[curMenu]`
`→ [i], getParameter("newline"));`

`for (int j=0; j<line.length; j++) {`

We use the newline value to calculate how many lines this submenu option will take up in the submenu, and then execute the following loop that many times.

49. `int w = fm.stringWidth(line[j]);`
`if (w > maxWidth) {`
`    maxWidth = w;`
`}`

Here we calculate the required width of the submenu based on the text to be displayed.

50. `menuItemRect[i] = new Rectangle();`
`menuItemRect[i].height = parse`
`→ (item[curMenu][i], getParameter`
`→ ("newline")).length * fm.getHeight`
`→ () + 2 * marginV;`
`maxHeight += menuItemRect[i].`
`→ height;`

Now we calculate the height based on the number of lines, and reset the maxHeight.

Applet 17.1 *continued*

```
                    Applet
int m = inMenu(hitArea, x, y);
if (m != curMenu) {
  curMenu = m;

  // A new menu is now active so compute
  → menuItemRect.
  if (m >= 0) {
    // Minimum width
    int maxWidth = 50;
    int maxHeight = 0;

    menuItemRect = new Rectangle
    → [item[curMenu].length];
    for (int i=0; i<menuItemRect.
    → length; i++) {
      String[] line = parse(item
      → [curMenu][i], getParameter
      → ("newline"));

      for (int j=0; j<line.length; j++) {
        int w = fm.stringWidth
        → (line[j]);
        if (w > maxWidth) {
          maxWidth = w;
        }
      }

      menuItemRect[i] = new
      → Rectangle();
      menuItemRect[i].height =
      → parse(item[curMenu][i],
      → getParameter("newline")).
      → length * fm.getHeight() + 2 *
      → marginV;
      maxHeight += menuItemRect[i].
      → height;
    }

    // Add one extra pixel for the left
    → edge.
    maxWidth += 2 * marginH + 1;
    if (down[m]) {
      y = Math.max(0, Math.min
      → (getSize().height-maxHeight-1,
      → dstPt[curMenu].y + srcRect
      → [curMenu].height-1));
    }
    else {
      y = Math.max(0, Math.min
      → (getSize().height-maxHeight-1,
      → dstPt[curMenu].y - maxHeight));
    }
```

Applet continues on next page

Applet 17.1 *continued*

```
                 Applet
        x = dstPt[curMenu].x + srcRect
     → [curMenu].width-maxWidth-1;
        for (int i=0; i<item[curMenu].
     → length; i++) {
           menuItemRect[i].x = x;
           menuItemRect[i].y = y;
           menuItemRect[i].width = maxWidth;
           y += menuItemRect[i].height;
        }
        getAppletContext().showStatus
     → (url[curMenu]);
      }
      repaint();
    }
    return;
  }

  // Returns the index of the rectangle in
  → rs containing x and y.
  // Returns -1 if either rs is null or x
  → and y is not in rs.
  int inMenu(Rectangle[] rs, int x, int y) {
    if (rs != null) {
      for (int i=0; i<rs.length; i++) {
        if (rs[i].contains(x, y)) {
          return i;
        }
      }
    }
    return -1;
  }
}
```

51. `maxWidth += 2 * marginH + 1;`

When the loop has completed, we add the desired horizontal margins to the `maxWidth`, plus one extra pixel for the left edge.

52.
```
if (down[m]) {
    y = Math.max(0, Math.min
 → (getSize().height-maxHeight-1,
 → dstPt[curMenu].y + srcRect
 → [curMenu].height-1));
}
else {
    y = Math.max(0, Math.min
 → (getSize().height-maxHeight-1,
 → dstPt[curMenu].y - maxHeight));
}
```

A submenu can be displayed either below the chosen menu option or above it. Either way, this code calculates the value of the y-position.

53. `x = dstPt[curMenu].x + srcRect`
`→ [curMenu].width-maxWidth-1;`

This calculates the x-position for the display of the submenu.

54.
```
for (int i=0; i<item[curMenu].
 → length; i++) {
    menuItemRect[i].x = x;
    menuItemRect[i].y = y;
    menuItemRect[i].width = maxWidth;
    y += menuItemRect[i].height;
}
```

For each item in the submenu, we save the x and y positions and the `maxWidth`, then increment y.

continued

55. `getAppletContext().showStatus`
→ `(url[curMenu]);`

We display the URL of the chosen submenu option on the browser's status line.

56.
```
int inMenu(Rectangle[] rs, int x,
→ int y) {
    if (rs != null) {
        for (int i=0; i<rs.length;
        → i++) {
            if (rs[i].contains(x, y)) {
                return i;
            }
        }
    }
    return -1;
}
```

The `inMenu()` method returns the index of the rectangle in `rs` containing x and y. If `rs` is null or x or y is not in `rs`, it returns −1.

And that's all there is to this nifty applet. Moving the cursor from option to option causes the `mouseMoved` event to be triggered, which then displays the applicable submenu.

WHERE TO LEARN MORE

While every author dreams that his or her book is everything that anyone would want to know about the subject, the truth is that Java is too complex a topic to cover completely in a book of this size and style. If what you've learned so far has you interested in learning more about Java, here are some resources to get you started.

Java on the Web

As would be expected with a language that started on the Web, there are numerous Web pages devoted to Java. Here are some sites that I've found to be worth a look.

Sun's Java site

`http://java.sun.com/` and
`http://developer.java.sun.com/`

The former is Sun's home for Java on the Web (**Figure A.1**). Because Sun developed Java, this is always the place to start for the latest and greatest information. When you want documentation on, for example, Java APIs, you know that here you're getting the word straight from the horse's mouth. While the main Java site is intended for everyone, the latter site is just for Java developers. Here you can find announcements and events, "What's New," and other information just for you.

Gamelan

`http://www.softwaredev.earthweb.com/java/`

Gamelan used to be the repository of many of the best applets on the Web (**Figure A.2**). It was acquired by EarthWeb, and was swallowed up into Developer.com. It's still a good place to find articles written about Java by those who are currently using it, and you can also find other people's applets that you can download and use on your pages (depending on the license). While it still keeps a place in my list of Java bookmarks, it's not the site that it used to be.

Figure A.1 Java's home on the Web at Sun.

Figure A.2 The Gamelan Directory, which used to be one of the best sites for applets on the Web, still has good stuff.

Figure A.3 JARS will rate your Java efforts and give you a snazzy badge to put on your site if you qualify.

Figure A.4 Café au Lait—Java FAQs, news, and resources.

The Java Review Service (JARS)

http://www.jars.com/

If, after reading this book, you write an applet that is just so new and wonderful you want the world to know about it, submit your page to JARS for evaluation (**Figure A.3**). Applets are judged on quality and innovation. If you make the grade, you'll get a link from their site to yours, and a badge you can display to show that you are now a Java wiz. You can even apply to be one of the judges!

Then again, if you're still looking for examples to help you make your applets sing and dance, you can also check out other people's code here to see exactly how the wizards did it.

Café au Lait

http://www.ibiblio.org/javafaq/

Every technology needs a FAQ (frequently asked questions) page; Java's can be found at Café au Lait (**Figure A.4**). This site is maintained by author Elliotte Rusty Harold, and includes a great list of Java news and resources, although the FAQ itself is somewhat out of date. If you're interested in XML, you can visit Café au Lait's sister site Café con Leche at http://www.ibiblio.org/xml where you'll find news and resources about all things XML.

Java Zone

`http://www.java-zone.com/`

The Java Zone (**Figure A.5**) is an informative site that is part of the DevX.com portal with tips, tutorials, and articles about Java (as well as many other languages and technologies). Be sure to filter their articles through their pro-Microsoft bias, though. Sourcebank, their Java source code library, has a handy search interface as well as browsable categories with hundreds of downloadable examples and applications.

IBM alphaWorks

`http://alphaworks.ibm.com/`

alphaWorks is a unique site provided by IBM. IBM's developers make their "alpha code" for newly developed technologies available for download before they are licensed or integrated into products. This gives you a chance to take a look at potential products from IBM for free during their development cycle. You must agree to the alphaWorks license agreement to get access to downloads, but it's a great place to find interesting and useful Java applications.

Figure A.5 DevX's Java Zone.

Figure A.6 JavaWorld—an online Java magazine from IDG.

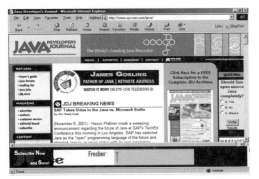

Figure A.7 The Java Developer's Journal in its online form.

Online Magazines

Early in Java's development, several of the usual magazine companies tried to start up new publications to serve the Java developer community. Most of them later fell victim to "Internet time"—in the lag between the articles being completed by the author and the magazine arriving in the readers' hands, weeks had passed, and those Web-savvy Java developers had long since read the news online. While a few Java publications are still selling print subscriptions, all of the following also have active Web sites.

JavaWorld Magazine

`http://www.javaworld.com/`

The last survivor of the big-time publishers' attempts at Java magazines, this is now an online-only publication from IDG (**Figure A.6**). Monthly and bimonthly columns include How-To Java, Java Developer, Cool Tools, Enterprise Java, Java 101, Java Q & A, and Java Tips.

Java Developer's Journal

`http://www.sys-con.com/java`

An annual subscription to the *Java Developer's Journal* is $50, or you can get a trial issue for $12 (**Figure A.7**). The digital edition is available to subscribers only, but many features and editorials are publicly available for viewing online.

Java Pro

`http://www.java-pro.com/`

Java Pro is another magazine with some of its content available online. Qualified applicants can get a free subscription to the print version of the magazine; for the rest of us, it's $28/year.

Integrated Development Environments (IDEs)

Where most languages have compilers, Java (strictly speaking) doesn't. Instead, Java has what are called Integrated Development Environments, or IDEs, which are used to turn your code into something that the computer can understand. Here are the major players (in no particular order).

Metrowerks CodeWarrior for Java, Professional Edition or Academic Edition

`http://www.metrowerks.com/desktop/java/`

If you want to write Java on the classic Mac OS, CodeWarrior is your only choice, but there's a version for Windows, also (**Figure A.8**). You can download a 30-day trial copy of the Windows version and check it out before you buy the complete package. For Windows 95 and later and Mac OS 8.6 and later.

Sun Microsystems Forte

`http://www.sun.com/forte/ffj/`

This is the IDE from the folks who brought you Java. The "Community Edition" is available for free, and the "Enterprise Edition" is available for a 60-day free trial. For Solaris 8, Windows 98 and later, and Linux.

IBM VisualAge for Java

`http://www.software.ibm.com/ad/vajava`

VisualAge for Java was the winner of the *Java Developer's Journal* Readers' Choice Award in 2001 (**Figure A.9**). There is a free "Entry Edition" that you can download to try it out. For Windows 98 and later and Linux.

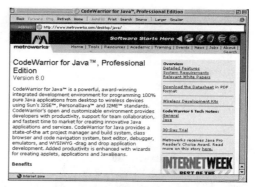

Figure A.8 CodeWarrior for Java is a great choice if you want to code on the Mac, particularly if you're still running Classic.

Figure A.9 VisualAge for Java (from IBM) was the reader's choice in *Java Developer's Journal* magazine.

INTEGRATED DEVELOPMENT ENVIRONMENTS (IDEs)

Figure A.10 Borland JBuilder is a product of Inprise.

Figure A.11 WebGain Visual Café is another visual development tool.

Inprise Borland JBuilder 6

`http://www.inprise.com/jbuilder/`

JBuilder was awarded "Best in Show" by the readers of *JavaPro* (**Figure A.10**) and is one of the few IDEs that can be run on a Mac (OS X only). You can also download a free "Personal" version of the previous version of JBuilder to use as long as you like (just not for commercial purposes). For Windows 2000 and later, Linux, Solaris, Mac OS X 10.1 and later.

WebGain Visual Café

`http://www.visualcafe.com/products/`
`visual_cafe/`

In March 2000, Symantec spun off a new company (WebGain) to focus on Java development tools, and Symantec Visual Café became WebGain Visual Café. It's still a good visual tool for Java development (**Figure A.11**). The Standard Edition is a great environment for learning Java. Visual Café provides productivity wizards and utilities as well as a two-way drag-and-drop interface that keeps the code and the visual designer always in synch, producing source code in real-time. For Windows NT/2000.

Apple ProjectBuilder

`http://www.devworld.apple.com/tools/`
`projectbuilder/`

If you own Mac OS X 10.1 or later, you've already got a copy of ProjectBuilder, Apple's multi-language IDE, as it's included with every full version of OS X. Combined with Apple's InterfaceBuilder (also included), it's worth a spin. For Mac OS X 10.1 and later.

INTEGRATED DEVELOPMENT ENVIRONMENTS (IDES)

Java Books

The book you're looking at now is just an introductory text—there's a lot more to this language! Here are a few of the best books to check out if you want to take the next step on the path to Java expertise.

Java in a Nutshell

Now in its third edition, this book has everything you always wanted to know about Java but didn't even know where to begin to ask. Written by David Flanagan, *Java in a Nutshell* is a great reference when you need the exact syntax of that one method.

Java Examples in a Nutshell

This book is a companion guide to the previous volume, and is also written by David Flanagan. While *Java in a Nutshell* is an excellent reference, it has virtually no examples. This book makes up for that lack, though the examples assume that you're starting with some programming background.

Core Java 2, Volumes 1 and 2

This book by Cay Horstmann and Gary Cornell has been fully updated for JDK 1.3 and has completely revised coverage of object-oriented development and Swing classes. It also has very good GUI coverage. Many people buy the first volume while they are learning Java and then get volume two when they want to learn more about enterprise Java development.

The Elements of Java Style

I find that I return to this book again and again. It is an excellent style guide. Your code will really benefit if you follow these suggestions—especially if you are working with other developers. Applying the principles in this little book will make your life easier as well as help you to write understandable and maintainable code.

Graphic Java 1.2, Mastering the JFC: AWT, Volume 1, and Graphic Java 2, Volume 2, Swing

The first volume in this set by David M. Geary tells you everything you need to know about the AWT, including an in-depth look at each of the layout managers. If you're working with the AWT, you'll need this book. If you plan to develop any kind of Java application with a GUI, you'll definitely want to own the second volume as well. In it, Geary starts from the ground and works his way up through every aspect of developing an interface with the Swing API.

Mr. Bunny's Big Cup o' Java

Yes, this book (by Carlton Egremont III) really does exist. In it, Mr. Bunny enters saying "Hello World!" and proceeds to attempt to teach Farmer Jake all about Java. While reading this book won't teach you (or Farmer Jake) much, it's great reading when taking short breaks from other, drier books. And you can be proud of yourself that you understand all the in-jokes for geeks.

Other books

This is by no means a comprehensive list of Java books. At this very moment, there are about 1000 books on Amazon.com that have been written about the Java language (and there will probably be a few more by the time you read this). I've listed just a few that I think are very good; I'm sure that as you fall more and more in love with the language, the Java section of your bookshelf will grow just as mine has.

Newsgroups

In the far distant past, there was one
`comp.lang.java` newsgroup, and virtually
overnight it became extremely busy.
Consequently, it was split up into many little
Java newsgroups, most of which are carried
by most news servers.

The following is a list of the newsgroups that
Google carries (**Figure A.12**). Your news
server may not carry all of these, but it may
also carry some that aren't here.

Figure A.12 The list of Java newsgroups offered by
Google Groups.

```
comp.lang.java
comp.lang.java.3d
comp.lang.java.advocacy
comp.lang.java.announce
comp.lang.java.api
comp.lang.java.beans
comp.lang.java.corba
comp.lang.java.databases
comp.lang.java.developer
comp.lang.java.gui
comp.lang.java.help
comp.lang.java.javascript
comp.lang.java.machine
comp.lang.java.misc
comp.lang.java.programmer
comp.lang.java.security
comp.lang.java.setup
comp.lang.java.softwaretools
```

✔ Tip

■ Usenet is not a friendly place for people
who are considered to be "newbies."
Asking what old-timers consider to be a
stupid question can bring nasty messages
in response ("flaming"). At a minimum,
always read a couple of days' worth of
messages before posting your first message, and always read the FAQ!

Figure A.13 Apple's home for Java development on the Mac.

Figure A.14 Who's suing whom this week? The Java Lobby sure knows who they think is in the right or in the wrong.

Cross-Platform Issues

The original promise of Java was "write once, run anywhere." Here are two sites that have little in common except a strong commitment to that philosophy.

Apple Java Developer pages

`http://devworld.apple.com/java/`

If you're developing Java applets or applications where you want Mac compatibility, you need to check out this site (**Figure A.13**). While Sun handles Java for Unix and Wintel systems, Apple has the sole responsibility for updating Java on the Mac. Consequently, it always seems to be a little behind and a little slow. However, you should at least try out your programs on the Mac to be absolutely sure that you've handled all the cross-platform issues. This site includes news and a link to Apple's java-dev email list.

The Java Lobby

`http://www.javalobby.org/`

These are the folks fighting the good fight for an open and standard Java (**Figure A.14**). For them, 99% pure Java just isn't quite good enough. This is an excellent resource site for finding out what all the fuss and lawsuits are about.

RESERVED WORDS

Reserved words are those words that have special meanings to a programming language. Therefore, they may not be used as names for variables, classes, or methods.

Most of the following words should be familiar from earlier parts of the book, though some either are outside the scope of this book or are words being reserved in anticipation of future usage.

Java's Reserved Words

These words are reserved by Java. While it's true that they are all lowercase and that Java, being case-sensitive, will allow you to name (for instance) a variable with a mixed-case version of any of these words, it's considered to be very bad programming style. At the least, it will make your code hard to understand and maintain.

abstract

Declares that a class cannot be instantiated.

boolean

A data type that can only be either true or false.

break

Used to escape early from a loop, or to skip the remaining case sections of a switch statement. Execution continues with the first line of code after the switch statement or loop.

byte

An 8-bit single-character data type.

case

Used in a switch statement to execute one of several sections of code depending on the value of a variable.

catch

Used to trap errors within a try block.

char

A 16-bit single-character data type.

class

A hierarchical collection of data and methods that act upon that data.

continue

Skips all following statements in a loop and continues with the next iteration of the loop.

default

Executes statements in a switch block if all cases within the switch block are false.

do

Used with a "while" to loop.

double

A double-precision floating point number.

else

Used within an if statement structure to execute a block of statements when whatever the if statement tests for evaluates to false.

extends

When one class extends another class, it inherits from that class.

false

A constant, which is always set to false.

final

When a class is declared final it cannot be inherited. When a method is declared final it cannot be overridden. Declaring a variable final makes it a non-modifiable constant.

finally

Forces a block of code to always be executed in a try...catch block.

float

A single-precision floating point number.

for

A loop with initialization, condition testing, and a statement to be run during each iteration.

`if`

Tests a condition and then executes a block of code when that condition is true.

`implements`

Defines a class as using an interface.

`import`

Makes Java classes available to the current class under an abbreviated name.

`instanceof`

Tests whether a variable is an instance of a particular class or implements a particular interface.

`int`

An integer number.

`interface`

Contains methods that are grouped together. Classes implement interfaces to use their methods.

`long`

A very large integer number.

`native`

Declares a function as external to Java. The method is implemented in a platform-dependent language such as C or C++.

`new`

Creates a new instance of an object, including allocating memory and initializing variables.

`null`

All instances of classes are initialized to `null` (a constant) until set up with a new command or assigned to an existing class.

`package`

A group of classes bundled together.

`private`

Only visible to the class that defined it.

`protected`

Only visible within the package that defined it.

`public`

Visible anywhere its class or package is visible.

`return`

Sends control (and sometimes variables) back from a method to its calling method.

`short`

A small integer number.

`static`

Static methods have one and only one instance per class, which is invoked through the class name.

`strictfp`

`strictfp` is a new keyword introduced for Java 2. It is used to ensure that certain `float` or `double` expressions conform to specific rules set out by the IEEE. Don't worry, you'll probably never have to use this, but if you do, be sure to check out the documentation on the `java.sun.com` site.

`super`

Accesses ancestor attributes that were over-ridden by descendant attributes.

`switch`

Executes one of several code blocks depending on the value of a variable.

`synchronized`

Only one thread is allowed to run in this method at a time.

`this`

Refers to the current instance of a class.

JAVA'S RESERVED WORDS

`throw`

Forces an error to occur.

`throws`

Indicates that this method can cause the thrown exception or error.

`transient`

A scratch variable for a class, which is neither saved with a class nor cloned to other instances of a class.

`true`

A constant, which is always set to `true`.

`try`

Sets up an error-catching block in which any errors caught are processed by `catch` and finally by code blocks.

`void`

This method does not return a value to its calling method.

`volatile`

This variable may be changed at any time, so no code optimization should be allowed.

`while`

Used with the `do` statement to perform a loop.

Words reserved but not yet used in Java

The following words have been reserved by Java, although they are not yet in use.

`byvalue`	`inner`
`cast`	`operator`
`const`	`outer`
`future`	`rest`
`generic`	`var`
`goto`	

Reserved method names

The following method names are reserved.

`clone`	`notify`
`equals`	`notifyAll`
`finalize`	`toString`
`getClass`	`wait`
`hashCode`	

Reserved characters

The following characters may not be used in variable names. Doing so will cause Java to try to evaluate the variables as statements, and you'll just end up with a mess on your hands.

+	*	(	;
-	|	)	?
!	-	{	,
%	/	}	.
^	<	[	
&	>	]	

THE JAVA
OBJECT HIERARCHY

As Java is an object-oriented language, its classes fall into a strict object hierarchy. This appendix lays out the classes and interfaces for each of the major Java packages.

In each of the following tables, objects in regular black text were introduced in JDK 1.0, objects in *black italics* were introduced in JDK 1.1, objects in red were introduced in JDK 1.2, and objects in *red italics* were introduced in JDK 1.3.

The java.applet Package

Table C.1

java.applet Classes and Interfaces

CLASS	ABSTRACT CLASS	INTERFACE	EXCEPTION
Applet	AppletContext	—	—
—	AppletStub	—	—
—	AudioClip	—	—

The java.awt Package

Table C.2

java.awt Classes and Interfaces

CLASS	ABSTRACT CLASS	INTERFACE	EXCEPTION
AWTError	*AWTEvent*	ActiveEvent	AWTException
AlphaComposite	Component	*Adjustable*	FontFormatException
AWTEventMulticaster	Graphics	Composite	*IllegalComponentStateException*
AWTPermission	Graphics2D	CompositeContext	—
BasicStroke	GraphicsConfigTemplate	*ItemSelectable*	—
BorderLayout	GraphicsConfiguration	*LayoutManager*	—
Button	GraphicsDevice	*LayoutManager2*	—
Canvas	GraphicsEnvironment	MenuContainer	—
CardLayout	Image	Paint	—
Checkbox	MenuComponent	PaintContext	—
CheckboxGroup	*PrintJob*	*PrintGraphics*	—
CheckboxMenuItem	Toolkit	*Shape*	—
Choice	—	Stroke	—
Color	—	Transparency	—
ComponentOrientation	—	—	—
Container	—	—	—
Cursor	—	—	—
Dialog	—	—	—
Dimension	—	—	—
Event	—	—	—
EventQueue	—	—	—
FileDialog	—	—	—
FlowLayout	—	—	—
Font	—	—	—
FontMetrics	—	—	—
Frame	—	—	—
GradientPaint	—	—	—
JobAttributes	—	—	—
GridBagConstraints	—	—	—
GridBagLayout	—	—	—

Table C.2 *continued*
java.awt Classes and Interfaces

CLASS	ABSTRACT CLASS	INTERFACE	EXCEPTION
GridLayout	—	—	—
Insets	—	—	—
Label	—	—	—
List	—	—	—
MediaTracker	—	—	—
Menu	—	—	—
MenuBar	—	—	—
MenuShortcut	—	—	—
PageAttributes	—	—	—
Panel	—	—	—
Point	—	—	—
Polygon	—	—	—
PopupMenu	—	—	—
Rectangle	—	—	—
RenderingHints	—	—	—
Robot	—	—	—
Scrollbar	—	—	—
ScrollPane	—	—	—
SystemColor	—	—	—
TextArea	—	—	—
TextComponent	—	—	—
TextField	—	—	—
TexturePaint	—	—	—
Window	—	—	—

The java.awt.color Package (introduced in JDK 1.2)

Table C.3
java.awt.color Classes and Interfaces

CLASS	ABSTRACT CLASS	INTERFACE	EXCEPTION
ICC_ColorSpace	ColorSpace	—	CMMException
ICC_Profile	—	—	ProfileDataException
ICC_ProfileGray	—	—	—
ICC_ProfileRGB	—	—	—

The java.awt.datatransfer Package (introduced in JDK 1.1)

Table C.4
java.awt.datatransfer Classes and Interfaces

CLASS	ABSTRACT CLASS	INTERFACE	EXCEPTION
Clipboard	—	ClipboardOwner	*MimeTypeParseException*
DataFlavor	—	FlavorMap	*UnsupportedFlavorException*
StringSelection	—	*Transferable*	—
SystemFlavorMap	—	—	—

The java.awt.dnd Package (introduced in JDK 1.2)

Table C.5
java.awt.dnd Classes and Interfaces

CLASS	ABSTRACT CLASS	INTERFACE	EXCEPTION
DnDConstants	—	Autoscroll	InvalidDnDOperationException
DragGestureEvent	—	DragGestureListener	—
DragGestureRecognizer	—	DragSourceListener	—
DragSource	—	DropTargetListener	—
DragSourceContext	—	—	—
DragSourceDragEvent	—	—	—
DragSourceDropEvent	—	—	—
DragSourceEvent	—	—	—
DropTarget	—	—	—
DropTargetContext	—	—	—
DropTargetDragEvent	—	—	—
DropTargetDropEvent	—	—	—
DropTargetEvent	—	—	—
MouseDragGestureRecognizer	—	—	—

The java.awt.event Package (introduced in JDK 1.1)

Table C.6
java.awt.event Classes and Interfaces

CLASS	ABSTRACT CLASS	INTERFACE	EXCEPTION
ActionEvent	ComponentAdapter	ActionListener	—
AdjustmentEvent	ContainerAdapter	AdjustmentListener	—
ComponentEvent	FocusAdapter	AWTEventListener	—
ContainerEvent	HierarchyBoundsAdapter	ComponentListener	—
FocusEvent	InputEvent	CopntainerListener	—
HierarchyEvent	KeyAdapter	FocusListener	—
InputMethodEvent	MouseAdapter	HierarchyBoundsListener	—
InvocationEvent	MouseMotionAdapter	HierarchyListener	—
ItemEvent	WindowAdapter	InputMethodListener	—
KeyEvent	—	ItemListener	—
MouseEvent	—	KeyListener	—
PaintEvent	—	MouseListener	—
TextEvent	—	MouseMotionListener	—
WindowEvent	—	TextListener	—
—	—	WindowListener	—

The java.awt.font Package (introduced in JDK 1.2)

Table C.7
java.awt.font Classes and Interfaces

CLASS	ABSTRACT CLASS	INTERFACE	EXCEPTION
FontRenderContext	GlyphVector	MultipleMaster	—
GlyphJustificationInfo	GraphicAttribute	OpenType	—
GlyphMetrics	LineMetrics	—	—
ImageGraphicAttribute	—	—	—
LineBreakMeasurer	—	—	—
ShapeGraphicAttribute	—	—	—
TextAttribute	—	—	—
TextHitInfo	—	—	—
TextLayout	—	—	—
TextMeasurer	—	—	—
TransformAttribute	—	—	—

The java.awt.geom Package (introduced in JDK 1.2)

Table C.8
java.awt.geom Classes and Interfaces

CLASS	ABSTRACT CLASS	INTERFACE	EXCEPTION
AffineTransform	Arc2D	PathIterator	IllegalPathStateException
Area	CubicCurve2D	—	NoninvertibleTransformException
FlatteningPathIterator	Dimension2D	—	—
GeneralPath	Ellipse2D	—	—
—	Line2D	—	—
—	Point2D	—	—
—	QuadCurve2D	—	—
—	Rectangle2D	—	—
—	RectangularShape	—	—
—	RoundRectangle2D	—	—

The java.awt.im Package (introduced in JDK 1.2)

Table C.9
java.awt.im Classes and Interfaces

CLASS	ABSTRACT CLASS	INTERFACE	EXCEPTION
InputContext	—	InputMethodRequests	—
InputMethodHighlight	—	—	—
InputSubset	—	—	—

The java.awt.image Package

Table C.10

java.awt.image Classes and Interfaces

CLASS	ABSTRACT CLASS	INTERFACE	EXCEPTION
AffineTransformOp	ColorModel	BufferedImageOp	ImagingOpException
AreaAveragingScaleFilter	DataBuffer	ImageConsumer	RasterFormatException
BandCombineOp	LookupTable	ImageObserver	—
BandedSampleModel	PackedColorModel	ImageProducer	—
BufferendImage	**RGBImageFilter**	RasterOp	—
BufferendImageFilter	SampleModel	RenderedImage	—
ByteLookupTable	—	TileObserver	—
ColorConvertOp	—	WritableRenderedImage	—
ComponentColorModel	—	—	—
ComponentSampleModel	—	—	—
ConvolveOp	—	—	—
CropImageFilter	—	—	—
DataBufferByte	—	—	—
DataBufferInt	—	—	—
DataBufferShort	—	—	—
DataBufferUShort	—	—	—
DirectColorModel	—	—	—
FilteredImageSource	—	—	—
ImageFilter	—	—	—
IndexColorModel	—	—	—
Kernel	—	—	—
LookupOp	—	—	—
MemoryImageSource	—	—	—
MultiPixelPackedSampleModel	—	—	—
PixelGrabber	—	—	—
PixelInterleavedSampleModel	—	—	—
Raster	—	—	—
ReplicateScaleFilter	—	—	—
RescaleOp	—	—	—
ShortLookupTable	—	—	—
SinglePixelPackedSampleModel	—	—	—
WritableRaster	—	—	—

The java.awt.image.renderable Package (introduced in JDK 1.2)

Table C.11
java.awt.image.renderable Classes and Interfaces

CLASS	ABSTRACT CLASS	INTERFACE	EXCEPTION
ParameterBlock	—	ContextualRenderedImageFactory	—
RenderableImageOp	—	RenderableImage	—
RenderableImageProducer	—	RenderedImageFactory	—
RenderContext	—	—	—

The java.awt.peer Package (As of JDK version 1.1, programs should not directly

manipulate peers)

Table C.12
java.awt.peer Classes and Interfaces

CLASS	ABSTRACT CLASS	INTERFACE	EXCEPTION
—	—	ButtonPeer	—
—	—	CanvasPeer	—
—	—	CheckboxMenuItemPeer	—
—	—	CheckboxPeer	—
—	—	ChoicePeer	—
—	—	ComponentPeer	—
—	—	ContainerPeer	—
—	—	DialogPeer	—
—	—	FileDialogPeer	—
—	—	*FontPeer*	—
—	—	FramePeer	—
—	—	LabelPeer	—
—	—	*LightweightPeer*	—
—	—	ListPeer	—
—	—	MenuBarPeer	—
—	—	MenuComponentPeer	—
—	—	MenuItemPeer	—
—	—	PanelPeer	—
—	—	*PopupMenuPeer*	—
—	—	*ScrollPanelPeer*	—
—	—	ScrollbarPeer	—
—	—	TextAreaPeer	—
—	—	TextComponentPeer	—
—	—	TextFieldPeer	—
—	—	WindowPeer	—

The java.awt.print Package (introduced in JDK 1.2)

Table C.13
java.awt.print Classes and Interfaces

CLASS	ABSTRACT CLASS	INTERFACE	EXCEPTION
Book	PrinterJob	Pageable	PrinterAbortException
Page Format	—	Printable	PrinterException
Paper	—	PrinterGraphics	PrinterIOException

The java.beans Package (introduced in JDK 1.1)

Table C.14
java.beans Classes and Interfaces

CLASS	ABSTRACT CLASS	INTERFACE	EXCEPTION
BeanDescriptor	—	AppletInitializer	InstrospectionException
Beans	—	BeanInfo	PropertyVetoException
EventSetDescription	—	Customizer	—
FeatureDescriptor	—	DesignMode	—
IndexedPropertyDescriptor	—	PropertyChangeListener	—
Introspector	—	PropertyEditor	—
MethodDescriptor	—	VetoableChangeListener	—
ParameterDescriptor	—	Visibility	—
PropertyChangeEvent	—	—	—
PropertyChangeSupport	—	—	—
PropertyDescriptor	—	—	—
PropertyEditorManager	—	—	—
PropertyEditorSupport	—	—	—
SimpleBeanInfo	—	—	—
VetoableChangeSupport	—	—	—

The java.beans.beancontext Package (introduced in JDK 1.2)

Table C.15

java.beancontext Classes and Interfaces

CLASS	ABSTRACT CLASS	INTERFACE	EXCEPTION
BeanContextChildSupport	BeanContextEvent	BeanContext	—
BeanContextMembershipEvent	—	BeanContextChild	—
BeanContextServiceAvailableEvent	—	BeanContextChildComponentProxy	—
BeanContextServiceRevokedEvent	—	BeanContextContainerProxy	—
BeanContextServicesSupport	—	BeanContextMembershipListener	—
BeanContextSupport	—	BeanContextProxy	—
—	—	BeanContextServiceProvider	—
—	—	BeanContextServiceProviderBeanInfo	—
—	—	BeanContextServiceRevokedListener	—
—	—	BeanContextServices	—
—	—	BeanContextServicesListener	—

The java.io Package

Table C.16
java.io Classes and Interfaces

CLASS	ABSTRACT CLASS	INTERFACE	EXCEPTION
BufferedInputStream	*FilterReader*	DataInput	*CharConversionException*
BufferedOutputStream	*FilterWriter*	DataOutput	EOFException
BufferedReader	InputStream	*Externalizable*	FileNotFoundException
BufferedWriter	OutputStream	FileFilter	InterruptedIOException
ByteArrayInputStream	*Reader*	FilenameFilter	*InvalidClassException*
ByteArrayOutputStream	*Writer*	*ObjectInput*	*InvalidObjectException*
CharArrayReader	—	*ObjectInputValidation*	IOException
CharArrayWriter	—	*ObjectOutput*	*NotActiveException*
DataInputStream	—	*ObjectStreamConstants*	*NotSerializableException*
DataOutputStream	—	*Serializable*	*ObjectStreamException*
File	—	—	*OptionalDataException*
FileDescriptor	—	—	*StreamCorruptedException*
FileInputStream	—	—	*SyncFailedException*
FileOutputStream	—	—	*UnsupportedEncodingException*
FilePermission	—	—	UTFDataFormatException
FileReader	—	—	*WriteAbortedException*
FileWriter	—	—	—
FilterInputStream	—	—	—
FilterOutputStream	—	—	—
InputStreamReader	—	—	—
LineNumberInputStream	—	—	—
LineNumberReader	—	—	—
ObjectInputStream	—	—	—
ObjectOutputStream	—	—	—
ObjectStreamClass	—	—	—
ObjectStreamField	—	—	—
OutputStreamWriter	—	—	—
PipedInputStream	—	—	—
PipedOutputStream	—	—	—
PipedReader	—	—	—
PipedWriter	—	—	—
PrintStream	—	—	—
PrintWriter	—	—	—
PushbackInputStream	—	—	—
PushbackReader	—	—	—
RandomAccessFile	—	—	—
SequenceInputStream	—	—	—
SerializablePermission	—	—	—
StreamTokenizer	—	—	—
StringBufferInputStream	—	—	—
StringReader	—	—	—
StringWriter	—	—	—

The java.lang Package

Table C.17

java.lang Classes and Interfaces

CLASS	ABSTRACT CLASS	INTERFACE	EXCEPTION
AbstractMethodError	ClassLoader	Cloneable	ArithmeticException
Boolean	Number	Comparable	ArrayIndexOutOfBoundsException
Byte	Process	Runnable	ArrayStoreException
Character	VirtualMachineError	—	ClassCastException
Character.Subset	—	—	ClassNotFoundException
Class	—	—	CloneNotSupportedException
ClassCircularityError	—	—	Exception
ClassFormatError	—	—	IllegalAccessException
Compiler	—	—	IllegalArgumentException
Double	—	—	IllegalMonitorStateException
Error	—	—	IllegalStateException
ExceptionInInitializerError	—	—	IllegalThreadStateException
Float	—	—	IndexOutOfBoundsException
IllegalAccessError	—	—	InstantiationException
IncompatibleClassChangeError	—	—	InterruptedException
InheritableThreadLocal	—	—	NegativeArraySizeException
InstantiationError	—	—	NoSuchFieldException
Integer	—	—	NoSuchMethodException
InternalError	—	—	NullPointerException
LinkageError	—	—	NumberFormatException
Long	—	—	RuntimeException
Math	—	—	SecurityException
NoClassDefFoundError	—	—	StringIndexOutOfBoundsException
NoSuchFieldError	—	—	UnsupportedOperationException
NoSuchMethodError	—	—	—
Object	—	—	—
OutOfMemoryError	—	—	—
Package	—	—	—
Runtime	—	—	—
RuntimePermission	—	—	—
SecurityManager	—	—	—
Short	—	—	—
StackOverflowError	—	—	—
StrictMath	—	—	—
String	—	—	—
StringBuffer	—	—	—
System	—	—	—
Thread	—	—	—
ThreadDeath	—	—	—
ThreadGroup	—	—	—

Table C.17 *continued*

java.lang Classes and Interfaces

CLASS	ABSTRACT CLASS	INTERFACE	EXCEPTION	
ThreadLocal	—	—	—	
Throwable	—	—	—	
UnknownError	—	—	—	
UnsatisfiedLinkError	—	—	—	
UnsupportedClassVersionError	—	—	—	
VerifyError	—	—	—	
Void	—	—	—	

The java.lang.ref Package (introduced in JDK 1.2)

Table C.18

java.lang.ref Classes and Interfaces

CLASS	ABSTRACT CLASS	INTERFACE	EXCEPTION	
PhantomReference	Reference	—	—	
ReferenceQueue	—	—	—	
SoftReference	—	—	—	
WeakReference	—	—	—	

The java.reflect Package (introduced in JDK 1.1)

Table C.19

java.reflect Classes and Interfaces

CLASS	ABSTRACT CLASS	INTERFACE	EXCEPTION	
AccessibleObject	—	*InvocationHandler*	*InvocationTargetException*	
Array	—	*Member*	*UndeclaredThrowableException*	
Constructor	—	—	—	
Field	—	—	—	
Method	—	—	—	
Modifier	—	—	—	
Proxy	—	—	—	
ReflectPermission	—	—	—	

The java.math Package (introduced in JDK 1.1)

Table C.20
java.math Classes and Interfaces

CLASS	ABSTRACT CLASS	INTERFACE	EXCEPTION
BigDecimal	—	—	—
BigInteger	—	—	—

The java.net Package

Table C.21
java.net Classes and Interfaces

CLASS	ABSTRACT CLASS	INTERFACE	EXCEPTION
DatagramPacket	Authenticator	ContentHandlerFactory	BindException
DatagramSocket	ContentHandler	DatagramSocketImplFactory	ConnectException
InetAddress	DatagramSocketImpl	FileNameMap	MalformedURLException
MulticastSocket	HttpURLConnection	SocketImplFactory	NoRouteToHostException
NetPermission	JarURLConnection	SocketOptions	ProtocolException
PasswordAuthentication	SocketImpl	URLStreamHandlerFactory	SocketException
ServerSocket	URLConnection	—	UnknownHostException
Socket	URLStreamHandler	—	UnknownServiceException
SocketPermission	—	—	—
URL	—	—	—
URLClassLoader	—	—	—
URLDecoder	—	—	—
URLEncoder	—	—	—

The java.text Package (introduced in JDK 1.1)

Table C.22
java.text Classes and Interfaces

CLASS	ABSTRACT CLASS	INTERFACE	EXCEPTION
Annotation	BreakIterator	AttributedCharacterIterator	ParseException
AttributedString	Collator	CharacterIterator	—
ChoiceFormat	DateFormat	—	—
CollationElementIterator	Format	—	—
CollationKey	NumberFormat	—	—
DateFormatSymbols	—	—	—
DecimalFormat	—	—	—
DecimalFormatSymbols	—	—	—
FieldPosition	—	—	—
MessageFormat	—	—	—
ParsePosition	—	—	—
RuleBasedCollator	—	—	—
SimpleDateFormat	—	—	—
StringCharacterIterator	—	—	—

The java.util Package

Table C.23
java.util Classes and Interfaces

CLASS	ABSTRACT CLASS	INTERFACE	EXCEPTION
ArrayList	AbstractCollection	Collection	ConcurrentModificationException
Arrays	AbstractList	Comparator	EmptyStackException
BitSet	AbstractMap	Enumeration	*MissingResourceException*
Collections	AbstractSequentialList	*EventListener*	NoSuchElementException
Date	AbstractSet	Iterator	*TooManyListenersException*
EventObject	*Calendar*	List	—
GregorianCalendar	Dictionary	ListIterator	—
HashMap	*ListResourceBundle*	Map	—
HashSet	*ResourceBundle*	Observer	—
Hashtable	*TimeZone*	Set	—
LinkedList	—	SortedMap	—
Locale	—	SortedSet	—
Observable	—	—	—
Properties	—	—	—
PropertyPermission	—	—	—
PropertyResourceBundle	—	—	—
Random	—	—	—
SimpleTimeZone	—	—	—
Stack	—	—	—
StringTokenizer	—	—	—
Timer	—	—	—
TimerTask	—	—	—
TreeMap	—	—	—
TreeSet	—	—	—
Vector	—	—	—
WeakHashMap	—	—	—

The java.util.jar Package (introduced in JDK 1.2)

Table C.24
java.util.jar Classes and Interfaces

CLASS	ABSTRACT CLASS	INTERFACE	EXCEPTION
Attributes	—	—	JarException
JarEntry	—	—	—
JarFile	—	—	—
JarInputStream	—	—	—
JarOutputStream	—	—	—
Manifest	—	—	—

The java.util.zip Package (introduced in JDK 1.1)

Table C.25
java.util.zip Classes and Interfaces

CLASS	ABSTRACT CLASS	INTERFACE	EXCEPTION
Adler32	—	Checksum	DataFormatException
CheckedInputStream	—	—	ZipEsception
CheckedOutputStream	—	—	—
CRC32	—	—	—
Deflater	—	—	—
DeflaterOutputStream	—	—	—
GZIPInputStream	—	—	—
GZIPOutputStream	—	—	—
Inflater	—	—	—
InflaterInputStream	—	—	—
ZipEntry	—	—	—
ZipFile	—	—	—
ZipInputStream	—	—	—
ZipOutputStream	—	—	—

DIFFERENCES BETWEEN JDKS 1.0, 1.1, 1.2, AND 1.3

D

Whenever a programming language is changed, programmers are forced to adapt. Not all the changes to the language concern the typical Java programmer; however, this appendix should help you understand the relevant changes between each version of the Java Development Kit (JDK).

In the first edition of this book, the most significant change from version 1.0 to version 1.1 was to the Java Event Model: the way that you make an applet respond to the user. The "new" Event Model was created to establish consistency so that Java could be more easily used with programming tools.

You might wonder why I've included a discussion of the old Event Model, especially since all examples in this book utilize the new model. The reason is that if you're writing for the Web, you can't guarantee visitors to your site will have the latest and greatest version of the Java Virtual Machine embedded in their browser. Although it may be hard to believe,

there are still many people surfing the Web using a browser that can only run Java applets using version 1.0 of the JDK. These people are a very small group (and the number continually grows smaller as they upgrade to newer browsers and operating systems). However, it may be important to you not to exclude these visitors from experiencing your applet, so the next section explains the differences between the old and new Event Models. If you're not worried about backwards compatibility of your applet, then you can safely skip the next section.

Other changes that have been made between versions 1.0, 1.1, 1.2, and 1.3 have introduced new capabilities to the language, so you won't have to make any changes to your code unless you want to. The main thing to remember is that these changes were made to help make programming easier, not to give you headaches.

The "Old" Event Model

If you find that you need (or want) to write applets that use the "old" Event Model, you'll need to understand the differences between the two.

The old event model relies on the use of the Event class. If you want your applet to respond to a user clicking on a button in the old model, for example, you would need to write a method called action, and then use the Event object that was passed to determine specifically whether the button you were interested in was pressed.

The new model requires you to make your applet into an ActionListener as well as registering each listener with the source of each event (as we have seen in the examples in this book). The old model doesn't require any of that, and is very simple and straightforward. It was great for very small applets (and still is, as a matter of fact). However, as programs grew larger it became very hard for programmers to determine which events belonged to which components, and this is one reason why the new model was introduced. Another reason that the model was changed is that the old model was bad for performance because the system had to check for every event regardless of whether it was relevant or not (i.e., whether there was any code that needed to be run for that event or not).

If you need to support both event models in the same applet, you can't just write code for both models in your applet and have the browser figure out what to do with it. Instead, you'll need to rely on the techniques described at http://java.sun.com/products/jdk/1.1/compatible/index.html. This will allow you to correctly send the right code to the right browser.

Handling a Button Press with JDK 1.0

```
public class ButtonApplet extends
→ Applet{

Button b;

public void init(){
  b=new Button("Press Me");
  add(b);
}

public boolean action(Event e, Object
→ arg){
  if(e.target instanceof Button)
  ...here is where you would
  → put the code to react to
  → the button press...
```

Handling a Button Press with JDK 1.1 and Above

```
public class ButtonApplet extends
→ Applet implements ActionListener{

Button b;

public void init(){
  b=new Button("press me");
  b.addActionListener(this);
  add(b);
}

public void
actionPerformed(ActionEvent e){
  if(e.getSource() instanceof
  → Button){
  ...here is where you would
  → put the code to react to a
  → button press...
```

Table D.1

Comparison of Method Names in JDK 1.0 and JDK 1.1 and Above	
JDK 1.0 METHOD NAME	JDK 1.1 AND ABOVE METHOD NAME
size()	getSize()
resize()	setSize()
location()	getLocation()
move()	setLocation()
enable(), disable()	setEnable()

Method names

Many of the methods that existed in JDK 1.0 were renamed in JDK 1.1. Although it is hard to see why this kind of change would be necessary, the new method names are more consistent. This makes programming easier, but it was really done so that Java could be manipulated by advanced programming tools. The term that is used in the Java documentation to mark a method as out-of-date is "deprecated."

Also added in JDK 1.1 were two large categories of methods called **accessors** and **mutators**. Accessors are methods that return the value of some variable. Mutators are methods that change the value of a variable. Accessors use the word "get" with the name of the variable appended, while mutators use the word "set" with the name of the variable appended, as shown in the examples in **Table D.1**.

These changed methods are found throughout the AWT, so be aware of them if you are modifying or updating an applet written for JDK 1.0. There is a more comprehensive guide on the Web at `http://java.sun.com/docs/books/tutorial/post1.0/converting/deprecatedAWT.html`.

Swing

Swing is a set of GUI (graphical user interface) components with a "Pluggable look and feel" introduced in version Java 1.2. It was written totally in Java, and is based on the version 1.1 Lightweight UI Framework. It uses the AWT as a foundation, but allows you much more freedom in designing and implementing your graphical interface. It lets you choose the "look and feel" of your applet based on a specific operating system (Motif, Microsoft Windows, Mac OS), or a uniform look and feel

continued

THE "OLD" EVENT MODEL

across all supporting operating systems (the "Java look and feel"). This is what is meant by the phrase "Pluggable look and feel." Unlike the interface components in the AWT 1.1 implementation, Swing components can be operated entirely from the keyboard (mouse-less operation). Swing also introduced some useful new interface components as well (such as tree view, list box, and tabbed panes). With the release of JDK 1.3, more new features have been added to Swing too.

The `java.sun.com` site has an excellent tutorial on how to create graphical interfaces with Swing components, which can be found at `http://java.sun.com/docs/books/tutorial/uiswing/index.html`.

JAR files

JAR files were introduced in version 1.1 and extended in version 1.2. JAR stands for "Java archive." You can use JAR files to package many Java class files or other resource files (graphics or sounds, for example) into one big file, with the extension ".jar" on the end. Most current browsers support JAR files, and you will learn how to put them into Web pages in the next section. There are several reasons to use JAR files:

◆ Files that are packaged together transfer more quickly over the Internet.

◆ It is easier to manage and track one big file than many small files.

◆ If files are grouped together, they can be manipulated as one unit (this is necessary for digital signatures).

◆ The archive format used in JAR files is the same as the one used in ZIP files. You can open a JAR file and take a peek inside by using any utility program that can read ZIP files (Winzip, PKZip, etc.).

Before the release of version 1.3, JAR files were cached on the visitor's machine when they were first downloaded. This caused some problems for long-running server applications. So, in version 1.3 of the JDK, there is a new "delete-on-close" option that can be used to correct this problem.

JDK 1.3 also supports *JAR Indexing*, which allows developers to break applet functionality into different JAR files so that only those files that are needed for a given run of that applet are actually downloaded.

You can find more information about JAR files at `http://java.sun.com/products/jdk/1.3/docs/guide/jar/`.

Internationalization

Java 1.1 introduced a new applet method called `getLocale()`. This method allows you to embed location-specific information (`java.util.Locale`) into your applet. Whenever someone runs the applet, their computer will automatically run the applet using the correct information for that locale. If all of the strings in an applet are internationalized, the applet will be accessible to Web viewers all over the world, not just in the country of origin.

Digital signatures

Another handy feature introduced in version 1.1 is digital signatures. This allows you to get out of the so-called "sandbox" that was discussed earlier in this book. When an applet is digitally signed, the user can be absolutely sure who wrote the applet, and that it hasn't been modified without the writer's authorization. With this knowledge, the user can then decide whether or not to trust applets to perform certain operations, such as accessing files from the hard drive. Using digital signatures is a little complicated. Without going into too much detail, here are the basic steps.

continued

THE "OLD" EVENT MODEL

To use digital signatures:

1. Apply to a public certificate authority (CA) for a key pair. For a list of CAs, open your browser's security console and look for a category called "signers." Go to the Web site of one of those signers for more information. Two of the more popular are Verisign and Thawte.

2. Create a key database. This was done using a tool called `javakey` in JDK 1.1 and is widely thought to be overly complex and buggy. Attempts to fix it actually made things worse, and the version of `javakey` that was released in JDK version 1.1.6 didn't even work at all. With the next release of the JDK (version 1.2), the tool was split into several new tools. The tool that now manages the key database is called `keytool`. Documentation for using it is available at `http://java.sun.com/docs/books/tutorial/security1.2/summary/tools.html`.

3. Sign the JAR file. This is done by using `javakey` in JDK 1.1, or `jarsigner` in JDK 1.2 and above.

In JDK 1.3, a new signature verification method has been added (FIPS) as well as providing support for Netscape-signed JAR files.

Using digital signatures is definitely not for the faint of heart; however, if you really need to use this feature, you can find all that you need to know at `http://java.sun.com/j2se/1.3/docs/guide/security/`.

Drag & Drop

Drag & Drop was introduced in version 1.2 of the JDK. It allowed for data transfer across native applications, applications written in Java, between Java applets, and within a single Java application. It didn't work very well (and not at all on the Linux implementation of the JDK). However, these problems have been fixed with the newest release of JDK 1.3, and now it works very well. It's handy in applications that utilize the Swing tree view. Everything you ever wanted to know about how to add Drag & Drop functionality to your applets can be found at `http://java.sun.com/j2se/1.3/docs/guide/dragndrop/`.

Javadoc

Javadoc is a really nifty tool from Sun for generating HTML documentation directly from Java source code. It was created by Sun for their own internal use while they were developing the Java language, but it was so useful that they decided to release it out into the world so we could all use it. The first version that was released was pretty crude, but it has become a fairly sophisticated tool as the Java language has become more and more popular. It's even included in the JDK, so you already have it!

Javadoc also allows special "at" tags (tags that begin with the @ symbol) to be included in comments that are treated differently by the engine when generating HTML. Javadocs are very useful when used to communicate how classes should be used without having to read the source code directly. This is great when you want to share your code with someone else, or if you've forgotten exactly how a particular class that you've written is supposed to be used. Since Java is written entirely *in* Java, Javadoc is used to generate the online documentation for the API. You can find it at `http://java.sun.com/j2se/1.3/docs/api/`.

You can generate documents that look as professional as the Java API by using Javadoc on your own source code. `http://java.sun.com/j2se/javadoc/` contains all the information that you need to use Javadoc on your source code as well as the Sun Style Guide for writing comments in the "Sun style."

THE "OLD" EVENT MODEL

Other changes

There have been a number of other changes and additions to the JDK, far too many to even mention in this appendix. However, some of these things might become useful to you as you continue to explore Java programming. You can read about all of the features in each JDK (starting with version 1.1) at: `http://java.sun.com/products/jdk/n.n/docs/relnotes/features.html` (replace `n.n` with the particular JDK version that you're interested in).

Looking forward

There is another upgrade in the works, JDK 1.4, which is still in beta at the time of this writing. Some of the features that are planned for the 1.4 release are regular expressions, secure sockets, and assertions. With native regular expressions, much of the cumbersome programming that has to be done to search within textual data will be greatly simplified. Support for secure sockets will allow developers to provide secure data communication between a client and a server running any application protocol (such as HTTP, Telnet, and FTP) over the Internet. Assertions provide a kind of programmer "self-check" against assumptions that have been made about a particular piece of code. Utilizing assertions in development and testing increases the possibility that your code is free of errors.

THE "OLD" EVENT MODEL

INDEX

Symbols

; (semicolon), in Java/JavaScript code, 41
{ } (curly braces), 40, 41, 71
[ ] (square brackets), 67
// comment indicator, 46
/* comment indicator, 46
$ (dollar sign), in variable names, 51
\ escape character, 56
& operator, 268
&& operator, 81, 268
+ operator, 60
= operator, 49
| operator, 268
|| operator, 81, 268
%> tag, 218
<% tag, 218, 230
<%= tag, 218, 219, 230
@ tag, 331
_ (underscore), in variable names, 51
*\ comment indicator, 46

A

Abstract Windowing Toolkit. *See* AWT
accessor methods, 327
acronyms, 11
action attribute, 186
ActionListener, 70–71, 72, 326
actionPerformed() method, 71, 72, 75, 127, 272
ActiveX, 247
AdjustmentListener, 72
Adobe GoLive, 249–252

adding applet tags with, 249–250
adding object tags with, 251–252
previewing applets in, 250
recommended books on, 243
Adobe GoLive 5 for Windows and Macintosh, 243
alert window, 185
align attribute, 31–32
alphaWorks, 296
ampersands, 81, 268
"and" operator, 81, 268
animated GIFs, 153
animation, 163–174
    displaying non-stop, 170–171
    double-buffering, 167–169, 205
    eliminating flicker in, 167–169
    Java's ability to handle, 153
    starting/stopping, 172–174
    with Swing, 205–208
    and threading, 163–166
AnimationPane class, 205, 208, 209
Apache, 219
Apple. *See also* Macintosh
    InterfaceBuilder, 299
    Java Developer pages, 303
    Java support, 2, 9
    ProjectBuilder, 299
applet tags
    attributes of, 23
    and passing information from JavaScript
        to Java, 183

applet tags (*continued*)
  placing applets on Web pages with, 22–23
  using Dreamweaver to add, 244–246
  using GoLive to add, 249–250
  using param tag in, 25
  Web browser considerations, 24
Applet6.class file, 208
applets
  building user interface for, 109–130
    (*See also* user interface)
  changing font characteristics in, 47–48,
    117, 118
  controlling flow of (*See* flow control)
  defined, 6
  digitally signing, 329–330
  drawing in, 97–101
  embedding location-specific information
    in, 329
  entering/displaying text in, 113–114
  examples
    biorhythm calculator, 205–208, 209–216
    butterfly, 104–107, 205–208
    deck-of-cards, 154–174
    four-function calculator, 269–276
    HelloWorld, 22–23, 190–191
    hierarchical menu, 277–292
    Tic-Tac-Toe, 253–268
    tinyScroller, 34, 35–37
  finding on the Web, 33–34, 294–296
  how they're presented in this book, xiii
  Java *vs.* Swing, 190
  layout considerations (*See* LayoutManagers)
  and older Web browsers, 9–10, 325
  passing parameters to, 25, 35–36, 44–45
  placing/positioning on Web pages,
    22–25, 27, 31–32, 97, 247
  putting borders around, 94
  responding to user input in, 70–72
  restricting to sandbox, 13, 329
  security considerations, 13
  setting background color for, 43
  threaded, 163–166
  transferring data between, 330–331
  uploading to server, 14
  using comments in, 46

Aqua interface, 133
archive files, 328
arrays, 67–68, 123, 160, 254, 262
arrow keys, moving image with, 104–105
arrows, in code examples, xiii
assertions, 332
"at" tags, 331
attributes. *See also* specific attributes
  applet tag, 23
  embed tag, 28
  object tag, 24
AWT, 20, 301

B

background color, setting applet's, 43
backslash (\) escape character, 56
biorhythm calculator, 209–216
body tags, 182
bold font style, 47, 117, 194
books, recommended
  Adobe GoLive, 243
  Dreamweaver, 243
  HTML, xi, 221
  Java, 300–301
  JavaScript, 6, 175
  JSP, 217
  servlets, 217
  Swing, 189, 301
Boolean values, 160, 254, 273
BorderLayout, 138–139, 144–145, 147–148, 195
borders
  applet, 94
  image, 158–159
Borland JBuilder, 299
braces. *See* curly braces
brackets ([ ]), 67
break command, 86, 87, 91
Brisbin, Shelly, 243
browsers. *See* Web browsers
butterfly applet, 104–107, 205–208
buttons
  creating, 152
  radio, 118–120, 197–199
  responding to user clicking on, 326
  size of, with Windows *vs.* Mac, 133, 145

D

data-entry errors, catching, 73–76
data transfer, 330–331
Date object, 209, 213
dayInCycle() method, 212
dayOfTheWeek array, 67–68
deck-of-cards applet, 154–174
defToolkit variable, 179
designers, Web, xi, xii, 4
destroy() method, 44, 237, 238
Developer.com, 294
developers, resources for Java, 294, 297, 299, 303
development environments. *See* IDEs
DevX.com, 296
digital signatures, 329–330
Digital Video Recorders, 3
displayText variable, 113, 114
displayVoteResults() method, 239
do/while loop, 84–85
document.writeln() method, 177, 180
doGet() method, 232, 233, 238
dollar sign, in variable names, 51
doPost() method, 233, 238
dot syntax, 16–17
double-buffering, 167–169, 205
Double class, 60
Double object, 63, 66
double primitive, 60, 65–66
Drag & Drop, 330–331
drawImage() method, 161, 169
drawing
   with drawRect() method, 158–159
   freehand, 100–101
   with mouse, 94–99
   in one dimension, 94–96
   in two dimensions, 97–99
drawing methods
   drawLine(), 95
   drawOval(), 99
   drawRect(), 99, 158–159
   drawRoundRect(), 99, 158, 161
   drawString(), 60
   fillOval(), 99
   fillRect(), 99

Dreamweaver, 243–248
   adding applet tags with, 244–246
   adding object tags with, 247–248
   extensibility features, 248
   recommended book on, 243
   viewing contents of applets in, 246
Dreamweaver 4 for Windows and Macintosh, 243
DVRs, 3

E

e-mail, contacting author via, xiv
EarthWeb, 294
editors, visual, 243
Egremont III, Carlton, 301
Elements of Java Style, 300
else statements, 77, 177
embed tags
   and Adobe GoLive, 251, 252
   attributes of, 28
   and checking for Java-enabled browsers, 177
   and Dreamweaver, 247, 248
   placing applets on Web pages with, 27
   and positioning of applets on Web pages, 31–32
   using with object tags, 247, 251, 252
encryption, password, 187
endPt variable, 95, 98, 101
equal sign (=), 49
errors, catching, 73–76, 165, 166
escape character, 56
Event class, 326
event handlers, 94
Event Model, Java, 325, 326
events, 70, 72
exceptions, throwing, 76, 110, 165
expressions, 229–230, 332
extends, 20
eXtensible Markup Language. *See* XML

F

false/true values, 160, 184–187, 254
FAQ, Java, 295
fillRect() method, 99
Flanagan, David, 300

N

name attribute, 35–36
name/value pairs, param tag, 25
names
  Macintosh file, 208
  method, 308, 327
  variable, 51, 308
navigator object, 176
NBTs, 3
Negrino, Tom, 6, 175
.NET platform, 3
Netscape. *See also* Web browsers
  enabling Java in, 30
  and Java history, 1, 175
  and Java versions, 9–10, 26
  and JavaScript, 5, 175
  and LiveConnect, 178, 180
  and LiveScript, 5–6, 175
  and public Java methods, 178
Netscape Communicator, 9
newNum variable, 273–274
news scroller applet, 33
newsgroups, 302
newText() method, 181–182
Next Big Thing, 2–3
null values, 45, 53
NumberFormatException, 76
numbers
  converting between strings and, 61–62
  converting between types of, 63–64
numeric variables, 58–59, 60

O

Oak programming language, 2
object hierarchy, 309–324
object tags
  adding with Dreamweaver, 247–248
  adding with GoLive, 251–252
  attributes of, 24
  and checking for Java-enabled browsers, 177
  and passing information from JavaScript to Java, 183
  placing applets on Web pages with, 24–25, 27, 247

using with embed tags, 247, 251, 252
  Web browser considerations, 24, 26, 27
objects
  combining, 16–18
  defined, 15
  documentation for, 15
  drawing, 97–99
  instantiating, 16
One Wolf WebArt, 34, 37
online magazines, 297
onLoad handler, 182
onSubmit handler, 186
"or" operator, 81, 268
OS X. *See* Mac OS X
ovals, drawing, 99
overriding methods, 44

P

packages
  defined, 20
  object hierarchy for specific, 309–324
paint() method
  and double-buffered animations, 169
  and drawing with mouse, 96, 98
  and HelloWorld applet, 40
  purpose of, 44, 51
  and Tic-Tac-Toe applet, 266
panels, 144–145, 146
param tags, 25, 35–36, 44
parameters
  passing, 35–36, 40, 44–45, 181–187
  using default values for, 36
parentheses, in methods, 16
parseInt() method, 120
Pascal, 7
passCheck() function, 184, 185–186
passing information
  from HTML to Java, 25, 35–36, 44–45
  from Java to JavaScript, 184–187
  from JavaScript to Java, 181–183
passwords
  checking validity of, 184–187
  one-way encryption of, 187
  protecting Web pages with, 110–112

Solaris, 8, 9, 26, 298, 299
special-effects applets, 33
square brackets ([ ]), 67
standards, Java, 303
start() method, 44, 172
startPt variable, 98, 101
startUp() function, 181, 182
startX/startY variables, 98, 99
status() method, 265, 267, 268
stop() method, 44, 172
string methods, 56–57
strings
    altering case of, 57
    converting between numbers and, 60,
        61–62, 120
    declaring, 50–53
    defined, 17, 50
    initializing, 50, 52
style guide, Java, 300
subclasses, 20, 66
submenus, 277
Sun Microsystems
    and hierarchical menu applet, 277
    IDE, 298
    and Java history, 2–3
    and Java versions, 9, 26
    Javadoc tool, 331–332
    and JavaScript, 175
    and Swing, 189
    and Tic-Tac-Toe applet, 254, 256
    and Web server software, 219
    Web site, 294
Sun Style Guide, 332
survey servlet, 234–242
Swing, 189–216
    animating images with, 205–208
    biorhythm calculator, 209–216
    contrasted with Java, 190
    creating checkboxes with, 194–196
    creating radio buttons with, 197–199
    creating shortcut keys with, 194
    purpose of, 189, 327
    recommended book on, 189, 301
    setting fonts with, 192–193
    setting "look and feel" with, 200–204, 327–328

tutorial, 328
    writing applets with, 190–191
switch/case statements, 88–91
Symantec, 299
syntax, Java, 300

T

tax calculator, 269
terminology, Java, 11, 15–20
text, entering/displaying in applets, 113–114
text areas, 125–127
text-effects applets, 33
text/javascript MIME type, 176
TextListener, 72, 114
Thawte, 330
this keyword, 45, 54–55
threading, 163–166
Tic-Tac-Toe applet, 253–268
tinyScroller applet, 34, 35–37
TiVo, 3
TLAs, 11
toLowerCase() method, 57
Tomcat, 219, 233
Toolkit, accessing default, 178–180
toString() method, 61
toUpperCase() method, 57
Towers, J. Tarin, 243
true/false values, 160, 184–187, 254
try/catch statements, 110, 165
try statements, 76
tutorials
    Java, 296
    Swing, 328
type attribute, 176

U

UI manager, 200, 203
underscore (_), in variable names, 51
Unix, 2, 9, 26
update() method, 44, 169
updateCount() method, 239
uppercase, displaying strings in, 57
URL variable, 110
Usenet, 302

`while` loops, 82–83, 242
`width` attribute, 22, 23, 24
`WindowListener`, 72
Windows
  IDEs, 298–299
  and Java 2 SDK, 8
  and Java font mapping, 42
  Java for, 2, 9
  and Java plugin, 26
  WYSIWYG tools, 246
WORA, 2, 217
World Wide Web, impact of Java on, 1.
    See also Web
Write Once, Run Anywhere, 2, 217
WYSIWYG tools, 243, 244, 246, 249

X

XML, 3, 229–230, 295
`xPos` coordinate, 205

Y

`yPos` coordinate, 205

Z

ZIP files, 328